Child Development for Child Care and Protection Workers

by the same authors

Child Neglect
Practice Issues for Health and Social Care
Edited by Julie Taylor and Brigid Daniel
Foreword by Olive Stevenson
ISBN 978 1 84310 160 4
Best Practice in Working with Children Series

The Early Years
Assessing and Promoting Resilience in Vulnerable Children 1
Brigid Daniel and Sally Wassell
ISBN 978 1 84310 013 3

The School Years
Assessing and Promoting Resilience in Vulnerable Children 2
Brigid Daniel and Sally Wassell
ISBN 978 1 84310 018 8

Adolescence
Assessing and Promoting Resilience in Vulnerable Children 3
Brigid Daniel and Sally Wassell
ISBN 978 1 84310 019 5

Engaging with Fathers
Practice Issues for Health and Social Care
Brigid Daniel and Julie Taylor
ISBN 978 1 85302 794 9

of related interest

The Child's World
The Comprehensive Guide to Assessing Children in Need
2nd edition
Edited by Jan Horwath
ISBN 978 1 84310 568 8

The Developing World of the Child
Edited by Jane Aldgate, David Jones, Wendy Rose and Carole Jeffery
Foreword by Maria Eagle
ISBN 978 1 84310 244 1

Good Practice in Safeguarding Children
Working Effectively in Child Protection
Edited by Liz Hughes and Hilary Owen
ISBN 978 1 84310 945 7
Good Practice in Health, Social Care and Criminal Justice Series

Child Development for Child Care and Protection Workers

SECOND EDITION

Brigid Daniel, Sally Wassell
and Robbie Gilligan

Foreword by David Howe

Jessica Kingsley *Publishers*
London and Philadelphia

Figures 2.1 and 2.2 are from *A Child's Journey Through Placement* by Vera Fahlberg © 1994 Vera Fahlberg and are reproduced with permission from British Association for Adoption and Fostering and Vera Fahlberg

Figures 2.5 and 7.2 are from *Understanding Children's Development* by Peter Smith and Helen Cowie © 1991 Peter Smith and Helen Cowie and are reproduced with permission from Blackwell Publishers

Figure 2.6 is from *Working with Adoptive Families Beyond Placement* by Ann Hartman © 1984 Ann Hartman and is reproduced with permission from Child Welfare League of America

Figure 3.1 is from *Attachment Theory, Child Maltreatment and Family Support* by David Howe *et al.* © 1999 D. Howe, M. Brandon, D. Hinings and G. Schofield and is reproduced with permission from Palgrave Macmillan

Figure 7.1 is from *Understanding Child Development* by Sara Meadows © 1986 Sara Meadows and is reproduced with permission from Taylor and Francis Publishers

Figure 8.1 is from *Children in Trouble* by Carol Hayden © 2007 Carol Hayden and is reproduced with permission from Palgrave Macmillan

Figure 8.2 is from *Every Child Matters* by the Department for Education and Schools © 2003 Crown Copyright and is reproduced with permission from HMSO

We are grateful to Blackwell Science and the *Journal of Child and Family Social Work* for permission to reproduce material from Daniel, Wassell, Ennis, Gilligan and Ennis (1997) 'Critical understandings of child development: The development of a module for a post-qualifying certificate course in child protection studies', *2*, 4, 209–220 in Chapter 2.

First published in 1999
This second edition published in 2010
by Jessica Kingsley Publishers
116 Pentonville Road
London N1 9JB, UK
and
400 Market Street, Suite 400
Philadelphia, PA 19106, USA

www.jkp.com

Library of Congress Cataloging in Publication Data
Daniel, Brigid, 1959-
  Child development for child care and protection workers / Brigid Daniel, Sally Wassell and Robbie Gilligan ; foreword by David Howe. -- 2nd ed.
    p. cm.
  Includes bibliographical references and index.
  ISBN 978-1-84905-068-5 (alk. paper)
 1. Child development. 2. Child psychology. 3. Child care workers. 4. Child welfare workers. I. Wassell, Sally. II. Gilligan, Robbie. III. Title.
  HQ772.D25 2010
  305.231088'3627--dc22
                        2010009500

British Library Cataloguing in Publication Data
A CIP catalogue record for this book is available from the British Library

ISBN 978 1 84905 068 5

Printed and bound in Great Britain by
MPG Books Group

Contents

Authors' Acknowledgements

For the first edition, Jim Ennis was responsible for bringing the writing team together and facilitating the book's development. Elaine Ennis also contributed many helpful comments. Sadly, since then Jim Ennis has died and we wish to pay tribute to his vision that made this book happen. Julie Barclay designed Figure 1.1 and Jane and Stan Gough helped with the typing. Thanks also to David and Gavin Willshaw and Chris Henderson for continued and ongoing encouragement and support.

Foreword

Whatever cards heredity deals, at birth each child has the genetic potential to become a unique, life-affirming individual. But how a particular genetic hand gets played, how the genes express themselves, depends so much on the quality and character of the environment as it presents itself, day by day, week by week, year by year. Nature and nurture interact in ways both wonderful and complex to make us who we are. Environments, particularly social environments, that are rich and responsive are most likely to help children realise their full potential. However, when the world is harsh and dangerous, cold and rejecting, bleak and empty, development suffers. Progress is impaired. Lives are disfigured. This, of course, is the world of the child care and protection worker.

To gauge deprivation and danger, child care workers need the yardsticks of normal development. How else do you know that what is happening to this child is beyond the pale, not to be tolerated? How else can you measure improvement? In their early years, young children develop rapidly. When all goes well, their competence grows at an extraordinary and thrilling rate. They have an appetite for life. In quick succession they learn to recognise, relate, control, smile, grasp, sit, crawl, laugh, walk, play, run, talk, share, count. One way to study children, therefore, is to chart these shared milestones. It is equally interesting, though, to consider children's individual differences. And although genes account for a good deal of our individuality, the social environment of parents, family and friends is an equally powerful force with which to reckon. Child care and protection workers can do nothing about genes, but they can assess the character of the environment, and they can attempt to change the quality of care-giving, the way a child views and reacts to friends, the poverty that places everyone under stress, and how a teacher might engage a child who has known nothing but neglect.

Modern ideas about children's development, including the way experience shapes the young brain, recognise that all of these elements interact in a continuous and dynamic way. Development takes place in a bewildering series of transactions between the individual and his or her environment. So, for example, a secure attachment and a cheerful temperament are likely to equip a young child well to take advantage of the next developmental opportunity that comes their way – play with peers, perhaps. Each transaction transforms current developments which in turn sets up new patterns of organisation that affect, and are affected by, subsequent experiences and opportunities in what is sometimes known as a transactional systems perspective. The child's evolving personality therefore interacts dynamically with the environment of parents, siblings, peers and teachers, projecting the individual along his or her unique developmental course. Developmentally speaking, each dynamic transaction can be for good or ill. Pathways can be optimal or sub-optimal. It is the job of child protection workers to study and understand each child with whom they work, all with a view to nudging him or her back on to one of life's more promising pathways.

These sketched ideas are drawn out in much richer detail by the authors of this welcome book. All three – Brigid Daniel, Sally Wassell and Robbie Gilligan – are experts in both children's development and the work of the child care and protection services. By knitting together an understanding of children's development and progress from infancy to adolescence with the concerns of child care and protection work, they have fashioned a book that is informed and informative, theoretically wise and practically useful. Major concepts such as resilience and vulnerability, risk and protection, context and care-giving, attachment and social ecology guide the reader along the many roads of possible development, some rocky, some smooth. Examples, key concepts and checklists keep ideas clear and thinking sharp. Readers will value *Child Development for Child Care and Protection Workers* for the wisdom that it brings and the guidance that it offers. And armed with the knowledge so neatly wrapped up in the pages of this very sensible book, the reflective practitioner will be well placed to make young lives that much better.

Professor David Howe
University of East Anglia
Norwich

CHAPTER I

Introduction: Framework for Understanding Child Development

Introduction

In this book we aim to provide practitioners with information to help with understanding key developmental processes through early years, school years and into adolescence. An understanding of the general parameters of development will assist with assessment of the specific developmental needs of individual children and the planning of intervention. All assessment requires balancing attention to 'norms' of development with the needs of the individual child. The underpinning theoretical framework for the book is attachment theory. A wealth of evidence has now accumulated attesting to the fundamental importance of secure attachment for healthy development. The concept of attachment and the importance of a child's relationships is explored in detail in Chapter 2. However, although attachment theory is our foundation, the book draws on a range of theoretical perspectives. In particular, a focus on attachment must not be equated with an individualistic approach that ignores the importance of wider influences upon development. In line with current assessment frameworks we advocate an ecological approach that considers factors at an individual, family, community and structural level (Department of Health 2000; Scottish Executive 2005).

Fundamental to the text as a whole is the assertion that, to be effective, child protection work (for example, investigating allegations of abuse, risk assessment, working with children identified as being at risk) must be informed by the same values as wider safeguarding and child care practice (for example, work with fostering and adoption, family support). Children whose development needs are not being met for whatever reason are in need of additional support – often the greatest risk to healthy development lies in neglect of basic needs. Thus, we caution against an artificial divide between children 'in need of support' and those 'in need of protection' (Department for Education and Schools 2003).

Across the UK and other jurisdictions with similar arrangements for the care and protection of children the last decade has seen huge policy changes in line with these concepts. The shift from the language of 'child protection' towards the language of 'safeguarding' in England signals a recognition of the importance of paying attention to the needs of all children. The assessment frameworks referred to above not only advocate an ecological approach, they promote the importance of looking at children holistically and considering cognitive, behavioural, material and emotional needs. Linked with this is the shift towards a far more explicitly multi-disciplinary approach to the recognition of and response to children who are in need of additional support and services. In particular, the key role of education and health professionals as part of the protective network around children is now undisputed. Indeed, the expectation in England is that 'everyone working with children, young people and families should have a common set of skills and knowledge' (HM Government 2005, p.4).

The challenges in safeguarding and protection are:

- to identify whether what would have been a child's normal pattern of development has been interrupted or disrupted in some way

- to establish whether the environment in which a child is living is likely to affect adversely their developmental path

- to find ways to maximise the possibility of a child attaining his or her developmental potential.

Supporting development towards potential

There are some universal characteristics of childhood that can be observed, the most obvious being the complete dependence on others at birth and in early childhood. The psychological and sociological study of children has yielded a vast amount of information about development. Many studies in the literature describe either stages of development or maturational tasks related to age. Those working in child care and protection must have some knowledge of such developmental milestones, but they cannot all be expected to be experts in all domains of development; rather, information needs to be pooled from across different disciplines and professions. For example, a teacher may well spot that a child's relationships with others are problematic, but will not be expected to analyse the child's attachment pattern. However, the teacher will be expected to supply detailed information about the child's learning style and stage of educational attainment.

Therefore this book provides an overview of the bounds of *healthy developmental pathways* clustered by age range, and informed by the grouping of practice issues. The material is set out so as to model a process of assessment that considers aspects of social, emotional, cognitive and, where appropriate, physical development (Chapters 6 to 8). This material is relatively unchanging – there are certain accepted developmental processes that research continues to confirm. However, there are greater expectations of the kind of emotional support that children have a right to expect; and there is greater recognition of the impact on development of family and social factors such as domestic abuse, parental mental ill health, parental substance abuse and violence within communities. The last decade has seen increased policy attention to parenting and support for parenting. Chapter 3 focuses on parenting in particular and care-giving more generally. It sets out the research about parenting styles and considers the factors that can support or impede parenting.

Each generation of children is also faced with different social challenges. For example, the last decade has seen a burgeoning of new technology, with its attendant advantages and disadvantages for children, and an increase in global movement of people, including unaccompanied children. Practitioners, therefore, need to be able to consider the universal features of fundamental developmental needs along with the overlaid impact of the wider context. There are no shortcuts: the basic principle is that a comprehensive assessment is required in order to plan effective intervention when a child is facing abuse and/or neglect.

Recognising potential

Throughout the book we will be stressing the importance of considering *each child as an individual*, with a distinct life history, within a unique set of current circumstances. It cannot be stressed too much that individual children vary. The fact that a child has not reached a particular stage that is 'average' for his age may be, but is not necessarily, an indicator of neglect, abuse or trauma. However, each child is born with *potential* and a successful childhood can be seen in terms of achieving that potential (see Figure 1.1).

Figure 1.1 Each child's potential to flourish in all domains needs to be supported

There can be different routes to this potential and different ways to encourage it. Some aspects of adult behaviour will support the development of potential, others will inhibit it and some aspects will have a negative effect. The experience of adverse life events and socio-economic deprivation may also affect development. The concept of potential is particularly useful when considering children with physical or intellectual impairments.

Thus each child, whatever their physical or intellectual capacity, has a potential which can be promoted. With information about what can be expected at any given age if a child's development is supported and healthy, it should be possible to assess the extent to which an individual child's potential has been undermined by adverse circumstances and events. Above all, it has to be recognised that if we do not expect much of the children we encounter then they are unlikely to flourish. Low expectations are especially damaging. Practitioners must take great care to avoid making assumptions about what a child can achieve based upon their background and where they live. They should also take great care not to accept lower standards of nurture for children just because of uncertainty about the best way to intervene.

Each day, practitioners are faced with children whose constellation of problems can be overwhelming. Some presenting problems perhaps have roots going back years, while others are due to current adverse life events and possibly abuse. At the same time the majority of families referred live in situations of extreme poverty and poor housing conditions. The practitioner is then faced with the task of intervening in the life of an individual child, with a distinct life history, within a unique set of current circumstances, while avoiding making the situation worse, and attempting to make it better. The key to promoting potential is the ability to assess the meaning of those past and current circumstances for the *individual* child.

The resilience matrix

Practitioners are often challenged by the complexity of *individual response* to circumstances. It is not uncommon for social workers to know children who have undergone very similar experiences but whose reactions are entirely different. So, for example, in response to sexual abuse by a step-father, one child may show prolonged problems such as extreme nightmares, clinginess to their mother, fear of all strangers and school refusal; while another child in response to similar experiences may show few ongoing signs of distress. Indeed, the lack of clear-cut relationships between incidents involving children and their symptoms is a major contributory factor in the difficulty of substantiating denied allegations of abuse.

To help with the application of a general understanding of developmental issues to the needs of an individual child we have developed the 'resilience matrix' (see also Daniel and Wassell 2002a, b and c). The matrix offers a framework to assist the practitioner to identify the range of positive and negative factors affecting a child. Once all these factors are mapped there can be greater understanding of how they interact to shape the unique needs of that child.

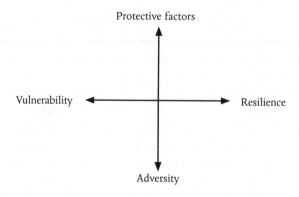

Figure 1.2 The resilience matrix, a framework for assessment and intervention to support healthy development

The matrix comprises two dimensions, one primarily intrinsic and one primarily extrinsic (see Figures 1.2 and 1.3). The first dimension is 'resilience and vulnerability'; the second is 'protective factors and adversity'.

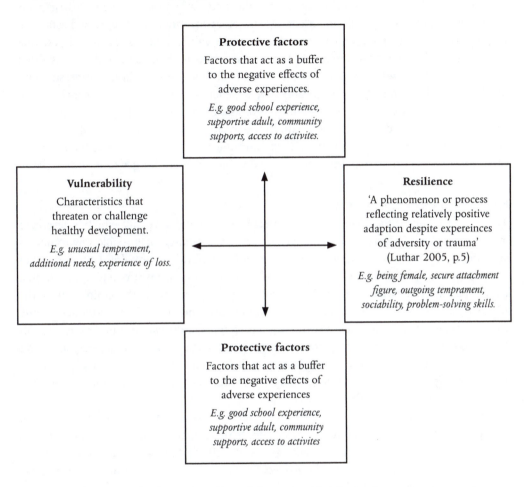

Protective factors

Factors that act as a buffer to the negative effects of adverse experiences.

E.g. good school experience, supportive adult, community supports, access to activites.

Vulnerability

Characteristics that threaten or challenge healthy development.

E.g. unusual temprament, additional needs, experience of loss.

Resilience

'A phenomenon or process reflecting relatively positive adaption despite expereinces of adversity or trauma' (Luthar 2005, p.5)

E.g. being female, secure attachment figure, outgoing temprament, sociability, problem-solving skills.

Protective factors

Factors that act as a buffer to the negative effects of adverse experiences

E.g. good school experience, supportive adult, community supports, access to activites

Figure 1.3 The resilience matrix with summary definitions and brief examples

Resilience and vulnerability

Each individual has his own level of resilience and vulnerability to stressful life events developed partly as a result of quality of attachments and other factors like individual temperament and experience of positive or negative life events. This dimension is considered in more depth in Chapter 4. When considering how to assess and support a child's development in the face of crisis, knowledge of factors of resilience is invaluable. A body of research has shifted the research emphasis towards an exploration of the factors intrinsic to an individual child that allow him to come through stressful life events relatively emotionally intact (Luthar 2005; Masten 1994; Rutter 2000; Werner 1990). So, for example, the child described above who appeared to show few ongoing problems may have had the resilience that comes from a secure attachment relationship.

The term 'vulnerable' is, itself, now contested, especially if it is used in a way that locates responsibility for factors within the individual – however, we use the term to denote the concept of elevated risk of poor outcomes as a result of adverse factors. We also recognise that children are not passive victims of events; rather, they are active participants in their lives and develop individual coping strategies that should be respected (Stainton Rogers 2001). So, to recognise factors that increase vulnerability is not to suggest that children should be treated as inherently fragile and unable to contribute to decisions about their lives. Having said that, the concept of vulnerability can help in the understanding of why some children suffer extreme and adverse reactions to negative life events. Indeed recognising vulnerability is an important part of assessing risk in child protection. So, for example, when considering the two children described above, the knowledge that the child showing ongoing problems has an insecure attachment relationship with her mother could go some way to explaining a heightened vulnerability to longer-term difficulties.

Protective factors and adversity

The second, related dimension is that of protective factors and adversity, which is described in more detail in Chapter 5. This dimension allows the range of possible environments and life events to be specifically assessed as either helpful or unhelpful to the child's development. So, for example, having a good school experience is protective for children whose lives are otherwise chaotic. Protective factors may directly buffer children from the effects of adversity – for example, the availability of a member of the extended family who offers refuge when a parent is drinking. Protective factors can also indirectly support development, for example the provision of parenting support can improve the child's experience of parenting. Protective factors may also help to nurture the factors in the child associated with resilience, for example access to a creative teacher who supports learning can help to improve a child's sense of self-efficacy.

At the other end of the spectrum are adverse factors – which may co-exist with protective factors. Living in poverty is an example of adversity. Similarly, racism is a form of adversity for a black child in Britain, against which the family can act as a protective bastion of defence (Robinson 2007). Adversity may be chronic, as in neglect from early years; or it may be acute, as in a sudden loss or a one-off experience of severe physical abuse. So the prevailing emotional and physical climate should be assessed as well as the experience of specific adverse events.

Assessment and intervention

This framework is designed as a simple tool to facilitate an assessment of the developmental progress of individual children and young people with whom we work. These children may be living in a variety of circumstances, many of them at home with one or both parents, some in newly constituted families with additional half-siblings, and others in substitute family care such as fostering or adoption, or in a residential setting.

It is crucial for intervention to be able to assess the interactional effects of the two dimensions. For example, what is described by Bee (1995) as the 'double whammy' of a vulnerable child in an adverse environment is what can lead to the poorest outcome. By the same token, a secure material environment is protective. Thus, taken together, these dimensions can act as a framework for the consideration of the overwhelming number of issues that may be affecting an individual child's development. In particular the model gives pointers to help with the recognition of protective aspects of a vulnerable child's environment and for recognising resilience in a child. The framework is also helpful for the assessment of the situation of a child with special needs. An individual child could, for example, have an impairment that renders him vulnerable to abuse, suffer the disability of living in an area where there is inadequate provision for children with special needs, but may have a resilient temperament and the protection of secure attachments. Figure 1.4 shows how the matrix can begin to be applied to different children.

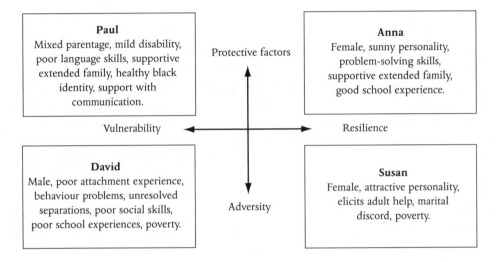

Figure 1.4 The resilience matrix with vignette illustrations

ANNA

From Figure 1.4 we can see that Anna is likely to have the best chance of healthy overall development. Not only is the fact of being female in itself protective, as boys are generally more vulnerable to stress, but also if Anna has a sunny, responsive personality and has learned social problem-solving skills, she will be well equipped to survive life's stresses. If she has additionally taken a healthy degree of responsibility for a sibling who perhaps has a disability, but does so in the context of a supportive extended family which is responsive to her needs, this may also be advantageous. If additionally she has had a good experience at school, this will stand her in good stead should she face other life stresses. Therefore, she has the advantages of a resilient personality, learned skills which equip her to face adversity, and a protective environment which ensures that her needs are met.

SUSAN

If we consider that, although Susan may face the adversity of living in poverty and additionally in a household full of marital discord, she is an attractive child who can elicit support from adults and children alike, this will be a buffer against the long-term effects of stress. Therefore, she has advantages which help her significantly in adversity.

PAUL

Paul is of mixed parentage, and, living in a predominantly white community, he may be vulnerable to the effects of racism. If he also has a mild disability which has affected significantly his development of language, he may be additionally vulnerable. However, if he lives with supportive members of his extended family who build his self-esteem as a black child, and resources have been found to focus on building his effective communication skills, his vulnerability may be reduced. This is dependent on the protective factors in his environment.

DAVID

David is clearly in the most vulnerable position as regards potential interruptions to his healthy development. He is the most obviously disadvantaged child because of a combination of stressors. If we imagine that not only is he vulnerable because of poor attachment experiences, but he also has long-standing behavioural problems, is falling behind at school and about to be excluded, we can see that he is already at risk of suffering from developmental delay or interruption. If he has additionally experienced adversity in that he lives in poverty and he has experienced numerous unresolved separations, we can see how his vulnerability might be increased. Not only is he more vulnerable but he has therefore also experienced many negative life events which are also likely to increase his vulnerability. Here we see the often powerful interaction between vulnerability and adversity as it may be that the more vulnerable a child, the more affected he or she may be by adverse experiences. Equally, the greater the persistent adversities, the more likely they are to render a particular child vulnerable.

Intervention

Throughout the book we provide many suggestions for intervention, but we suggest that the framework can offer a map of the aims of intervention. When considering the key concepts of resilience, adversity, vulnerability and protective factors as they are illustrated throughout the text, issues of relevance may emerge in relation to an individual child or young person with whom you are working which may help to clarify the focus of intervention.

In essence, the aim is to move children from the left part of the matrix to the right and from the bottom to the top. Overall, the more factors that can be located in the top right quadrant the better. In the example of Paul above, for example, we need to identify ways in which we can build his resilience and reduce his vulnerability, for example by offering him a warm attachment experience and increasing his social skills. In addition, we may be able to consider whether any of the circumstances of adversity can be reduced or removed and protective factors in the environment either harnessed or introduced. For example, an appropriate school placement and supportive adults managing Paul's difficult behaviour adeptly may be factors that could combine to help him to develop problem-solving skills and higher self-esteem. The level and nature of intervention will therefore depend upon the degree of vulnerability and levels of adversity balanced against the resources in his family community and professional support system which can be harnessed to address them.

Activity 1.1

Draw the resilience matrix on a large piece of paper. Consider a child or young person with whom you are working. Note down all the significant intrinsic and extrinsic factors that you are aware of at appropriate points in the four quadrants. Look at the overall picture and consider what it tells you about the balance of positive and negative features of the child's life. It may be helpful to undertake this task as a joint exercise with all the key practitioners working with the child and to revisit it after a period of intervention as a way to monitor any improvements.

In the course of the exploration of various factors which influence both the vulnerability and resilience of individual children, key themes emerge which it is helpful for the practitioner to bear in mind throughout.

- It is the *impact* of the event or set of life circumstances which dictates the way in which a particular child is likely to be affected.

- While the chronology of events is of importance, of even greater salience is the age and stage of development at which these events occurred, as the child's responses will be influenced by their cognitive capacity to make sense of these events.

- It is the particular coincidence of individual personality factors, the nature of supportive relationships available to the child or young person and his relative vulnerability or resilience at the time, as shaped by the influence of past history, which is most likely to inform the child's need for support.

- We should be not only providing what each child needs at the time, but anticipating what they might need in developing for themselves a coherent story of life events and circumstances at later stages of development. This can be invaluable in influencing parents' and carers' preparedness to identify and support the child's later needs for additional help.

Conclusion

It is hoped that this approach can rekindle some hope for workers in a profession where it can be hard to retain a sense of optimism about the potential for positive outcomes for some of the children encountered. As Werner (1990) states:

> The life stories of resilient individuals have taught us that competence, confidence and caring can flourish, even under adverse circumstances, if young children encounter persons who provide them with a secure basis for the development of trust, autonomy, and initiative. (p.113)

CHAPTER 2

Developing Relationships

Introduction

This chapter will set out the underpinning theoretical framework for the book. We will explore attachment theory and draw out issues of particular interest for all professionals working with children and their families.

Why attachment theory?

Originated by Bowlby (1969) and further developed by Ainsworth *et al.* (1978) this theoretical framework helps all practitioners to make sense of the development and behaviours of children and young people. These theorists developed a view that a close relationship with at least one responsive and reliable adult is vital for healthy development. The child learns about his emotions through repeated *reciprocal* interactions with a small number of care-givers. Through a process of sharing of emotion with his attachment figure/s the child learns how to recognise, understand and express his own feelings. The presence of a responsive care-giver helps the young child to *regulate* his feeling states so that he is not overwhelmed. Bowlby emphasises in his early work the child's experience of a warm, intimate and continuous relationship, rather than emphasising the fact that it must be the child's biological mother who offers this 'secure base'. He also stresses the importance of a relationship with a sensitive and attuned attachment figure as the key to the mental and developmental progress for the child in all domains. We shall explore attachment theory as a framework for understanding key influences upon a child's healthy development for a number of reasons, listed below.

- The experience of at least one 'good enough' attachment relationship is crucial for healthy development in all domains.

- Practice frameworks drawn from attachment theory are helpful in *assessing* interaction within close relationships and understanding the emotional exchange between important adults and the child.

- Careful, open-minded assessment can be used sensitively across cultures by practitioners who are alert to considering *which* adults are important to the child, rather than assuming that this is necessarily always the mother figure. This renders the theory relevant for a wide range of care-giving situations.

- Theoretical application of attachment theory includes the consideration of an important *network* of relationships important to the child, rather than assuming the centrality of one key figure.

- Attachment theory incorporates the notion of the child as *initiator* of interaction, as an active agent in their emotional lives.

- It helps professionals working with children to attune to different patterns of *response* and *initiatives* in children who develop survival strategies in circumstances of less than adequate care-giving.

- It helps the professional to identify the *impact* of particular styles of care-giving.

- It includes an awareness of the vital importance of the parent/carer's own attachment history in promoting security.

- It provides a useful model for moving from *assessment* of the child's attachment behaviours to the identification of appropriate *interventions* for building more secure attachments which offer a secure base to the child.

- It includes the consideration of the importance of sibling and peer attachment relationships throughout childhood.

- It emphasises the significance of early interaction with care-givers for the development of crucial areas in the child's brain which facilitate social understanding, both of the child's emotions and those of others.

- It provides a framework of analysis which can be used as a basis for building new attachments in kinship care or stranger placements.

- It helps to illustrate the driving forces behind offending and antisocial behaviours.

- It is closely linked with theories of resilience and attribution theory and can therefore be used both to identify and build upon existing strengths in the child and also to understand the child's *pattern of thinking* about himself and others, as well as understanding his *feelings*.

Attachment theory asserts that is there is a biological imperative for infants to form attachments and that they exhibit *attachment behaviours* in order to promote feelings of security. In this sense attachment behaviour can be viewed as *survival behaviour*. The theory relates the quality of such early attachment relationships to emotional functioning throughout life. That is, it asserts that the development of the self as a socio-emotional being is mediated through relationships with other people, which in turn are mediated through communication.

Attachment theory also relates language, cognitive and moral development to the quality of early attachment relationships. Therefore, an understanding of the theory of these developmental dimensions should provide a good basis for assessing the possible effects on the child's development of insecure attachment relationships. Identifying the child's style of attachment, most helpfully through *description* of their behaviours, is helpful to all professionals working either to enhance existing attachment relationships or to promote new relationships in alternative care-giving settings, whether in kinship or stranger placements.

Definition and functions of attachment relationships

Fahlberg (1994) quotes Kennell in her definition of attachments as 'an affectionate bond between two individuals that endures through space and time and serves to join them emotionally' (p.14). She emphasises that a healthy attachment relationship helps a child to:

- retain a full intellectual potential
- sort out what they perceive of the world
- think logically
- develop a conscience
- become self-reliant
- cope with stress and frustration
- handle fear, worry and anxiety
- develop future relationships
- reduce jealousy.

Healthy attachment relationships serve two fundamental purposes:

- to reduce anxiety in the child
- to promote healthy exploration and learning.

Insecure attachment relationships are linked with many interruptions and distortions in healthy development. Among the problems commonly identified resulting from insecure attachments can be difficulties with:

- the child's ability to regulate his own emotions
- healthy conscience development
- impulse control
- positive self-esteem
- social interactions with others
- cognitive skills such as understanding cause and effect
- trusting others
- the development of a whole range of different skills.

Key components of attachment theory

Humans appear to have a basic propensity to make intimate emotional bonds. Bowlby stresses a biological need to seek and maintain contact with others, an impulse to maintain closeness, and the need for a particular person if distressed. This process begins in infancy and continues throughout life. Bowlby drew on ethological theories which stress the importance of considering behaviours developed to adapt to a particular care-giving environment. The biological readiness to make these bonds in order to establish a sense of security is balanced with the need to explore the world. For the purposes of child protection the human environment of close relationships is crucial.

The attachment system

The goal of the child within close relationships, commonly referred to as the *attachment system*, is to feel safe, secure and protected. The child develops a repertoire of proximity-promoting attachment behaviours. These can include, in infancy, vocalising, crying, smiling and reaching out, for example. Attachment behaviour may gain the care-giver's attention in a positive way but aversive attachment behaviours, such as crying, serve also to bring the care-giver close to soothe the child. Practitioners are commonly involved in assessment of attachment behaviours as indicators of the degree to which the care-givers involved in the child's intimate care are able to offer the necessary responsiveness to promote a secure base for the child's healthy exploration of his environment.

The care-giving system

This system is represented by the care-giver's initiatives and responses to the child which shape the nature and quality of care. The attachment figure needs to be attuned to the child's signals and respond in an accurate and timely way. Therefore, the quality of care offered by attachment figures has a very significant part to play in the child's feelings of security. Crucial to the establishment of the secure relationship is the care-giver's capacity to attune to the child's signals, to think about the meaning of the child's behaviour and to respond in a way that will soothe the child and communicate messages about their availability at times of anxiety (see Figure 2.1).

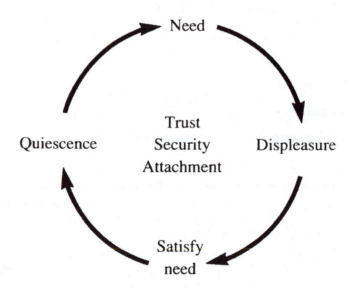

Figure 2.1 The 'arousal–relaxation cycle' (Fahlberg 1994), showing a successful interaction between a care-giver and child, as initiated by the child

The degree to which the care-giver is able to attune to the child's signals and to respond appropriately influences the primary level of security in the child. Also important for the formation of a secure attachment is the care-giver's ability to keep the child's needs consistently 'in mind' and to reach out to the child, promoting positive interactions and self-esteem (see Figure 2.2).

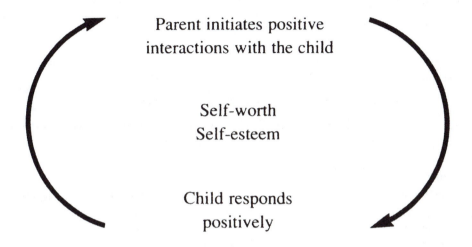

Figure 2.2 The 'positive interaction cycle' (Fahlberg 1994), showing a successful interaction between a care-giver and child, as initiated by the adult

Therefore, crucial in the promotion of secure attachment is the care-giver's capacity to think about the child's behaviour and to be able to consider and respond to the child's thoughts and feelings. Assessing attachment interactions is a key skill for all professionals involved in work with vulnerable children and their families. Observation of cycles of behaviour between the child and care-giver, attachment behaviours and care-giving initiatives and responses is helpful, not only in assessing the nature and level of the child's security within primary attachment relationships, but also in formulating work to protect the child from neglectful or abusive care-giving and to enhance relationship security within the existing or new attachment relationships.

The exploratory system
When the child feels secure with his care-givers, his energies can be freed to focus on exploration. An attuned care-giver will actively support exploration, being available as a secure base for the child should they become anxious (Schofield and Beek 2006).

Practice points
When assessing attachment relationships it can be helpful to consider the following questions:

- To what degree does the presence of the care-giver reduce the child's anxiety?

- Is the child preoccupied with the attachment figure or is he able to explore his environment in a healthy way?

Crucial here in a healthy attachment relationship is the observation of the balance between *attachment* behaviours and *exploratory* behaviours.

Activity 2.1

Consider the situation of children being looked after by foster carers or in residential settings.

- How might the above concepts be helpful in understanding some of the range of behaviours shown by such children?

- What messages for practice can be taken from the concepts?

Hints for answers

Children in care are likely to be living away from the person to whom they have their *primary attachment relationship*. If this is the case, every effort must be made to promote regular and meaningful contact. For a child with no primary attachment relationship intervention needs to be focused on helping him or her to develop one.

The most obvious manifestation of *proximity seeking* would be running home. Children who make frequent attempts to run home may need support in finding other ways to maintain proximity, perhaps by using a telephone. The level of contact would also need to be considered as it may be insufficient for the child.

The link between the presence of a *secure base* and active exploratory behaviour may explain why some children being looked after away from home are reluctant to take part in what are planned as fun activities. This would indicate that attention should be paid to the child's need for security.

Expressions of grief and anger are manifestations of *separation protest*. They need to be recognised as a natural part of attachment behaviour. See Chapter 4 for a detailed discussion of separation and grief.

The theory of *internal working models* suggests that children develop a template for relationships based on early attachment experiences. This pattern may then form the basis for their interactions with others. So, for example, children who are used to making aggressive demands in order to be noticed may transfer that behaviour to carers. This area will be discussed in detail in Chapter 8.

Young people may approach leaving care in different ways. Some may be determined to be totally independent in a way that suggests problems with *mature dependence*. Others may react with the opposite extreme of *immature dependence*. These patterns underline the crucial importance of early planning for a young person's transition to adulthood.

Recent developments in the neuro-biology of emotional development

Schore (1994) describes the way in which the experience of the relationship with the responsive care-giver not only provides the basis for emotional regulation but also the physical development of the brain. He emphasises the way in which the experience of attunement in the care-giver's responses and initiatives increases the development of the limbic system in the brain, promoting healthy socio-emotional development. It is through this experience that the very young child learns to understand about his own emotions and intentions and, gradually, the feelings of others.

The work of Perry (1995) illustrates the implications of poor early attachment experiences for healthy brain development. He describes the way in which the infant and young child's brain develops, the brain stem developing first, to be followed by the mid-brain, limbic system and cortex. He emphasises the way in which emotional reactivity, affiliation and attachment occur between the care-giver and the child, directly affecting the development of the child's mid-brain and limbic system.

When commenting on the child's experience of the lack of attunement, Hughes (1997) comments:

> the infant who experiences a lack of attunement perceives the pre-verbal self as being basically flawed, and thus he feels empty, helpless and hopeless. Without having the mirroring mother to regulate and integrate his emerging affective self, he is left a victim of his own poorly related impulses, affects and psychological-behavioural-biological state. (p.28)

Hughes emphasises the way in which experiences of maltreatment negatively affect healthy brain development for many abused or neglected children, negatively influencing their ability to regulate their emotions and to develop and sustain trusting relationships. These key ideas about the way in which maltreatment affects the development of healthy attachment relationships and other areas of development will be pursued in Chapter 6. He focuses not only on the emotional impact of trauma, but also on crucial effects on the child's capacity to *think* about their own experiences and to render them coherent. This approach is particularly helpful when supporting children with disorganised attachment styles in alternative placements. Further development of the therapeutic model can be found in Hughes (1997, 2009).

Selective attachment relationships are not necessarily dependent on physical care but rather upon the capacity of the care-giver to attune to the child's needs, offering sensitive responsiveness particularly at times of stress or threat. On the basis of early attachment experiences an *internal working model* develops which will act as a template, script or recipe for other relationships. Attachment behaviours continue through life and develop from immature dependence on care-givers to mature dependence on friends and partners.

The work of Howe *et al.* (1999), in particular, greatly enhances our understanding, not only of different styles or patterns of attachment behaviour in the child, but adds to our understanding of the link between the care-giver's attachment style and care-giving behaviour upon the child's internal working model of attachment (see Figure 2.3).

INSECURE ATTACHMENT PATTERNS

	Avoidant	Ambivalent	Disorganised
Carer provides child with:	• rejecting • inconsistent • indifferent • hostile • cold • conditional • controlling	• insensitive • chaotic • underinvolved • inconsistent • anxious • uncertain • not rejecting or hostile • unpredictably responsive	• frightening • frightened • helpless • abdicating responsibility • abuse/serious deprivation
Child's response:	Attempts to become independent and emotionally autonomous – to parent himself. • defended • emotions inhibited • self-sufficient • independent • inhibited emotions • anger and fear	Fearful he will not get what he needs so intensifies attachment behaviour. • clingy/whining • inhibited play and • exploration • dependent • combination of need and anger • watchful • coercive (?)	Irresolvable conflict of wanting to approach the attachment figure who is also the source of anxiety. • frozen • fear/compliance • fear/rage • controlling aggressive • attachment figure either frightening or frightened
Strategies child brings to new placement	• has learned not to ask for care-giver's help in times of need and distress • acts as if nothing is wrong when in distress	• acts with exaggerated need and anger when distressed • makes carer feel inadequate to soothe or meet the child's needs	• avoids being cared for – behaves as if carer is a source of potential neglect, danger or helpless need. • tries to remain in control bossy, angry, rageful, aggressive, seductive
Carer's response:	Carer may feel unwanted and back off, ignore the child or 'deactivate' their care-giving.	Carer may feel exasperated/exhausted. May react with threats of giving up on such a demanding relationship, which is emotionally charged but low on satisfaction.	Carer may feel helpless and angry, and in extreme cases may feel like abdicating role of care-giver.

Figure 2.3 Attachment patterns (adapted from Howe 1995)

This framework underlines the crucial importance of the care-giver's own early experience of attachment security and specifically the consideration of the degree to which the adult has *reflected* on these relationships as an important aspect of assessment and work. This draws from the work of Main (1991) and Crittenden (1995) and enhances our appreciation of the significance of the adult's own early experiences of attachment. This, in turn, helps the practitioner to identify particular circumstances in which a focus on therapeutic work for the adult in promoting a 'coherent story' of their own experiences may be necessary, alongside work on the adult–child relationship, in order to enhance attachment security for the child. See Chapter 3 for more detail on issues of adult attachment.

As can be seen from Figure 2.4, Howe, in his framework for the application of attachment theory, also emphasises the importance of the assessment of the nature and quality of care-giving offered to the child. This can be assessed either through naturalistic observation of aspects of care-giving or through deliberately structured opportunities, for example the provision of a meal or night-time settling routine.

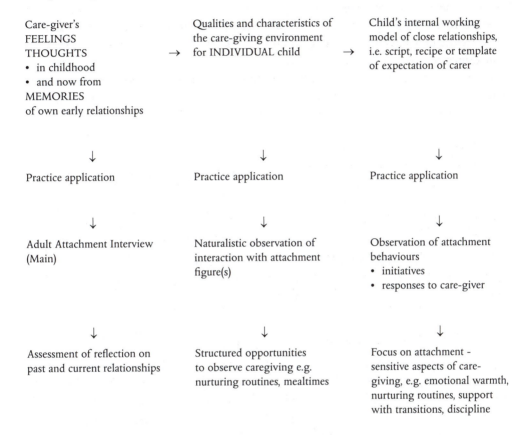

Care-giver's FEELINGS THOUGHTS • in childhood • and now from MEMORIES of own early relationships	→	Qualities and characteristics of the care-giving environment for INDIVIDUAL child	→	Child's internal working model of close relationships, i.e. script, recipe or template of expectation of carer
↓		↓		↓
Practice application		Practice application		Practice application
↓		↓		↓
Adult Attachment Interview (Main)		Naturalistic observation of interaction with attachment figure(s)		Observation of attachment behaviours • initiatives • responses to care-giver
↓		↓		↓
Assessment of reflection on past and current relationships		Structured opportunities to observe caregiving e.g. nurturing routines, mealtimes		Focus on attachment - sensitive aspects of care- giving, e.g. emotional warmth, nurturing routines, support with transitions, discipline

Figure 2.4 A framework for the application of attachment theory (adapted from Howe 1995)

Several key aspects of care-giving are particularly relevant for assessment:

- the nature and quality of nurturing routines
- the child's experiences of emotional warmth
- support for the child in transition
- comfort through separations and losses
- non-punitive management of discipline
- support for mastery and self-esteem
- comfort when the child is ill, hurt or sad.

Observation of parent–child interaction around these issues illustrates both the strengths and weaknesses within the child's experiences of care-giving and, from this base line assessment, work can be focused to enhance the child's attachment security. As can be seen from Figure 2.4 the nature of the parent's own early attachment experiences and the degree to which they have reflected upon them, and the nature and quality of the care-giving offered to the child, shape the experiences upon which the child will build a pattern or style of attachment behaviour in the context of a particular relationship, learned from their history of care-giving.

Much research based on attachment theory directly aims to further an understanding of the factors that contribute to difficulties in parent–child relationships. For example, the empirical work of Ainsworth, Bell and Stayton (1971) has been built upon significantly by Howe (1995) and others in exploring the significance of different care-giving environments, and notably the *quality* of predictable responsiveness to the child in influencing the child's attachment security.

Attachment styles

Ainsworth first identified different patterns or styles of attachment behaviour in infants which were indicative of either secure or insecure attachment. A strong association exists between the experience of secure attachment and healthy emotional development. An understanding of the theoretical and empirical connections between patterns or styles of attachment behaviour and healthy development helps professionals when assessing the quality of a child's relationships. The link with the aims of child protection and safe-guarding work here is clear, namely to protect children from situations where care-givers, who may often be the main attachment figures, cause harm to their children, either by commission or omission.

These patterns of attachment behaviour in the child correspond to the clarifications of adult attachment security (see Chapter 3). These behaviours reflect the internal working model, script, recipe or template of relationships and the child's 'survival' strategy in the context of the style of care-giving. For example, the securely attached child is able to rely upon consistent emotional warmth, non-punitive discipline and attuned responsiveness in circumstances of anxiety, separation or transition. Positive initiatives towards support of mastery and attainment also build self-esteem and self-efficacy.

It can be seen that experiences of attuned care-giving not only promote feelings of trust and a positive view of the care-giver, but also promote positive feelings of self-esteem and efficacy within the child. The secure child, therefore, not only expects adults to be supportive and responsive but also has a positive view of him- or herself. Many children, however, develop insecure attachment behaviours as a consequence of less responsive care-giving.

Ainsworth first identified insecure patterns of attachment behaviour through an experiment involving toddlers being observed with their mothers in a strange situation. This involved the child being observed with his mother, during brief separation from the mother, in the presence of a stranger and a reunion with his mother. She found that children's responses appeared to fall into different kinds which illustrated the style of attachment between adult and child.

While about two-thirds of the children showed behaviours consistent with secure attachments (also known as type B), others showed responses which indicated insecure attachment. She subdivided insecure attachments into type A, known as 'anxious avoidant', and type C, 'anxious resistant', also known as ambivalent. From further studies an additional pattern has been identified known as type D, 'disorganised/disoriented' attachment style. Notably, Ainsworth's early studies were carried out with mothers, as was most of the subsequent work on early attachment.

Secure attachment (type B)

Whereas those children identified as having secure attachment actively explored when their mothers were present, they were upset on her departure, ceasing exploration; they showed strong interest in interacting with her and establishing closeness to her when she returned. They clung to her in the presence of a stranger. Securely attached children were able to rely on their mother's behaviour which was positive, sensitive and encouraging of close physical contact.

Anxious avoidant insecure attachment (type A)

Toddlers demonstrating this style of attachment showed little distress on separation and avoided contact with their mother on return, some children ignoring her. They reacted to a stranger in the same way as the mother. Typically the mother's behaviour is described as relatively cold and at times angry and rejecting. Notably, in these relationships the child was rewarded by parental approval for independent self-caring behaviours, denying his need for comfort and reassurance. These children *reduced* their attachment behaviours.

Anxious, resistant or ambivalent insecure attachment (type C)

These toddlers were anxious before separation from their mother, very upset during separation and ambivalent during renewed contact, both seeking and resisting contact. Although the mother's behaviour appeared warm, she was less sensitive to the child's signals, commonly responding at inappropriate times. These children intensified their attachment behaviours in an attempt to retain the attachment figure's responses.

Disorganised, disoriented insecure attachment (type D)

These toddlers showed contradictory behaviour patterns, for example gazing away while being held, demonstrating resistance and avoidance and unusual expressions of negative emotion.

While the child with secure attachment can rely on the parent's availability and responsiveness, and feel safe to explore and play in the carer's presence (demonstrating a healthy balance between attachment behaviours and exploratory behaviours), children with insecure attachment behaviours demonstrate either a preoccupation with the adult's presence (type C) with reduced capacity to explore, or appear to have learned not to rely upon reliable responses, seeking to be independent (type A).

The behaviour of a child with a disorganised attachment style (type D) can be difficult to interpret yet commonly these children show a confusing combination of approach and avoidance behaviours in the presence of their attachment figure and may display one, or a combination, of the following behaviours:

- aggressive, controlling or coercive behaviour

- compulsive, compliant behaviour

- a pattern of compulsive care-giving.

It is important to consider ways in which the care-giving offered to the child may indicate that the care-giver is either *frightening* or *frightened*. As Schofield and Beek (2006) comment:

> it is always important to identify where fear may have played a part in the child's experience, since fear contributes to disorganisation and can produce particularly persistent difficulties in learning to trust. Fear may be as powerfully present in histories of neglect as in histories of abuse, but may yet be overlooked. (p.234)

When fear is considered as a component of the relationship, either as a result of the frightening behaviours of an abusive care-giver, or through demonstrations of helplessness, the child is left in a primitive state of anxiety, unable to rely on the attachment figure as the source of security. It is helpful for the practitioner to bear in mind the possibility that the attachment figure who is helpless or powerless, either through circumstances of domestic violence or indeed problems of mental illness or substance abuse, can be as anxiety-provoking to the child as the frightening parent who is unpredictably abusive and unavailable. Schofield and Beek (2006) encourage the practitioner to focus on collecting evidence from a range of sources when describing the child's capacity to explore and to use a selective attachment figure as a secure base.

These experiences of care-giving influence not only the child's view of their attachment figure, but also of themselves:

1. The child with a secure attachment style has positive feelings and expectations about him- or herself and others.

2. The child with an avoidant style feels unloved but self-reliant and has negative expectations of others.

3. The child with an ambivalent style negatively values him- or herself, experiencing others as potentially available but unreliable and unpredictable.

4. The child with a disorganised style has negative feelings about him- or herself and experiences others as both frightening and unavailable. (Adapted from Howe et al. 1999, p.25)

Whereas children with an insecure ambivalent style (type C) tend to develop a positive view of the attachment figure and a negative view of themselves, children with an insecure *avoidant* style (type A) develop a positive view of themselves and negative expectations of the attachment figure. These children have internalised a view of their attachment figure as relatively unresponsive, specifically at times of anxiety and distress, and, as a survival strategy, have developed a tendency to be self-reliant, to learn to contain their distress and not signal their emotional needs.

It is crucially important for the practitioner not to confuse insecure avoidant children with these learned responses with children who are genuinely healthily resilient. As noted by Schofield and Beek (2006):

> an insecure avoidant child who seems to bury himself in playing or activities may appear to be confident to explore, but does not acknowledge feelings or seek comfort. This child is unable to use the adult as a haven of safety and often plays in ways that would be less rich than secure children whose anxieties are allayed by available parenting. Such children may be seen as 'resilient', a common assessment error, or said to have no attachment. (p.324)

Rather than focusing on seeking to categorise the child's behaviour in a way which may not be helpful to colleague practitioners, they suggest 'the task then is to make sense of the evidence communicated in ways that other professionals can understand or that can help the care-givers make sense of what may be going on' (p.324). They emphasise that applying a label to the behaviour may be less helpful than describing the behaviour in detail and explaining how that strategy may have emerged in response to certain kinds of care-giving.

In particular, observing the child's attachment behaviour carefully when with his care-giver in circumstances when he feels particularly *anxious* can be especially helpful in clarifying the level and nature of security available to the children within the relationship. This child may be falsely identified as having a 'strong' attachment to his attachment figure when in fact the relationship is not providing a secure base for the child. The description of an attachment relationship as strong may imply the presence of a healthy attachment when this may be far from the case.

Downes (1992) describes an additional type or style of attachment that is not quite the same as those described above. In this type, the child has an anxious *preoccupation* with the availability of the carer. This is clearly an insecure type of attachment with anxiety as a crucial element and careful observation of the child who appears to be persistently preoccupied with the availability of his carer, with little exploratory behaviour, may indicate that, far from it being a strong attachment, the child is less than secure.

Schofield and Beek (2006) emphasise the greater importance in assessment of distinguishing between organised and disorganised attachment styles. It is crucially important for practitioners in their observations to identify the child who is so negatively affected by the care-giving environment that he is unable to find an organised strategy of response. Their behaviour may appear both confused and confusing as they may be forced to rely upon a care-giver who is either frightening or helpless and thus unable to offer comfort and security. It is poignant that the child with a disorganised style of attachment (type D) will have both a negative view of themselves and a mistrustful view of others. Once again, careful observation of the child's attachment behaviours with their care-givers can help in the identification of children who are most severely compromised by poor quality care-giving which is either neglectful or abusive.

Although assessment of the security of the child's relationship with different attachment figures is a crucial starting point, it is necessary to use careful observations of interaction to inform:

- the level of risk to the child

- the child's fundamental unmet needs in the relationship

- a move beyond assessment to focused work, either on

  ○ enhancing the current relationships available to the child *or*

  ○ identification of strategies focused upon increasing the child's ability to turn towards subsequent carers.

Activity 2.2

Observe the interaction between a parent or significant carer and a child of any age.

1. Describe the child's initiatives towards the adult and the child's responses to the adult's initiatives.

2. Describe the adult's initiatives towards the child and the adult's responses to the child's signals.

3. What might this tell you about the degree to which the child has learned to rely on the attachment figure?

It is helpful for the practitioner to remember that the child is likely to have available to him or her a network of attachment relationships and careful observation can illustrate the strengths and security offered to the child through each relationship. We may find, for example, that a child has a relatively secure attachment to a member of the extended family, rather than a parent figure. This can be protective of healthy development and is an important consideration when assessing the strength of family resources available to the child at home.

It may be, for example, that the child is most securely attached to an older sibling, rather than a parent figure. While it is not reasonable to expect another child, however attuned and responsive, to meet the primary attachment needs of a younger sibling, the warmth in the relationship may well have protective elements for the child's later recovery. Nevertheless, the child's need for a sense of primary security in a relationship with a reliable, responsive and attuned adult is of primary significance. A strong and nurturing relationship with a sibling will be important in considerations of care planning.

Assessment of sibling attachments

Sibling relationships have long been known to have great significance, not only for early development, but also through to later adult life. Dunn (1993) emphasises the importance of close relationships between children and highlights the significance of dimensions of these relationships other than primary security, for example warmth, shared humour and connectedness.

Practitioners are often called upon to structure assessments for the strength and nature of attachments between siblings and a useful framework is offered by Lord and Borthwick (2001). Of particular value is the Sibling Relationship Checklist which explores the detail of dimensions of behaviours between pairs of siblings (Department of Health 1991). This framework encourages close observation and analysis of many dimensions of the sibling relationship, denoting one sibling as child A and the other as child B. First, the worker or carer is encouraged to consider the initiatives and responses of child A towards child B (and then *vice versa*) in relation to key attachment behaviours. These behaviours include:

- expressions of warmth and affection
- empathic behaviour towards the sibling
- shared rituals/routines of play
- signs of attunement
- aggression or competition
- many other aspects of the relationship.

This is a well-tested framework which can act as a lens through which the initiatives and responses of each child towards the other can be analysed. The framework invites not only consideration of the fundamental features of interaction, but also elicits particular examples of such behaviours, and their observed frequency. Crucially the framework identifies not only positive aspects of interaction, but also dimensions such as the nature and degree of rivalrous behaviour, and can elicit descriptions of behaviours which are persistently dominating or even abusive.

It is helpful that the framework invites an analysis of circumstances in which, for example, one child is so competitive with the other that they both interfere with the nurturing of their siblings and, in consequence, fail to signal their own needs clearly, focusing the carer's attention on the rivalrous antagonistic behaviours.

While it is an important practice, in principle, to keep siblings together in the same care-giving environment wherever possible, there are some circumstances in which warm and close sibling relationships have not been developed, for example because of intense competition for the care-giver's attention in neglectful circumstances. Whereas siblings may have acted as a comfort to one another in circumstances of adversity, in specific cases we may identify patterns of domination and/or abuse which need to be considered in the formulation of a safe care-giving plan for each child.

Careful assessment may identify the relationships which illustrate the negative effects of poor quality care-giving on the sibling relationship. These assessments are vital both for

- structuring effective protective work for individual children who may have been abused or neglected, and

- identifying reparative work focused on the sibling relationship to alleviate the negative effects of unhelpful dynamics inherited from life at home.

It may be helpful to consider the following framework when assessing sibling relationships and their implications for work and care-planning:

- to reflect first on the clarification of the unmet needs of each child

- to assess carefully the nature and strength of attachments within each sibling pairing

- to consider the dynamics within the larger sibling group

- to consider the wishes and feelings of each child.

The child's temperament

A further key influence in the development of attachment is the individual temperament of the child; for example, Chess and Thompson (1977) identify three types of temperament:

- an *easy* child usually seems happy, readily establishes routines, but can also adapt to new experiences

- a *difficult* child cries a lot, will not settle to a routine and does not adapt well to changes

- a *slow to warm up* child is more passive, negative and less adaptable than the easy child.

Notably, a mismatch of temperament between the carer and the child can be a source of some enduring difficulties. It is possible to recognise problems in parent–child relationships which can be pinpointed to such lack of fit. Sometimes simply using this form of analysis can help when assessing attachment problems that may have developed from very early on. It can also help explain why a parent may have difficulties in their relationship with one of their children, but not another. This issue is returned to again in Chapters 3 and 6.

Endurance of attachment patterns

There is evidence that a pattern of attachment established during childhood can be enduring and may eventually become a feature of the way the child, young person or adult interacts with other people. In other words, the internal working model which develops as a result of early interactions influences later relationships. For example, the quality of the care-giver's behaviour at six months predicts attachment behaviour at three years, even towards another sibling. Children presenting a secure attachment relationship are less likely to show high dependency on the carer in social interactions with other children at four to five years. Those with insecure patterns are more likely to show less positive attitudes with peers and increased behavioural and social difficulties (Sroufe and Fleeson 1988). There is debate about the extent to which internal models are open to change as a result of later experience. However, the potential for change through therapeutic insight, for example, reflected in the approach of Hughes (2009) for supporting children who have experienced emotional trauma, is based on the belief that different experiences of relationships of a more secure nature provide an avenue for intervention.

Some hazards of uncritical use of attachment theory

Attachment theory has been the subject of extensive theoretical exploration and multi-cultural empirical research. This has enhanced understanding of the importance of multiple attachments for children's development, as well as the extent to which children's emotional needs can be met within different family structures. However, despite these refinements, ideas based on popular misconceptions of attachment theory can and have been used in a way that is oppressive of different cultures and of women.

Bowlby's work has been most influential in the development of attachment theory (Bowlby 1969), and it was his original emphasis on the role of the mother as the primary attachment figure that has been used by those who hold the maternal relationship responsible for all aspects of the child's development. Despite Rutter's influential critique of the influence of maternal deprivation (Rutter 1981) which asserts that the quality of the attachment relationship is more important for the child's healthy development than the need for the mother to be the primary attachment figure, this ideology still pervades much child development research. It is still frequently mothers who bear the brunt of social work intervention and, as Swift (1995) points out in a study of child neglect, 'in both popular and professional understanding, the mother's quality of attachment and, by implication, her quality of care are connected to her child's development all through life' (p.97).

Similarly, attachment theory can be linked with an assumption that the traditional 'nuclear family' provides a superior child-rearing environment. This in turn can devalue cultural and ethnic variety in family structure, despite the evidence that children can develop successfully in many different family structures. The political and majority emphasis continues to be on a Western model of the nuclear family which is not the experience of many children – for example, many children are cared for by extended family members who are part of their attachment network, relying on them to meet their basic needs alongside parent figures (Gambe *et al.* 1992).

Describing the importance of early close relationships is not the equivalent of prescribing the nature of family structure. Although young children can be seen to possess universal needs for nurturing, these can be met in many different ways (Devore and Schlessinger 1987). One study found that children of six different cultures demonstrate the same universal characteristics of dependence, but that the length of time they remain dependent varied according to culture, as did the extent to which those other than the mother met some of their dependency needs (Whiting and Edwards 1988).

In summary, practitioners need to be respectful and sensitive towards varied patterns of care-giving influenced by the cultural norms within different communities. The key consideration is the assesment of whether or not basic needs are reliably met.

The aim of the book, therefore, is to draw ideas from child development research as relevant for practice in such a way as to retain the important element of attachment theory for understanding the development of individual children, without reinforcing the emphasis on the exclusive role of mothers or upon the 'traditional' nuclear family. The book emphasises the approach of Garbarino (1980) in asserting that when assessing the emotional development of children the starting point must be the *child's experience* of adult behaviour.

Social network theory and the ecological approach

Assessment must explore the layers of influence upon the developing child. While attachment theory can be used as the basis for understanding individual development, emphasis must also be given to the resources in the environment within which relationships are established. By the same token, it is essential to explore the extent to which close attachment relationships and high quality care-giving can mediate the impact and influence of the wider environment on children.

> The framework for the assessment of a child's protective environment will need to acknowledge the part played by the state and society in general, the part played by the community within which the child (or children) live and the part played by the individual family in mediating access to formal and informal resources and support for both child and carer. (Boushel 1994, p.179)

The ecological approach emphasises the need to take account of the child's attachment network in assessment. For each child there may be a large number of possibilities for development of healthy attachment relationships. The nature of attachment may differ with different adults. It is also helpful to consider the nature of the child's relationships with peers and siblings, commonly referred to as the *affiliatory system*. We need to consider the child's affiliatory system in parallel with his attachment behaviour and care-giver's responses. Lewis argues that children demonstrate a dual system of needs for both peers and adults from the beginning of life (1994). It may be more helpful to see peer (and sibling) relationships as developing in parallel with parent relationships, not simply building on a primary relationship.

Social network theory enables a broader perspective to be taken on a child's human environment. Historically it has not always been assumed that mothers should provide full-time care, and women have often been economic providers as well as parents. Historical and cross-cultural research shows that infant rearing has always been shared with other adults and often with other children (Goldsmith 1990; Scarr 1990). Research shows no differences in rates of secure attachment to mothers between infants in full-time day care and those at home. The crucial consideration is that positive secure attachment is facilitated by attentive, responsive care-giving, whether by mothers or others (Scarr 1990). Work on fathers' roles has also demonstrated that fathers can have a direct influence on development. One study reported that children brought up in families where fathers stayed at home and took the principal caring role demonstrated secure attachment behaviours in relation to their fathers (Geiger 1996). This is supported by Dunn's extensive work on the child's relationships with those other than the parents, and especially relationships with siblings, describing how even very young children have a sophisticated social understanding and awareness and are sensitive to other people's moods (Dunn 1993).

An ecological approach requires that the child never be assessed in isolation and as such is consistent with an ecological view of child development as advanced by Bronfenbrenner (1989). This approach recognises that children do not grow up in a vacuum. Instead, each child can be seen to be in the centre of a number of concentric circles (see Figure 2.5). Immediately surrounding the child are *microsystems* which comprise family, or alternative family, and others with whom the child has most immediate, direct contact. Attachment networks as described above are examples of microsystems.

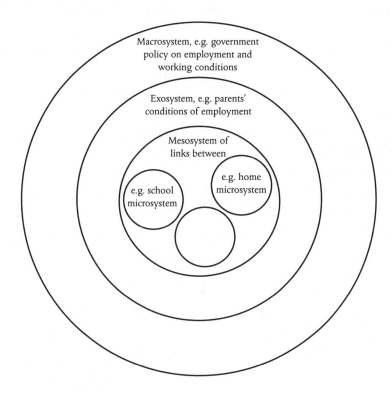

Figure 2.5 Bronfenbrenner's (1989) ecological framework (from Smith and Cowie 1991)

In turn the microsystems are embedded within *exosystems* which have a direct influence upon the child. Examples of exosystems would be the parent's work place or parent's friendships. The *macrosystem,* which has influence over exosystems and microsystems, comprises the wider political and cultural context. The economic situation, type of housing, ethnicity and so on would all be part of the macrosystem.

All these layers of influence help to shape the child's development, directly and indirectly. Ethnically sensitive practice is entirely consistent with an ecological approach that strives to improve the extent to which the material and social environment meets a person's individual needs (Devore and Schlessinger 1987). As emphasised in a code of practice considering issues of race and child protection

> ethnicity is a concept which belongs to everyone. All practice should be seen in the context of class, race and gender, which in combination will show the uniqueness of all experience. Ethnically sensitive practice is not a 'sideline' or an addendum – it needs to permeate practice at all times and at all levels. (Baldwin, Johansen and Seale 1989/90, p.19)

The ecological approach to child development suggests that detailed assessment of all aspects of a young person's situation, which includes consideration of all levels, including the wider impact of adversity such as racism and material resources, is essential to the planning of intervention with children and young people. This assessment must begin with the young person and their past and current experience. A useful focus is upon an analysis of the *impact and meaning* of life events, relationships and circumstances upon the individual child.

Activity 2.3

1. Consider a child on your caseload.
2. Using the social network approach, map out each important relationship the child has. If helpful, use the ecomap provided (Figure 2.6).
3. Note what needs of the child are being satisfied by these different relationships.
4. Consider the implications for the child and adult when only one person is available to meet all the child's needs.

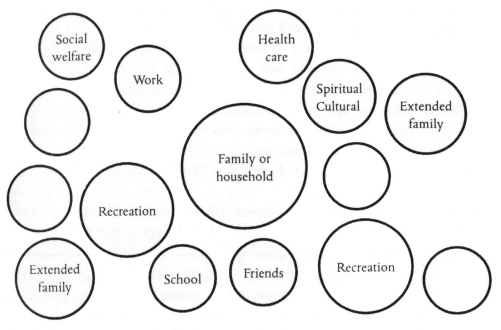

Fill in connections where they exist. Indicate nature of connections with a descriptive word or by drawing different kinds of lines: ———— for strong, -------- for tenuous, ++++++ for stressful. Draw arrows along lines to signify flow of energy, resources etc. → →
Identify significant people and fill in the empty circles as needed.

Figure 2.6 The ecomap can be a useful tool for mapping out the important relationships in a child's life (Hartman 1984)

Summary

This chapter sets out the reasons for using attachment theory as an underpinning theoretical approach. This does not mean that other theoretical approaches do not have much to offer to practice. However, the contention of this book is that the majority of children encountered by practitioners working in child protection/safeguarding and child care have difficulties which can be attributed to attachment issues. Many children have encountered troubled, insecure relationships with their main carers and many have experienced loss of important people.

Moreover, attachment theory can offer insight to guide intervention. For children who need to be looked after away from home, attachment theory can help us to understand both the impact of separation from important people and the processes involved in making new relationships. There is no substitute within effective multi-agency practice for the detailed observation and careful analysis of the child's attachment relationships and their impact on all domains of development. In turn, the influence of each ecological layer around the child should be considered. This analysis can then be used as a basis for effective intervention, in structured interventions to enhance existing attachment relationships or by the necessary removal of the child from situations in which he or she is experiencing significant harm. For those children who cannot remain at home or return, the analysis can also guide interventions in offering the child reparative attachment experiences.

Key messages

- A healthy attachment with at least one reliable and responsive adult is crucial for many aspects of healthy development for children and young people.

- Children may establish a network of attachment relationships which may differ both in style and levels of security offered to the child.

- Healthy attachment is characterised by a balance between attachment and exploratory behaviour.

- The assessment of attachment behaviours is revealing of the security of the particular relationship.

- Healthy attachment is promoted by secure care-givers who are 'mind minded' or, in other words, able to attune to the child's feelings, thoughts and needs and to offer sensitive responsiveness.

- This helps children not only to begin to understand their own emotions and thoughts but also to develop an awareness of the feelings of others, thereby promoting both healthy emotional and social development.

- Experiences of abuse or neglect are strongly linked with insecure attachment behaviours.

- Careful analysis is needed to assess accurately the *impact* of the style of care-giving on individual children.

- Crucially, experiences of abuse and neglect have negative effects not only on emotional security but also on neuro-biological development of the brain, particularly in very young children during the first two years of life.

- Negative effects can be seen, however, not only in the early years and in early developmental progress, but also in later development.

- These experiences of maltreatment interfere with the child's ability to regulate emotion and they have many other negative effects on other domains of development, particularly social, moral and cognitive development.

- It is more helpful for the practitioner, from careful observation, to *describe* rather than merely attempt to categorise the child's behaviours in order to illustrate clearly the child's unique adaptation to their particular history of care-giving.

- While it is helpful for assessment to focus upon elements of insecurity within the child's primary attachment relationships, of more particular relevance, particularly for reparative care, is whether or not the child has an *organised* or *disorganised* style of attachment response.

- Children with insecure relationships may often appear to be preoccupied with their attachment figure, heightening their attachment behaviours; however, it is vital that, if the relationship does not offer primary security to the child, it is not described as 'strong'.

- Resilient children are most appropriately described as those who have been able to rely on at least one adult to respond to their needs, equipping them to ask for help and support when needy or anxious, rather than learning to be unhealthily self-reliant and pseudo-independent.

- Understanding the child's *internal working model* can help in developing strategies for repairing existing attachments and/or in selecting and supporting placements in kinship, fostering or adoptive care.

- It is helpful for practitioners from all disciplines to be aware of abusive or neglectful patterns of care-giving which can produce disorganised behaviours as these children are among the most vulnerable.

- It is important also for all practitioners to attend to the impact of maltreatment on the child, especially responses of either:
  ○ a tendency towards hyper-arousal and vigilance *or*
  ○ dissociation.

- Therapeutic efforts can helpfully be focused on:
  ○ helping children to learn to understand and regulate their own emotions through experiences of attunement with an alternative attachment figure and/ or therapist, and
  ○ helping children to make sense of their thoughts about their experiences, in other words to develop a coherent narrative of their lives and experiences.

- It is important to remember that even very young children are often active agents in their own relationships and that their individual temperamental style acts as a powerful influence within their primary attachment relationships, particularly when there is a 'lack of fit' with their parents' care-giving style.

- Efforts to enhance the security of the child's attachment relationships can usefully be focused on deliberate strategies to meet the child's unmet needs, particularly his emotional needs.

- Sibling relationships and those with peers (affiliative relationships) are of great importance in healthy child development and careful assessment of the dynamics of individual sibling pairs should be a focus of effective assessment.

- Care should be taken by professionals to avoid unhelpful cultural bias in their assessment of families from different ethnic groups and to avoid sexist approaches to families of different constellations, for example same-sex parents.

- Fathers have much to offer children in their contribution to care-giving, to daughters as well as sons.

- Whatever the care setting, and whoever the parenting figures, it is the *quality* of care which is important, rather than the identity of the care-giver.

- Even in circumstances of highly compromised care-giving, new therapeutic approaches based on an understanding of attachment theory can offer hope to practitioners in structuring opportunities for either enhancing existing attachments or for offering reparative care-giving in other settings.

CHAPTER 3

Parenting and Care-giving

Introduction

In this chapter we will set out research about different styles of parenting, outline what children need from care-givers, and offer frameworks for assessment and intervention. The chapter will also contain a consideration of different aspects of support for parenting and explore current material about what kind of care-giving support is most helpful. There will also be a consideration of key components of the process of change in parents and care-givers towards care-giving which meets the child's needs and provides greater security.

We shall also consider some of the insights which can be drawn from attachment theory into the significance of the care-giver's own childhood experience of attachment for the quality of care-giving they offer to individual children. This chapter is linked directly with the previous chapter (see Figure 2.4).

Parenting and care-giving

Parenting is a complex and diverse process and has far-reaching implications. Although the links are complex, research has established associations between childhood experiences and adult health and well-being, with evidence to suggest that much adult distress can be traced to adversity in childhood (e.g. Rutter and Rutter 1993). It is important to stress that 'parenting' need not necessarily be carried out by biological parents. When considered from the point of view of the child, the important issue is not *who* carries out the parenting, but the *nature and quality of care* received.

As suggested in the previous chapter, there is a potential for attachment theory to be used to support assumptions that the nurturing of children should be carried out by the mother. In fact, a considerable amount of the parenting literature makes an implicit or explicit assumption that parenting is carried out by the mother. For example, in a study of health visitor and social work intervention, Edwards (1998) found that, although male figures were often present in the home, they were not included in the discussions about the children. The focus of work was the mother, and both parents were given the subtle message that parenting was in fact mothering. This assumption is perhaps most evident in practice with neglect. Because referrals for physical neglect are often centred upon issues of nurture, this is often equated with mothering and it is mothers who are labelled 'neglectful' (Swift 1995).

Practitioners will meet children who are cared for in families of many different constellations. For example, more children may be cared for by lone fathers than in the past. Daniel and Taylor (2001) include contributions from practitioners working with fathers in different settings and consider the very positive influence of fathering at different stages of development. Lamb (2004) offers recent findings and reflections on the role of fathers in child development.

Recent research into outcomes for children growing up in lesbian and gay households considers developmental impacts, longer-term outcomes, family relationships, mental health, peer relationships and psycho-sexual development (Patterson 2005; Tasker 1999; Tasker and Golombok 1997). The findings suggest that it is not the sexuality of care-givers which is the most significant variable but rather the quality of relationships offered to the child. 'It is what happens within a family, not the way families are composed, that seems to matter most' (Golombok 2000, p.101).

The message for practice is that the child's needs must be held as the central focus, whoever is undertaking the care-giving tasks. No assumption should be made about who is, or who should be, the main carer. It may be, for example, that one person takes the primary responsibility for the care of the child, but the tasks are shared. It may be that the mother is the main carer, but equally it could be a father or member of the extended family. An open-minded attitude is essential when looking for alternative carers for children whose biological parents are unable to care for them. Practice must be respectful of different cultural traditions of care-giving.

The role of the parent or care-giver

Even though children's needs can be met by several people, comprising the attachment network, there are aspects of parenting that have been shown to be more helpful than others in supporting the development of the child's potential. We shall consider the role of the care-giver in meeting three fundamental needs of every child.

The provision of a secure base

The previous chapter stressed the importance of a secure base of at least one 'good enough' attachment relationship in order to support healthy child development in all domains. It is through the adult–child relationship that parents provide this secure base, which, according to Dowling (1993), should include:

> an understanding of the child's wish for proximity, attention and responsiveness, not as naughty, demanding or unreasonable, but as a developmental expression or his or her need. The more this need is rejected, or unmet, the more the demand will increase, and eventually it will be expressed in the form of symptoms...

> [and]...a recognition [that] the commonest source of children's anger is the frustration of their desire for love and care and their anxiety commonly reflects the uncertainty as to whether parents will continue to be available. (p.406)

A coherent story

The child also needs a coherent story about early attachment experiences in order to feel secure. This story should be able to incorporate both positive and negative experiences and helps the child to integrate his or her *feelings* about their experiences with their *thoughts*. This process, supported by the care-giver, can help the child to deal with all kinds of adversities, for example traumatic sudden losses, within an attuned, supportive process of developing a narrative which makes sense to the child.

Predictability of care

A fundamental need for children of all ages is predictability of care as uncertainty about the secure base is powerfully undermining of a fundamental sense of security. Having addressed issues linked with a secure base in the previous chapter, focusing in particular on the internal working model formed within the child as a result of her experiences of care-giving, when considering influences upon care-giving, it is helpful to reflect upon the adult's own early attachment history.

The links here with attribution theory become clear as we consider that, as human beings, with a need to make sense of our experiences, we not only have *feeling* responses to what occurs in our lives, but also develop a pattern of *thinking*. It is helpful to consider, not only the impact of early attachment experiences of the parent or care-giver themselves, but also patterns of thinking or attribution drawn from these experiences which can have a bearing upon the quality of care-giving offered to a particular child.

The care-giver's experience of early attachment

Since the original work of Main and Goldwyn (1984) who developed the Adult Attachment Interview, there has been increasing interest in the association between the inter-generational links between the security of the parent's childhood experience of attachment and the security which they are able to offer to their own child as a care-giver. The Adult Attachment Interview is an hour-long semi-structured interview which explores parents' descriptions of their own early attachment relationships in childhood, exploring memories which either support or contradict the descriptions of past and current relationships with parent figures and with their own children. The focus is on three key areas:

- experiences of loss, separation and rejection
- experiences of emotional upsets, hurts and sickness
- experiences of love and acceptance with each care-giver.

This protocol was developed to assess the way in which adults organise attachment-related thoughts, feelings and memories. The assessment of the interview *discourse* or narrative depends less on the precise *content* of what is said, but more on the way in which the story is told and whether it is coherent, or otherwise. Those adults who have not yet reflected upon their childhood history and made sense of their feelings associated with early insecure attachment experiences are more likely to remain insecure in their attachment status, increasing the likelihood of their children also having insecure attachments.

The adult classification for attachment security generally corresponds to insecure childhood patterns, although they may not necessarily be continuously linked (see Figure 3.1).

	Secure – Autonomous	Avoidant – Dismissing	Ambivalent – Preoccupied Entangled	Disorganised – Unresolved
Infancy	Secure	Insecure avoidant	Insecure ambivalent – Resistant	Insecure Disorganised Disoriented
Toddlerhood – Preschool – School age	Secure optimal	Defended – Disengaged	Dependent – Deprived Coercive	Controlling Confused
Adolescence – Adulthood	Autonomous – Free to evaluate	Dismissing	Preoccupied – Entangled Enmeshed	Unresolved Loss/Trauma Disorganised
Parenting style	Secure base	Rejecting	Uncertain	Helpless

Figure 3.1 Attachment behaviours and patterns across the lifespan (adapted from Howe et al. 1999)

Later experiences of more positive attachments in later childhood or adulthood, particularly those which offer an opportunity for reflection, can provide a chance for adults to develop a coherent story of their early lives, and for them to offer more secure attachment for their children than they themselves received in childhood. These adults may be described as having an 'earned secure' style (style B).

In summary, adults with a B style offer a coherent narrative or story and can represent and tell the story, including feelings, and integrate new experiences into their story. Adults with a C style tell stories which are over-elaborate, enmeshed and overwhelmed by experience. Adults with an A style tell stories which cling to rules and rigidity and emphasise cognition, rather than emotion, and finally adults with a disorganised style present a very confusing account which lacks coherence.

There are clear implications for practice in the quality of the account of childhood presented to the worker, from whatever discipline. The sensitive practitioner can gain much useful information about the potential for parents with different styles of attachment to offer secure parenting to their child from paying close attention to the way in which they present the story of their own history in attachment terms.

This has implications for interventions with parents with many unresolved issues from the past as can become clear from their account of their history, who may be less likely than others to benefit merely from parenting skills training. In particular, those parents who clearly live with acute unresolved traumas from their own history may well need an opportunity for guided reflection within a therapeutic relationship in relation to their own early unaddressed traumas, either prior to, or in parallel with, work to address their parenting skills. The worker's attunement to the nature and quality of the adult's account of their childhood can combine usefully with the assessment of the nature and quality of the care-giving offered to an individual child to give pointers to necessary interventions required to offer safety and security to individual children.

Assessing the quality of care-giving

When assessing child–parent/care-giver interactions the following questions may be helpful:

- Does the parent respond to the child's signals of need? If so, how appropriate, timely and predictable are their responses?

- Does the parent reach out to the child? If so, how constructive, attuned and supportive are these initiatives?

Alongside holding these questions in mind, Howe *et al.* (1999) quote Ainsworth *et al.* (1971) in exploring four dimensions of parenting which can be useful for assessment of parent/care-giver–child interaction. The labels for these dimensions need to be used with caution and should not automatically be used to imply deliberate action. Rather, they describe patterns of interaction.

Sensitivity versus insensitivity

Some parents are able to recognise their children's needs and respond in a timely and appropriate manner. 'Insensitive' parents, by contrast, fail to read their child's signals, being focused more on their own thoughts and feelings, needs and wishes.

Acceptance versus rejection

'Accepting' parents recognise the legitimate developmental demands of their children, notably being able to accept expressions of anger in their children; 'rejecting' parents more often resent the demands that their children make upon them, particularly emotional demands. Their children's dependency may arouse anxiety and distress, leading to expressions of rejection, anger or lack of affection.

Cooperation versus interference

While some parents are able to acknowledge and support their child's need for autonomy, promoting a cooperative relationship (which in turn results in experiences of mastery for their child), other parents are unable to take such cooperative approaches, behaving in a more controlling and interfering manner, in ways which can be abrupt, impatient or even aggressive.

Accessibility versus ignoring

While some parents remain emotionally available to their children and alert to their needs, others are preoccupied and absorbed in their own concerns and may fail to notice their child's signals of need and are less likely to promote secure attachment. The dimensions of sensitivity, acceptance, cooperation and accessibility are closely linked with secure attachment. By contrast, the more negative indicators of insensitive, rejecting, interfering or ignoring behaviour are linked with different types of insecure attachment (Howe *et al.* 1999).

The influence of particular parenting styles

Baumrind (1972) identified four parenting styles which may be summarised as follows:

- *Authoritative parenting* is warm but firm. It sets standards for behaviour but within the capabilities of the child and matches his or her level of development. Autonomy is valued, but responsibility is taken for the child's behaviour. Discipline is rational, with discussion and appropriate explanation. Such parenting has been shown to be associated with children who display more psycho-social competence and who are warm, affectionate, altruistic, responsible, self-assured, creative, curious, successful in school and more likely to have more positive self-esteem.

- *Authoritarian parenting* establishes obedience and conformity. Discipline is punitive and absolute, without discussion. The child is expected to accept rules without question. Independence is not encouraged and their development as an individual is not supported. This approach is associated with children who are more dependent, passive, less socially adept, less self-assured and less intellectually curious.

- *Indulgent parenting* is accepting of most behaviour. Discipline is passive and there are few demands placed on the child. Control is seen as an infringement of the child's right to freedom. It is associated with children who are less mature, more irresponsible, conforming to peers and lacking in leadership.

- *Indifferent parenting* in its extreme is neglectful. Life and discipline are centred on adult needs. The child's interests are not considered and her opinion is not sought. The child's activities are not routinely supervised. It is associated with children who are impulsive and who show delinquent behaviour.

Authoritative parenting is generally accepted to be the most helpful to the development of a child's potential and may be identified through careful observation of care-giving behaviours.

Framework for assessment

Reder and Lucey (1995) have outlined a very helpful framework for the assessment of parenting, adapted below.

Parent's relationship to the role of parenting

- What is the parent's knowledge and attitude towards child-rearing?

- Do they provide basic essential physical care?

- Do they provide age-appropriate emotional care?

- Do they encourage secure attachment through responsive, sensitive responses and initiatives?

- Do they accept responsibility for parenting behaviour?
- Do they accept responsibility for protectiveness?
- Do they acknowledge problems and accept the need for change in parenting behaviour?
- Do they acknowledge the impact of their own behaviour on the child?

Parent's relationship to the child

- Do they view the child as a separate person?
- What are the feelings of the parent towards the child?
- Do they have empathy for the child's predicament?
- Are the child's essential needs given primacy over the parent's desires?

Family influences

- What is the parent's awareness and attitude towards their own parenting experiences in childhood?
- Do they have a supportive (non-dependent) relationship with their partner?
- What is the child's involvement, if any, in the family's discordant relationships?
- How sensitive are the parents to relationship stresses?
- What is the meaning of the child to the parents?
- What is the child's contribution to parenting?
- What is the child's attitude to the care-takers?

Interaction with the external world

- What is the nature and range of the parent's support network?
- How would you describe their relationships in the past and at present with professionals?

Potential for change

- Do they acknowledge the problems?
- Do they have concern for the child?
- Do they accept responsibility for their contribution?
- Do they recognise the need for outside help?
- Do they wish for things to be different?
- Do they have an ability to view others as potentially helpful?
- What have been their previous responses to being helped?

- What have been their responses to previous interventions? (Adapted from Reder and Lucey 1995, pp.8–13).

This framework is not only useful as a basis for reflection by the individual practitioner engaged with a family, but can also provide a useful structure for collecting observations and information from professionals involved on an inter-agency basis in crucial assessment work.

Helpful aspects of parenting

While consideration of the care-giver's parenting style is clearly relevant, it is not sufficient to consider the parent's behaviour alone when judging parental impact, as it is the child's *experience* of the parental behaviour that will affect their emotional development (Garbarino 1980). The influence of temperamental variations between children is relevant here and it would be over-simplistic to be too prescriptive about parenting. The key factor is the importance of the nature of the *fit* between the child's needs and the parental response.

However, Cooper (1985) suggests that all children, from all cultures, require:

- basic physical care

- affection including physical and emotional intimacy

- security which includes consistency of routines, stability and continuity of care

- the stimulation of innate potential to encouragement and praise

- guidance and control

- age-appropriate responsibility

- age-appropriate independence to make their own decisions, tailored to the child's ability and understanding of the consequences of such decisions.

Parenting at different stages of development
Infancy

Attachment theory stresses the centrality of the nature of communication between the carer and the child as a basis for trust, security and positive attachment of the child. Although Trevarthen and Aitken (2001) emphasise the role of the baby as an active partner in communication and interaction, in infancy the meshing of communication is principally under adult control. In summary, infants require carers who offer:

- attuned responsiveness

- attentiveness

- emotional warmth

- stimulation towards exploration

- a capacity to understand the child's feelings, demonstrated in a 'mind minded' attitude.

These issues are explored further in Chapter 6.

School age

During the school years, children's lives expand socially, emotionally and intellectually, as will be developed in the content of Chapter 7. The parenting role has to adapt to consider greater flexibility of response to the developing child. As children move into and through their school years they need:

- continued nurturing through predictable routines

- the encouragement of internalised control

- increased use of induction and reasoning

- encouragement with schooling

- consistent discipline

- expressions of warmth

- encouragement of socialisation with peers.

Adolescence

In Chapter 8 the maturational tasks of adolescence are explored and, in that context, positive aspects of the adolescent–parent relationship are considered in some detail. This includes the complexities of caring for adolescents in foster care. In summary, adolescents need:

- empathy from their carers

- parents or carers who see things from their point of view

- constructive discipline, rather than criticism and restraint

- positive communication

- active and warm involvement

- encouragement towards cooperation and collaboration

- flexibility of approach in negotiating solutions

- positive support for social development

- encouragement of mastery and achievement.

Aspects of parenting which undermine healthy development

In Chapter 5 the damaging effects of some aspects of parenting will be explored as a form of adversity. Such adversity can range from emotional and physical neglect, either with or without deliberate intent, to abusive and cruel acts by those in the parenting role. Several research studies have noted the specific combination of *low warmth* and *high criticism* as particularly damaging for children (DHSS 1995). While some parents appear to be deliberately cruel to their children, many children are harmed by their parents' inability to appreciate or understand their needs, often fuelled by the nature and quality of the parents' own early experiences or the existence of parallel stresses in their own lives. However, whatever the contributory causes, experiences of maltreatment, either neglect or abuse, are likely to have an undermining effect on one or a combination of the child's:

- development

- behaviour

- self-esteem

- attachment security.

When assessing an individual child's unique predicament, it is useful to hold these dimensions in mind when considering the *impact* of a particular style of parenting on the individual child. As suggested by Howe *et al.* in their overall framework (1999), an assessment of the nature and quality of care-giving and its effects on the child will be central in informing interventions (see Figure 2.4).

Activity 3.1

Using Figure 3.2, outline parenting behaviours which, in your view, express a healthy response to each of the child's needs at each age, for example affection: cuddling, rocking; stimulation: encouragement of speech by talking to the child.

Attribution theory and its relevance for parenting

Attribution theory encourages reflection on the part of the practitioner on the parent's patterns of thinking about individual children. Attribution theory is considered more fully in Chapter 4. Assessment of indications of the *meaning* of each child to parents or care-givers can inform the degree of risk to a child and guide deliberate interventions to alter or shift negative attributions, in particular. For example, individual children may carry particular negative meaning for a parent, arising from particular aspects of the history of the relationship.

In some circumstances the particular *qualities* or *characteristics* of the child may have a negative meaning for the parent, leading them to behave in an abusive or neglectful manner. For example, a child who resembles a rejected spouse or partner *may* lead to a parent behaving in an abusive or rejecting manner towards the child. Equally, aspects of the parent's own history, as already explored in terms of unaddressed traumatic early childhood experiences for the adult, may lead to difficulty for the parent in understanding and responding appropriately to the child's ordinary developmental needs.

The child may have been conceived or born in difficult circumstances and this may influence the parent's patterns of thinking about the child, resulting in negative behaviours and attributions. Careful assessment of this issue is important as the meaning of the child to parents or care-givers can highlight issues of potential risk of significant harm to the child – more useful and important information on this can be found in Reder and Lucey (1995).

Parenting responses to children's needs

Age	Physical needs	Affection	Security	Stimulation of innate potential	Guidance and control	Responsibility	Independence
Birth to one year							
Toddler							
Primary/ early school							
Middle years							
Adolescence							

Figure 3.2 A table to help guide assessment of parenting responses to children's needs at different stages

It may well be that it is not only negative attributions which carry risk to the child's development and well-being, as the *favoured* child may well be at risk, in some circumstances, of negative developmental effects, if, for example, as a result the child is indulged and is provided with inadequate ordinary behavioural boundaries.

Crucially, the parent's *attributions* or patterns of thinking about the child, combined with their *feelings,* can powerfully influence *behaviours* towards the child, significantly affecting the patterns of initiatives and response to the child within the care-giving environment. Clearly the relevance of this area of assessment is the degree to which parenting *behaviours* will have an impact on the child's sense of security and also her sense of self-esteem.

The impact of poverty

Ghate and Hazel (2002) found that parents living in impoverished environments are likely to suffer more from physical ill health than the general population and to have a higher risk of suffering from depression. Parents with physical and mental health difficulties were found also to be more likely to have a child with challenging behaviour. The *cumulative* stressors of low income, poor housing and a greater likelihood of lone parenthood need to be considered by practitioners when offering support. As Daniel and Rioch (2007) comment: 'The current position tends to coalesce around an interactional model whereby poverty is seen to interact with other psychological, social, emotional and inter-personal problems to drag parenting down' (p.437). In keeping their children safe in high risk communities, parents have more limited choices.

Family support intervention

Major stressors upon parents arise from the experience of poverty which can seriously undermine an individual parent's capacity to meet their children's needs. Support should have the aim of offering help at the right time, from the right people and in the right place (Utting 1995). Pointers about the most effective kind of support can be drawn from a range of research in the evaluation of large-scale preventative projects in the provision of support via means of agencies and specific parenting projects.

Prevention programmes

The greatest concern for professionals is the impact of abusive parenting and a wide range of family support services are designed with the focus of preventing abuse (Mostyn 1996; Parton 1995). From their work in Britain in collaboration with parents, Baldwin and Spencer (1993) suggest that effective prevention projects need to focus on aspects of:

- family support, including practical and emotional support
- social supports, including safety in the community
- partnership strategies which invite participation and ownership by parents.

Cohn Donnelly (1997) summarises the kind of parenting support that has been found to reduce the likelihood of abuse and improve child outcomes:

- early intervention, either home based or centre based

- a duration of at least six months and possibly up to several years

- support offered close to (or before) the birth of a baby

- intense support, at least once a week if not more frequently

- comprehensive input, not just focusing on parenting skills

- help offered by workers whose personality is warm and accepting.

Thompson (1995) stresses the importance of detailed assessment of the *kind* of support that is needed, because, as he has cautioned, not all social contact is automatically helpful. For example, some social supports encourage neglectful or abusive parenting strategies and, for some parents, contact with the extended family may be characterised by arguments, criticism and stress, and be undermining to parenting ability.

Crittenden (1996) suggests that families can be categorised according to their ability to assess their own state of need, to seek appropriate services and to make adaptive changes. This categorisation could be a useful guide for assessment when a situation seems blocked or stuck. Again, it is important to be cautious about labelling and stigmatising parents. These categories describe patterns which can be used to guide assessment, but practitioners need to avoid alienating parents by overtly categorising them.

- Parents who are *independent* and *adequate* and who can competently assess the needs of family members and find resources to meet those needs and make changes.

- Parents who are *vulnerable to crises* and who are capable of independent functioning but may temporarily need help and advice and may need some months of support.

- Parents where the situation is *restorable* who are potentially independent but may require two to five years of well-planned support.

- Parents who are *supportable* and who are unable to make changes needed quickly enough to meet their children's needs, but can manage if supported with services on a long-term basis.

- *Inadequate* parents who are not able to offer their children enough to meet their needs even with intensive support.

An example of the application of these categories in practice arises in cases of physical neglect. Many children are referred for concern about neglect within families that seem to have difficulty in making use of support. The parents often feel unable to make changes in their parenting style, and also feel that no one can help them. As Crittenden (1996) comments, parents

> not only see themselves as powerless, but they perceive everyone else as powerless. Because they believe everyone is powerless, they believe that effort to achieve goals is futile. Even accepting an offer of a reward for certain kinds of effort…appears useless if one believes that no one has the power to make things happen. (p.163)

Developing an appreciation of these patterns of attribution in some parents should help practitioners to understand why support offered is not necessarily automatically welcomed. In these circumstances, the intervention needs to focus first on enabling parents to shift their perceptions of their own inability to change, for example by starting with much smaller changes than multiple, global requirements.

It is also often the case that children who are neglected are in families that could be characterised as either 'restorable' or 'supportable'. The intervention literature clearly indicates that long-term support is needed if real improvement is to be made for children experiencing neglect (Gaudin 1993). The judgements will be case specific but must be monitored closely to avoid the problems of either unhelpful delay and 'drift' for the child or further significant harm.

What helps in programmes for work with parents?

Barlow (1999), when considering 18 studies of parent education programmes, concluded that those which combined a *behavioural approach* with *problem-solving* were most effective. Cognitive behavioural approaches focus upon patterns of thinking which in turn affect parenting behaviours. This reflects the focus in attribution theory upon the significance of the parent's thoughts and the meaning of the particular child (Reder and Duncan 1995). Approaches which combine these features include the following:

- The Mellow Parenting Programme (www.acamh.org.uk)

- Video Interactive Guidance (www.cpdeducation.co.uk/veroc)

- Triple P – Positive, Parenting Program (www.triplep.net)

- The Webster-Stratton Programme (Webster-Stratton 1999) – this programme is underpinned by learning theory, but also includes a careful focus on a collaborative and engaging approach to work with parents and guided positive nurturing and behaviour management.

Key principles of parenting support work are summarised by Daniel and Rioch (2007), as follows:

- relationships offered to parents with workers are crucial

- successful engagement of parents is based upon skills of empathic relationship building

- parents need to be respected if they are to be supported in building on strengths

- parents often need services that include practical supports and focus on effective problem-solving

- offering a *range* of services is important

- where there are multiple problems they need multiple solutions

- reducing parents' negative attributions towards themselves and their children is an important aim, particularly in safeguarding and protection work.

Structuring interventions in parenting

Careful observation of parent/child interaction can inform work with parents to enhance their awareness of their child's needs and responsiveness. For example, a parent may not pick up on the child's signals, may interpret these signals inaccurately and/or may respond in an unhelpful, delayed or even punitive manner. Work to enhance the parent's attunement to the child's signals and to develop a series of appropriate strategies in response may well be helpful in increasing the child's trust and feelings of security.

A focus on the parent's initiatives towards the child can be helpful in identifying negative initiatives, for example inappropriate control or criticism, and can also identify an absence of positive initiatives (see Figure 2.2). Strategies need to be aimed at:

- attuning parents to the child's cues or signals of need

- developing their repertoire of age-appropriate *responses*

- modelling and rehearsing anticipation and positive *initiatives*

- promoting *pleasurable* exchanges.

In structuring the focus of interventions it will be helpful to make an assessment of the parent's state of mind in relation to attachment – gained from analysis of their account of their own attachment experiences; and observation, wherever possible, of care-giving behaviours combined with observations of the children's attachment behaviours (Howe *et al.* 1999).

Assessment of parental motivation to change

Where there are problems in care-giving which have resulted either in neglect of the child's needs or in abusive treatment (whether by intention or omission) parental motivation to change is a crucial issue for assessment. A very helpful model is offered by Horwath and Morrison (2001) which builds upon Prochaska, DiClemente and Narcross's Comprehensive Model of Change (1992). Prochaska *et al.*'s model is familiar to many practitioners and contains five stages of change, as follows:

- contemplation

- determination

- action

- maintenance

- lapse.

Morrison (1998) offers useful guidance to practitioners during the crucial stage of 'contemplation', identifying seven steps in work with parents towards accepting the need for change in their parenting *behaviours*. The identification of required behaviours focused on meeting the child's unmet *needs* can be helpful in measuring change. In addition, two blocks to change are identified:

- pre-contemplation

- relapse.

Lapse and relapse

DiClemente (1991) distinguishes helpfully between lapse and relapse as part of the process towards sustained change. Whereas *lapses* can occur when there is a crisis and there may be a temporary problem, it is vital that parents are prepared by being offered a *lapse* strategy usually involving professionals and other support networks. Positive learning can be gained and commitment renewed on the basis of closely supported and monitored re-evaluation, reminders of positive strategies and incremental successes. It is vital, however, that the work is undertaken within a timescale to meet the child's needs for security and not extended indefinitely. These matters should be anticipated and built into the process of review of care planning. By contrast, *relapse* is defined as 'a return to unwanted behaviour – in some cases abuse of a child – which may have serious consequences for the family's future' (p.105). The skills of the working team around the family will be pivotal in ensuring the continued safety of the child in the process of learning and change for the parents/care-givers.

Strategies for enhancing the quality of care-giving

Schofield and Beek (2006) set out a useful framework offering five particular areas for enhancing the secure base available to a child. It is drawn principally from practice in substitute care placements in fostering and adoptive families and may also be relevant to practice with children placed in kinship care placements. The framework considers the following areas for reflection and intervention:

- being available – helping children to trust

- responding sensitively – helping children to manage their feelings and behaviour

- accepting the child – building self-esteem

- cooperative care-giving – helping children to feel effective

- promoting family membership – helping children to belong.

This approach is useful to practitioners in focusing on areas of *positive initiatives*. This framework can be particularly helpful in enhancing the quality of care-giving for children who are unable to return home to their birth parents and models, through careful consideration of these five aspects of the child's life and the development of deliberate positive initiatives to begin to repair the impact of past experiences of insecure attachment and to harness the strengths and resources of new care-givers.

Practitioners may find it helpful to focus positive parenting initiatives within areas of the child's life which are particularly sensitive to the promotion of more secure attachment, among others, as follows:

- provision of consistent *nurturing routines*

- frequent expressions of *emotional warmth* and reassurance

- support for the child in *transitions*

- provision of comfort through *separations*

- being responsive to the child at times of *anxiety*, sadness or stress

- provision of non-punitive age-appropriate *discipline*

- confident management of in-family *disputes*, either between adults or between siblings

- support for *mastery* and achievement of the individual child.

Practice points

- A working agreement is an extremely helpful tool to ensure that parents are clear about expectations of them.

- The stages of the work must be clear with information about the worker's role at all points of the work, e.g. the worker may be actively involved in modelling change at an earlier stage, removing themselves at the later stage of work when they are reminding parents, rather than working directly with them on strategies.

- Precise descriptions of 'behaviours', which are not expressed in jargon, will be very helpful when establishing a partnership with parents.

- Feedback about progress at all stages will be a parent's right.

- Timely review of progress will allow for any necessary changes to the process and ensure that unhelpful and harmful drift in planning is avoided.

- For particular groups of parents, e.g. those with mental health difficulties or those with learning disabilities, appropriate careful assessment and support will be necessary, often involving adult services.

- Early assessment of parents with learning disabilities by appropriate qualified professionals from adult services can help to clarify:
  ○ realistic expectations of the parent
  ○ appropriate methods of work informed by the assessment of the parent's needs and learning style
  ○ realistic timescales for change.

- A respectful, sensitive approach to work with parents from different cultures will be vital to good practice.

Assessing and working with disabled adults as parents

Research conducted by Olsen and Tyers (2004) identifies key principles of good practice in work with disabled parents. These include:

- promoting parental choice and control

- focusing on how barriers to fulfilment of the parenting role can be tackled

- offering support which involves good joint working strategies between social services, health, housing, education etc. and guidelines supported by clear anti-discriminatory policy

- promoting a partnership approach both across teams and with parents.

The recommendations reflect research conducted from a 'social model' of disability perspective. A positive open-minded focus on ways in which the agencies can collaborate to facilitate parenting to meet the child's needs wherever possible by their disabled parents is the key message for practitioners.

Assessing and working with parents with learning disabilities

Schofield (quoted in Howe 1996) poses a crucial set of questions for practitioners when working with parents with learning disabilities:

> Do cognitive deficits which might be thought to cause difficulties in mastering practical tasks also contribute to problems in establishing secure attachments, or do other aspects of personal circumstances and history combine with the cognitive deficit to cause difficulties in parenting? Or is the learning disability irrelevant to the causation of the problems but perhaps important to how help should be offered? (p.37)

These questions emphasise, therefore, the importance of the influence of childhood attachment experiences and relationships for parents with learning disabilities. A crucial issue to be considered is to what degree the parent's own attachment history drives continuing concerns about their capacity for attunement and responsiveness in secure care-giving.

Assessment of children in need and their families from minority ethnic groups

When assessing parenting capacity and the care of minority ethnic children, Banks (2001) stresses the importance of workers not compromising the quality of assessment and the clarity of focus on the needs of the child. The criteria should be culturally relevant and, most important, child-centred. He emphasises the additional needs of minority ethnic children, for example in relation to personal care and dietary considerations. He also emphasises the need for the child to receive their care-giver's support in dealing with experiences of racism.

Banks urges an examination of workers' attitudes and summarises key practice points as follows:

- 'What is culturally implicit should be made explicit' – the worker is encouraged to discover this in an open-minded discussion with the family.

- Workers must be clear about the legal context in which any concerns arise.

- Workers must ensure they have adequate skills, knowledge and understanding. Banks cautions against value-based assumptions and racist or ethnocentric attitudes in workers.

- The approach must support the child's 'psychological and physical connectedness with their respective communities, with no attempt to apologise for the family's cultural beliefs and behaviour'.

- He urges that cultural understanding should be balanced with an awareness of structural inequalities in issues of power within the assessment.

- He cautions against 'a preoccupation with the exotic and unusual, while other salient factors are ignored'.

- He supports a context of clear policy and procedural guidelines, crucially involving anti-oppressive and anti-racist training, linked with desirable measurable outcomes for the child.

- Finally, he encourages an assessment that 'recognises cultural difference without making the assessment subjective', underlying the importance of supervision for practitioners. (Banks 2001, p.147)

Activity 3.2

Thinking of an individual child living at home or accommodated, identify three fundamental or basic unmet needs.

1. What changes are required for the child's needs to be met?
2. What parenting *behaviours* would we wish to promote in meeting the child's needs?
3. How will progress be measured?

Key messages

- Families of many different constellations, for example lone parents and same-sex carers, can offer attuned care-giving which promotes healthy development. The crucial factor for the child's well-being is the quality of care-giving.

- All children need a secure base of attachment relationships, a coherent story of life events, relationships and circumstances, and predictability of care if they are to develop to their full potential.

- Parents' or care-givers' early experiences of childhood attachment relationships are relevant considerations in assessing the child's predicament and informing appropriate interventions.

- Those children most at risk of harm are those parented by adults whose early traumas are unaddressed as care-giving is often negatively affected by these issues.

- Even those care-givers with experience of trauma and loss may achieve an 'earned secure' state of mind in relation to attachment, if they have been able to reflect and/or benefit from later positive relationships.

- Therapeutic interventions with parents on early loss and trauma can be successful in enhancing the quality of care-giving.

- Parents with an authoritative style are most likely to promote healthy development in all domains.

- The application of attribution theory can be relevant when assessing care-givers, birth parents, kinship carers and substitute carers, for example, if focused on 'the meaning of the child' to the care-givers.

- Work towards effective change must:
  ◦ outline the changes needed to meet the child's unmet needs
  ◦ assess parents' willingness and ability to change
  ◦ emphasise *behavioural* changes necessary from care-givers
  ◦ include regular feedback
  ◦ be conducted in a timely fashion to avoid drift for the child.

- Parenting assessments should assess and work with the parent's capacity to:
  ◦ acknowledge problems
  ◦ understand the effects on the child
  ◦ empathise with the child's predicament.

- Systems for monitoring progress in enhancing responsiveness and measuring the impact on the child are crucial.

- It is important to examine the nature of social supports available to parents to ensure that they enhance positive parenting rather than supporting harmful patterns.

- Child and adult services must work together in parenting assessments and this may be especially important in work with parents with physical disabilities, learning disabilities, mental health problems or substance misuse issues.

- When working towards change the *impact* of the parenting on the child may be measured through examining changes in:
  ◦ behaviour
  ◦ enhanced developmental progress
  ◦ improved self-esteem
  ◦ greater attachment security.

- Culturally sensitive, child-focused work with parents from different cultures is necessary if families are not to be marginalised and if children are to be protected.

CHAPTER 4

Resilience and Vulnerability

Introduction

In Chapter 1 we set out the resilience matrix and explained how it can be used as an overall framework to help with assessing the impact of a range of factors upon a child's development and with planning intervention (see also Daniel and Wassell 2002a, b and c; Gilligan 2001, 2009a). In this chapter will we explore the concepts of vulnerability and resilience in more depth (see Figure 4.1). We will give a critical overview of each concept and analyse in detail a number of vulnerability factors that are likely to be encountered in practice, and set out some of the ways to counter their negative impact upon development. We shall especially focus on ways to foster a sense of inner security, and ways to ameliorate the impact of loss. As we stated in Chapter 1, the dimension of vulnerability and resilience aims to capture a range of intrinsic or internal characteristics of an individual. The extrinsic dimension of adversity and protective factors will be explored in more detail in the following chapter. However, in practice the divisions are not as precise as this because there is, of course, considerable interaction between internal and external factors.

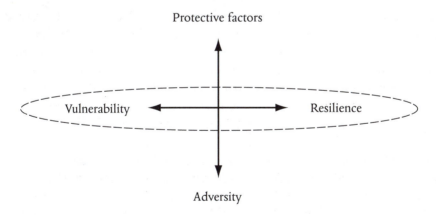

Figure 4.1 Resilience matrix, showing chapter focus

Resilience

A popular definition of resilience has been Fonagy and colleagues' – '*Normal* development under difficult conditions' (1994, p.231). A number of people have highlighted the extent to which resilience, as a concept, has been misunderstood, especially with the notion that there is an all-or-nothing aspect to being 'resilient' and that it is a fixed trait, when the evidence, in fact, suggests that it is a more relative phenomenon. Rutter (2000) has summarised the current evidence thus:

> children's resistance to stress is relative, rather than absolute; the origins of stress resistance are both environmental and constitutional; and the degree of resistance is not a fixed individual characteristic. Rather resistance varies over time and according to circumstances. (p.651)

These aspects are summed up in Luthar's definition, where resilience is taken to be 'a phenomenon or process reflecting relatively positive adaptation despite experiences of adversity or trauma' (2005, p.6). Gilligan's description of resilience is also helpful because it introduces the notion of 'thriving' and encourages us to remember the concept of *potential*, also described in Chapter 1: 'qualities which cushion a vulnerable child from the worst effects of adversity in whatever form it takes and which may help a child or young person to cope, survive and even thrive in the face of great hurt and disadvantage' (Gilligan 1997, p.12).

The research into the factors associated with resilience is now very extensive and the factors that have been identified as contributing to resilience are also numerous. There is considerable agreement now that resilience is associated with the presence of protective factors in three categories of:

- psychological/dispositional attributes

- family support and cohesion

- external support systems. (Friborg *et al.* 2003)

Werner's substantial longitudinal study identified a range of factors associated with resilience at each of these levels (Werner 1990). Her findings and subsequent research coalesce around some key factors including three fundamental factors of security of attachment, self-esteem and self-efficacy (Gilligan 1997). The factors she identified are summarised below within an ecological framework.

Resilience factors within the individual child
INFANCY

Werner (1990) comments, 'Resilient infants tend to have predictable temperamental characteristics which elicit positive responses from other people' (p.100). Resilient infants and toddlers:

- are active, affectionate, cuddly, good-natured, responsive and easy to deal with and have a capacity for self-expression

- have experienced a secure attachment and learned to trust in its availability

- have a supportive family member

- have a pronounced sense of autonomy and social orientation

- are described as alert, cheerful, responsive, self-confident and independent

- are advanced in communication, mobility and self-help skills

- are more advanced in social play than vulnerable toddlers
- have developed a coping pattern that combines autonomy with an ability to ask for support when needed.

These characteristics are also predictive of resilience in later years.

PRE-SCHOOL YEARS
Resilient pre-schoolers:

- have well-developed communication and problem-solving skills which the child is able to put to good use
- are sociable but also independent.

MIDDLE CHILDHOOD
Stress-resistant primary schoolers:

- are well-liked by peers and adults
- are reflective rather than impulsive in thinking style
- feel they can influence their environments positively
- are able to use flexible coping strategies, including humour
- are adept at recruiting surrogate parents, even if not blood relatives.

Gender also has a role to play at this stage in development.

- Resilient *boys* are emotionally expressive, socially perceptive and nurturant.
- Resilient *girls* are autonomous and independent.
- Resilient *children* display flexible coping strategies which promote mastery over adversity rather than reactions in a rigidly sex-stereotyped manner.
- Overall, *girls* are generally more resilient to stress and trauma than boys.

ADOLESCENCE
Resilient young people are those who:

- are more responsible and achievement-oriented
- prefer structure in their lives and have internalised a positive set of values
- have a more positive self-concept
- are more appreciative, gentle, nurturing and socially perceptive than their more vulnerable peers
- are characterised by pronounced social maturity and a stronger sense of responsibility
- have belief in their own capacity to control their fate

- by pre-school stage were healthily autonomous with an ability to enlist support
- have repeated successful experiences of overcoming stressful situations (often with the support of others)
- have a sense of self-efficacy and confidence
- can select what they need from their environment and make good use of it
- change or restructure a situation
- are optimistic and hopeful.

Factors in the family situation that help to nurture resilience

Some of the factors in the family context could be considered to be 'protective factors' and will be re-visited in the next chapter. We have, in Chapter 3, set out a range of factors that can help to support the development of secure attachment – a key factor in nurturing resilience. Our focus here is on the factors within the family environment that can also help to nurture those internal characteristics in a child known to be associated with resilience. Resilience-promoting caring environments provide:

- an opportunity to establish a close bond with at least one person who has provided stable care and adequate and appropriate attention (secure base) in the first year of life
- affectionate ties with alternative care-givers, e.g. grandparents, who may support parents and provide the child with alternative nurturing
- involvement in sibling care-giving, either as the giver or the recipient, which can be a major preventive factor for vulnerable children; the availability of some supplementary support from an adult is a crucial determinant of whether older siblings will help or hinder younger ones.

SOCIALISATION PRACTICES

Key characteristics of the home environment have been identified in respect of boys and girls as particularly protective of healthy development. Resilient girls are reared in households combining:

- an absence of over-protection
- an emphasis on risk-taking
- reliable emotional support.

Resilient boys are reared in households combining:

- greater structure
- rules
- parental supervision

- the availability of a male as a healthy role model

- encouragement for emotional expression.

REQUIRED HELPFULNESS

Productive roles of responsibility for the child, associated with close family ties, are protective.

FAITH

A belief in a broader value system can help the child to persist in problem-solving or in surviving a set of challenging life circumstances. A sense of 'coherence' in their experience gives the child a feeling of rootedness, the conviction that life has meaning and an optimistic focus.

Resilience factors in the community
FRIENDS

The capacity to make and sustain friendships is protective and a source of comfort and support.

SCHOOL

Even if not gifted, resilient children can put their abilities to good use. School is often an effective refuge for children under stress or those who have experienced abuse. Teachers can shape both academic attainment and positive self-concept and esteem.

FOR GIRLS

The nurturing and fostering of responsibility builds strength and resilience.

FOR BOYS

Structure and control helps them to develop an 'internal locus of control' which fosters social and intellectual development.

Activity 4.1

Focusing on your work with an individual child or young person, please consider, in the light of Werner's framework, the following questions.

1. How might you decrease the child's exposure to key risk factors and stressful life events?
2. Identify potential strengths in (a) the individual child, (b) the family context and (c) the wider community.
3. Outline suggestions as to how these might be harnessed to support the child.

Potential pitfalls of uncritical use of the term 'resilience'

The extent to which the concept of resilience has been embraced in policy and practice is a testament to perceptions of its strengths. However, it has been subjected to some critique. For example, some young people who appear to be resilient may in fact be internalising their symptoms and showing 'apparent resilience' (Luthar 1991). Children who appear to be doing well can be labelled as 'resilient' and therefore be denied the support that they need.

Although individualism is not an inherent aspect of the concept of resilience, its translation into practice does tend to become individualised (Rigsby 1994). The tendency for social work practice with vulnerable children to overlook structural issues and fail to address them effectively has been highlighted by Jack (2000, 2001). It is impossible for any one practitioner to address all ecological levels; however, the current multi-disciplinary context opens up many opportunities to target all ecological levels.

The lack of research into the effectiveness of resilience-based intervention is also a significant gap. Much of the recent empirical research into resilience has focused on refining understanding of the concept of resilience: for example, about which factors confer protection only in the presence of adversity and the exact pathways of effects. However, with the surge in 'resilience-based' practice, it is crucial to carefully monitor the effectiveness of any intervention strategies aimed explicitly at boosting a child's resilience in the face of abuse and neglect.

Intervention

Bolger and Patterson's (2003) longitudinal study of 107 maltreated children suggested that maltreated children are unlikely to show resilient adaptation because:

- their families fail to provide the experiences that support normal development

- maltreatment co-occurs with other environmental threats

- disturbances in the family relationships act as a conduit for distal stresses

- their environment lacks protective factors.

Neglect is associated with:

- poor attachments

- low self-esteem

- low self-efficacy

- poor cognitive development.

The careful assessment of factors of resilience in individual children, their family relationships and wider community networks is important for shaping intervention. Care is needed in making sure that avoidance of dependency relationships, an attitude of 'I'm fine, I don't need anyone' or a persistent tendency to be self-parenting are not mistaken for resilience as a basis of healthy dependence. Some children and young people develop skills in keeping adults at a distance by learning to mask and cover up their underlying distress. Their needs are more likely to go unnoticed, especially if they have siblings who are very demanding or whose behaviour signals their needs more explicitly.

Given that one of the most helpful areas for intervention with individual children and young people is that of building healthy resilience, it is useful for the practitioner to have a framework from which to begin to consider strategies for work with the individual child. Practitioners are frequently engaged in work which builds strengths in the child and it may merely be a question of giving added emphasis to this work and involving the child or young person themselves in developing the ideas which may add to the impact of positive strategies. It may be helpful to question the assumption that the social worker is always the person who offers all the direct support as other adults in the child's life may be better placed to sustain these efforts over time. Recruiting someone already known to the child or a befriender to act as a mentor can be an alternative way of offering continuity of concern and interest and tracking progress and success and mastery. Gilligan (1997) identifies six key areas of focus which can form the basis for clarifying initiatives for work:

- Encouraging purposeful contact with family members and other key adults from the child's past.

- Encouraging positive school experience.

- Encouraging friendships with peers.

- Actively fostering interest, involvement and talents in sport, music, hobbies or cultural pursuits.

- Helping the child to rehearse, dissect and discuss problem-solving and coping skills and strategies.

- Promoting pro-social qualities in the young person. (pp.7–8)

Precisely because a resilience-led approach depends on a very detailed, individual and specific plan for intervention for each child every plan will necessarily be different. However, the research into factors associated with resilience has led to the development of a number of similar guiding frameworks for intervention via a range of protective factors. Rutter's (1987) framework suggests that practice:

- should alter or reduce the child's exposure to risk

- should reduce the negative chain reaction of risk exposure

- should establish and maintain self-esteem and self-efficacy

- should create opportunities.

Masten's (1994) framework suggests that practitioners should aim to:

- reduce vulnerability and risk

- reduce the number of stressors and pile-up

- increase the available resources

- foster resilience strings
- alter or reduce the child's exposure to risk.

And Benard (2004) suggests the need for the child to experience:

- caring relationships
- high expectations
- opportunities to participate and contribute.

It is also important to focus on factors that are 'modifiable modifiers', that is, they can be changed, like self-efficacy, rather than being relatively fixed, like gender (Luthar 2005).

Masten and Coatsworth (1998) provide an overall framework for intervention by suggesting that prevention and intervention design can be:

- risk-focused, for example public-health programmes such as those aimed at preventing low birth weight and projects aimed at reducing the stressors associated with transition between primary and secondary education
- resource-focused, for example adding extra assets for children or improving access to resources, especially when risks are intractable
- process-focused, for example improving attachment, self-efficacy and self-regulation.

Yates and Masten (2004) suggest that the most effective intervention programmes involve all three: 'These multi-faceted paradigms attempt to reduce modifiable risk, strengthen meaningful assets, and recruit core developmental systems to enhance positive adaptational processes within the child, the family and the broader community' (p.10).

An important focus for work may be:

- to decrease exposure to key risk factors and stressful life events and, wherever possible, in addition
- to increase the number of available protective factors, for example building competencies and social support.

Vulnerability

The concept of vulnerability has been subject to some critique because of the danger of 'victim-blaming' and of ignoring the structural factors that may be impacting upon the child and family. However, in this book we are using the term 'vulnerable' to describe the situation where a child is at elevated risk of compromised development because of either innate characteristics or because of the impact of adverse factors. When assessing a child's developmental trajectory it is vital that the practitioner identifies potential vulnerabilities so that they can ensure that protective factors are put in place at the level of the individual, family and/or wider community. Factors that might render a child vulnerable to abuse and neglect and/or to not weathering ordinary adversities, and veering off a healthy developmental path, can be separated into:

- some intrinsic characteristics in the child which might render him more vulnerable

- those vulnerabilities imposed by parents' views or expectations of the child.

Alongside these general factors, the particular age of the child and developmental stage may render the child particularly vulnerable.

Babies and infants
INTRINSIC CHARACTERISTICS OF THE CHILD

Babies and infants who fit the following descriptions of their characteristics may be more vulnerable:

- the child who is born too soon – an unplanned or unintended pregnancy

- the child who is born with developmental difficulties, in particular various sorts of disabilities

- the child who is arrhythmic, i.e. the child who cannot be helped to settle into any predictable rhythm or routine

- the child who cries and cannot be comforted

- the child who cannot sleep or disturbs the parent frequently, waking during the night in particular

- the child with an unusual temperament – especially the child who is either very active or very passive, and the child who will not accept being held.

THOSE VULNERABILITIES IMPOSED BY PARENTS' VIEWS OR EXPECTATIONS OF THE CHILD

Babies and infants fitting these descriptions may be more vulnerable:

- the child who is born of the 'wrong' sex, i.e. where the sex of the child disappoints parental expectations and hopes

- the child who resembles a hated partner or spouse.

Alongside these general factors, the age of the child and developmental stage may render the child particularly vulnerable. Babies can be particularly prone to all kinds of abuse and neglect because of their total dependence on adults and their vulnerability to specific physical trauma, for example shaking injuries. The child who is between 6 months and 18 months is especially vulnerable to effects of separations because he has 'selected' or identified his primary carers and therefore experience loss in a pervasive sense. The child between these ages who experiences multiple caretakers may well be especially vulnerable to a difficulty in establishing a secure base. What is clearly protective for a child at this age and stage is to have experienced at least one good attachment in his early years.

Pre-school stage
INTRINSIC CHARACTERISTICS IN THE CHILD

- At the pre-school stage, the child is likely to take on some sense of responsibility and personal connection with negative life events, particularly if they are separated at this time. Children are more likely to attribute blame to themselves and this will render them more vulnerable to the effects of future separations and may threaten their confidence in their 'secure base'.

- The fact that the child at this stage will be challenging authority figures through healthy autonomous behaviour may render him at risk of physical abuse or emotional abuse.

- The child who feels unsafe to explore and insecure in his attachment may cling to or follow the carer in an irritating manner, provoking abuse.

- If the issues of autonomy and independence are not well managed at this stage, they may well re-emerge in a salient way in adolescence. However, this then provides an opportunity for re-working these issues in a healthier manner.

THOSE VULNERABILITIES IMPOSED BY PARENTS' VIEWS OR EXPECTATIONS OF THE CHILD

- The child at this stage of development should be exploring his environment – therefore if he is either under-protected or over-protected, his development may suffer.

- The lack of healthy boundaries increases the likelihood of behaviour problems that can spiral out of control.

The school-age child
INTRINSIC CHARACTERISTICS IN THE CHILD

- The child who is subject to developmental delay and the child who needs special help at this stage, especially to enter school, may be particularly vulnerable. Therefore the child who is sensitised to separations may not manage this milestone well.

- The child who is aggressive or who has persistent behaviour problems will struggle.

- The child who makes no demands for his emotional needs to be met, i.e. is passive and unresponsive, as he does not enlist adult support, can be overlooked.

- The child who is slow or unable to learn, who has particular learning difficulties which are not identified, is vulnerable.

- The child who is struggling intellectually at school is vulnerable because this has particular knock-on effects on social and emotional development as well as intellectual functioning.

THOSE VULNERABILITIES IMPOSED BY PARENTS' VIEWS OR EXPECTATIONS OF THE CHILD
Children who fit the following descriptions are more vulnerable:

- the child who is isolated as part of a closed family system

- the child who is scapegoated, in particular the child who is the focus of negative responses and initiatives from parents among siblings who are more clearly valued

- the child who is different in any way, in particular the child who may be identifiably different in racial terms within a predominantly white society, particularly those children who are of mixed parentage.

Adolescence
INTRINSIC CHARACTERISTICS IN THE CHILD

- The young person who has learned no planning or problem-solving skills may well be vulnerable as he or she is unable to protect him- or herself or ask for adult support in a healthy manner.

- Children with established behaviour problems which have not been addressed and/or patterns of disturbed behaviour, especially conduct disorder in boys, will have often already encountered difficulties in nursery settings as well as in primary and secondary school as their behaviour sets them apart from their peers. They are more likely:
  - to have trouble in making and keeping friends
  - to find it hard to develop a pattern of learning
  - to gravitate towards other children or young people in trouble partly as a reflection of their view of themselves, as well as through attraction to the excitement this peer group offers
  - to be more vulnerable to disruptions in schooling which is a setting invaluable for providing resilience in late adolescence and in the transition to adulthood.

- The young person with poor self-esteem or sense of self-efficacy is less resilient.

- The young person who is part of an under-achieving or anti-authority group with limited choice of other peers is vulnerable.

THOSE VULNERABILITIES IMPOSED BY PARENTS' VIEWS OR EXPECTATIONS OF THE CHILD
During adolescence children who fit the following descriptions are more vulnerable:

- the young person who is disapproved of or blamed for family problems: the scapegoat may believe there is no point in trying as he cannot effect any improvement in his circumstances

- the young person who is pressed to take on too many family responsibilities, in particular the 'parental' child

- the child who has no support for his developing independence

- the child who is not nourished in terms of his or her questions and confusions about his or her sexual identity and orientation

- the young person who has no continuity of confiding relationships at a stage of development when the 'secure base' is particularly necessary once more

- the young person who is frequently separated from important people, such as attachment figures, peer connections and school links, with no support in addressing these moves and changes, and no help in making sense of the continuity and coherence of their own life story.

Parental factors

Certain factors within parents' own experience or relationships and circumstances may add to an individual child or young person's vulnerability. Examples of this include:

- the child who lives with parents who are depressed or have significant long-standing psychiatric problems which affect the parent–child relationship or safety and nurturing of the young person (especially significant if long-standing mental health problems remain unidentified)

- the child who witnesses long-standing marital discord with no resolution

- the child who lives in a household where there is domestic violence

- the child whose parents separate, especially if these separations are unpredicted and repeated.

Continuing friction between parental partners post-separation and a poor post-separation environment for the child or young person are especially significant as are tensions or even violence or abuse in contact arrangements after divorce. The child of parents under particular long-term stress may be additionally vulnerable where there is a parent:

- with no warm, confiding relationship of his own

- who was poorly nourished himself in emotional terms

- who had a particularly difficult time at the developmental stage which their child has now reached

- with poor knowledge of child development and therefore unclear expectations and with a need for help to learn what it is reasonable to expect of a child and what stimulation and opportunity the child needs

- with significant intellectual limitations who has no support with the parenting tasks

- with significant drug or alcohol dependency which negatively affects their emotional availability

- who has poor problem-solving and planning skills and may be devastated by every setback

- who is caught up in a violent relationship or series of relationships with violent partners.

Absence of community supports

The availability of certain community supports may be invaluable in building resilience and providing some protection for an individual child/young person within his family setting. Conversely, the absence of such supports can significantly increase the individual child's vulnerability. Among the most significant issues within this domain of the child's life are:

- the absence of any extended family support; this is particularly exacerbated where there is active disapproval from family members

- poor housing, which places stress on adults and children

- money worries or significant poverty

- a lack of support groups for the parents within their local community with no relief at all for the parent from the strains of the parenting task

- the lack of available early intervention services within the community

- poor mental health diagnosis and ineffective treatment of parents' problems or an individual child's depression or other psychiatric problems

- racism within the local community where the child is either black or of mixed parentage

- isolation from ethnic community supports which might be preventative in terms of building the strengths of parents, children and young people in combating racism

- unhelpful conflicts within different support systems surrounding any particular family, which are especially unhelpful in situations of abuse and/or neglect where the helping systems may mirror the conflicts within the family.

We see many situations in our practice which may call into question the degree of emotional nurturing available to an individual child within his or her home setting. We may, for example, observe a parent shouting loudly at a child, or treating him in a physically rough manner. What remains to be explained is the often surprising variability in the effects that this kind of treatment has on individual children. This might lead us to wonder how we can identify most readily those children who may be particularly vulnerable to the negative effects of life's stresses, for example marital violence, separation and maternal depression. Research can tell us something about combinations of stresses which are likely to render a particular child more vulnerable. However, in terms of intervention, there is no substitute for detailed, careful observation of the effects of a particular environment and all its influences on a child and a sensitive awareness of that child's experience of his environment and relationships. If we can identify those children who are particularly vulnerable as early as possible, it is likely that we can then focus intervention more precisely, so as to harness any potential for resilience within the child and within his close environment.

Activity 4.2

Think of an individual child or young person and consider what has happened to this child, e.g. abuse, neglect or multiple separations.

1. What messages has this child taken from these experiences e.g. 'my behaviour is too difficult to handle' or 'I'm not lovable'?

2. What pattern of attachment behaviours might we identify?

3. What messages is the child communicating in these behaviours, e.g. 'it's not safe to come close' or 'adults can't be trusted'?

4. What healing messages do we want to communicate?

5. How might we do this (a) in nurturing routines, (b) in non-punitive behaviour management, (c) in direct work with the child, (d) in family work, (e) in purposeful arrangements for contact for separated children, (f) in strategies for building strengths?

Promoting a sense of security via the parent–child relationship

In Chapter 2 key ideas about the importance of attachment relationships for children and young people have already been explored. The idea of a secure base as a focus for promoting and sustaining the development of a feeling of security and well-being underlines an examination of a child's attachment relationships as highly significant, both in assessment and in work with individual children and adolescents either remaining at home, placed with foster families or in residential units. It is important to assess the level of security within the child's primary attachment relationships and, from a 'baseline' analysis of interaction, strategies can be formulated to enhance the quality of care-giving.

Specific approaches have been developed which offer programmes of work, either with an individual focus or on a group basis. These include programmes involving the use of video, for example Video Interactive Guidance, which have been developed within some local authorities (Macdonald and Lugton 2006). Other programmes include opportunities for parents to reflect on their own childhood attachment experiences, in parallel with work on the parent–child relationship (e.g. the Mellow Parenting Programme – www. acamh.org.uk).

Fife Council (unpublished, 2006) in Scotland has developed a framework for a Working Agreement with parents within which, either working with parents when their child is still at home to prevent removal, or within contact sessions for accommodated children, the following areas are considered:

1. The identification of a maximum of three hitherto unmet needs of the child, one of which must be an emotional need, upon which to focus efforts to enhance parental

responsiveness. For example, Mary has an unmet need to know that her mother and father love her.

2. The second step involves clarifying what needs to change in the parents' behaviour for the child's needs to be met. For example, for mother and father to show more love and affection to their daughter.

3. The third step identifies specific desired behaviours from parents within observed sessions. These are described in simple language, without unhelpful jargon, and should be culturally sensitive. For example, how the mother and father might greet Mary when she first arrives in contact with further detail of initiatives that the parents could take of a loving nature in each session.

4. The fourth aspect of the agreement identifies precisely the help that parents can expect from workers at each stage. For example, it may be that Mary's parents will need substantial guidance about the required behaviours in some detail, perhaps including rehearsal and role play.

This apparently simple agreement has the advantage of a clear focus on the child as the starting point; the identification of behaviours designed to meet the child's needs can then be more easily measured in order to indicate progress.

The agreement allows for different stages of the work:

• During the *assessment* stage, desired behaviours are identified from the assessment of the 'baseline' of interaction.

• The *work* stage can then involve several sessions, adjusted according to the requirements of the specific case, with the worker demonstrating behaviours or strategies guiding parents towards positive initiatives.

• The *reminder* stage involves cueing, reminding and prompting parents in order to consolidate new learning. The worker will be less actively involved but nevertheless still supportive.

• The *observation* stage involves the worker stepping back from interaction in order to observe any substantive changes in behaviour.

A working agreement, if negotiated with parents with openness, honesty and sensitivity, can:

• enhance the possibility of parental cooperation through clear and respectful consultation

• promote partnership through the transparent nature of the contract including comprehensible language

• help parents to understand precisely what is being asked of them

• provide opportunities for observation of behaviours as indicators of change

• keep the focus for reviewing progress upon the unmet needs of the child.

Use of this framework has resulted in the following advantages:

- enhancing the parent–child relationship in situations where previously the *purposes* of contact had been rather vague

- providing opportunities for parents to experience success and thereby encouraging them to work towards a return home for an accommodated child or to enhance the care-giving for a child at home

- clarifying situations in a timely fashion where parents are unable or unwilling to make changes in their parenting.

Promoting a sense of security via sibling relationships

While not denying the security dimension of healthy attachment relationships with carers, Dunn (1993) expands our understanding of the broader world of the child's close connections. The relationship between brothers and sisters holds potential for support at times of stress, but also for additional isolation and rejection for a few children who experience themselves as outsiders or scapegoats within a sibling group (Kosonen 1997). For example, practitioners are familiar with children who appear more closely attached to siblings than to anyone else. We meet children who care for one another or who are even the main caretakers for a sibling group. Although we often view this scenario with concern, the caretaking role may bring some advantages to a child despite the early burden this represents.

We strive wherever possible to make and maintain joint sibling placements so that we can minimise any further stress of separation. Day or foster carers and residential staff need to be sensitive to the fact that this caring role, however inappropriate it may seem, may well be central to the child's current sense of self-esteem and identity within the family. Care should be taken to encourage the child to relinquish this in a gradual way, with a clear acknowledgement of the child's caretaking instincts.

Some children are clearly the scapegoats within a sibling group, constantly criticised and undermined by their parents' attitudes and responses. Rutter and Rutter (1993) comment upon the particular predicament of such children as they regard them as more vulnerable in a family where all the children suffer some neglect or abuse. Dunn and Plomin (1990) suggest:

> It may matter very little whether children are brought up in a home that is less loving or more punitive than average whereas it may matter a great deal that one child consistently receives less affection or more criticism and punishment than his brother or sister. (p.49)

Dunn and Plomin further found in their studies that 'those children who received less affection and more control than their siblings tended to show more problem behaviour' (p.48). Clearly, this is a particular group of children we need to identify, support and monitor with special attention.

Practice point

What emerges as especially significant is the *rejection* experienced by a child, particularly when he or she lives with the constant daily comparison of his carers' more positive (or merely less negative) behaviour towards a sibling. A second factor of major impact and significance is the experience of not mattering to anyone, having no-one in their lives to whom they are of importance. Some children who are not naturally *persistent* in their attempts to reach out to adults in the hope of their needs being understood and met may 'give up' and hide their own needs. These children, especially if they are compliant and 'easy to manage' or keen to please, may hide their needs even in placements away from home, and practitioners need to be aware of underlying neglect and its potential longer-term impact.

The Sibling Relationship Checklist (Department of Health 1991), also referred to in Chapter 2, can be helpful in identifying the focus for intervention when practitioners are wishing to concentrate on building and supporting positive elements of a sibling relationship. It can also be used to clarify the strength and nature of sibling attachments, also a vital issue in planning accommodation or longer-term placements.

Disabled children and young people: resilience and vulnerability

The developmental challenges facing disabled children and their families are summed up in a recent UK Government report:

> It has traditionally been the case that disabled children are likely to have poorer outcomes across a range of indicators compared to their non-disabled peers, including lower educational attainment, poorer access to health services and therefore poorer health outcomes, more difficult transitions to adulthood, and poorer employment outcomes. Families of disabled children are less likely to have one or both parents in work, and are more likely to suffer from family break up. Siblings of disabled children may also be more likely to suffer from emotional and behavioural problems, for example through sleep deprivation. (HM Treasury and Department for Education and Skills 2007, pp.11–12)

The report is one of several associated with a national policy aimed at tackling these disadvantages – *Aiming High for Disabled Children*. The underlying principles are as applicable to practice as to national policy:

- Disabled children will have the same opportunities to develop and fulfil their potential as all other children.

- Families with disabled children will get the support they need, when they need it.

- Universal children's services will be more genuinely inclusive of disabled children, including those with complex needs.

- Disabled children will be at the heart of the ongoing change programme for children's services. (p.10)

Maltreatment of disabled children

The evidence that disabled children are at elevated risk of abuse and neglect is extensive; however, an assumption of inherent vulnerability has also been challenged. Cross *et al.* (1993) are clear about the importance of recognising maltreatment of disabled children; but they also point to the 'created' vulnerability that comes from a range of social factors including lack of structural supports, poor access to many services and stereotypical and discriminatory attitudes. When considering the developmental needs of disabled children, therefore, it is crucial to assess all factors at all ecological levels that may contribute to a heightened risk of compromised development rather than focusing only on the impact of the impairment.

Until relatively recently the abuse of disabled children was largely unrecognised and unreported. In a landmark publication Westcott and Jones (1999) brought together the previous three decades of research and concluded with confidence that disabled children are more vulnerable to abuse and neglect than non-disabled children. Several of the studies they reviewed focused on the extent to which the abuse may have caused the impairment, for example brain injury as a result of being shaken as an infant — an important issue to which professionals must remain alert. Noting that the evidence tells us as much about attitudes towards disability as about abuse they describe a shift from the concept of disabled children as 'abuse provoking' towards an ecological and social model that considers the dynamics of the interacting factors associated with elevated risk. Citing Westcott (1993) they suggest:

> Specifically, disabled children were judged more vulnerable since they experienced: greater physical and social isolation (including institutional care); a lack of control over their life and bodies (e.g. insensitive and/or intrusive medical interventions); greater dependency on others (including the provision of intimate care); and problems in communication (including, for example, a lack of vocabulary to describe abuse in some alternative communication systems). (p.501)

They herald a move towards a combined social and ecological model of prevention at the personal, professional and organisational levels and stress the importance of multi-disciplinary assessment that draws on the skills of those with specialist knowledge and communication skills.

A more recent review indicates that disabled children in the UK and other countries are still at greater risk (Miller 2002):

> From an analysis of over 40,000 children in an American city Sullivan and Knutson (2000) found that disabled children were 3.4 times more likely to be abused or neglected. They were 3.8 times more likely to be neglected; 3.8 times more likely to be physically abused; 3.1 times more likely to be sexually abused; and 3.9 times more likely to be emotionally abused. Overall, 31% of the total disabled children in this research had been abused. (p.1)

They go on to collate a range of factors that increase vulnerability to abuse:

- Society devalues and disempowers disabled people. Attitudes lead to a created vulnerability.

- Disabled children and their families face many barriers to their full participation in society which limits their capacity both to contribute towards and access community resources and services, including preventative services.

- There is a lack of awareness among carers, professionals and the general public of the vulnerability of disabled children and the indicators of abuse.

- People hold beliefs that disabled children are not abused or beliefs that minimise the impact of abuse. These can lead to the denial of, or failure to report, abuse.

- There is a general lack of communication and consultation with disabled children over their experiences, views, wishes and feelings and the lack of choice and control they have over many aspects of their lives.

- Lack of appropriate or poorly coordinated support services can leave disabled children and their families unsupported and physically and socially isolated. Isolation is widely considered to be a risk factor for abuse.

- There is a structural and skills gap between professionals working with disabled children and those in child protection leading to barriers to an effective child protection system.

- There is a lack of comprehensive and multi-agency assessment and planning in relation to indication of need at an early stage. This leads to both a failure to promote the child's welfare and a failure to identify early indications of possible abuse.

- Assumptions are sometimes made about disabled children, e.g. their mood, injury or behaviour. This can result in indicators of possible abuse being mistakenly attributed to the child's impairment.

- Disabled children's dependency on an abusing carer can create difficulties in avoiding or communicating about abuse especially if this is a key person through whom the child communicates.

- Some disabled children may have learned from their care or wider experience to be compliant and not to 'complain'.

- There is a lack of effective sex education or safety and awareness work with disabled children.

Disabled children may:

- receive intimate personal care, possibly from a number of carers, which may increase the risk of exposure to abusive behaviour

- have an impaired capacity to resist or avoid abuse

- have communication difficulties or lack of access to an appropriate vocabulary which may make it difficult to tell others what is happening

- not have someone to turn to, may lack the privacy they need to do this, or the person they turn to may not be receptive to the issues being communicated

- be inhibited about complaining because of a fear of losing services

- be especially vulnerable to bullying and intimidation

- be more vulnerable than other children to abuse by their peers. (p.2)

Neglect of disabled children

Neglect is discussed further in Chapter 5, but with regard to disabled children specifically, Kennedy and Wonnacott (2005) give a very useful overview of some of the key practice issues to consider in relation to the neglect of disabled children. They take a social model of disability as their starting point, but also highlight the need to assess parental capacity. As with all children, neglect can impact on all aspects of development, but there is a danger that compromised development for disabled children is blamed on the impairment, not neglect. Practitioners can focus on the provision of practical support and be distracted from noticing when there is a breakdown in or absence of care. At all times practitioners need to be asking themselves what may be contributing to neglect at the level of environment, service provision, family circumstances and social attitudes. They acknowledge that there can be a paradox in the message that disabled children need to be considered simultaneously as no different from other children, but also as having additional needs. The important message for practitioners is that they need to apply the same care to assessing developmental needs in all domains and consider whether the children are attaining *their* potential. In particular, secure attachments are as important for disabled children and must be respected and considered when making plans for respite care. Practitioners must avoid falling into the trap of accepting a standard of care for a disabled child that they would not for one without an impairment. For example, it is all too easy to assume that being underweight is a result of the impairment, but it could also be due to lack of sufficient or appropriate nourishment. Disabled children should also have opportunities to take part in activities – their needs for stimulation can be neglected due to mobility issues or 'over-protection'.

Disabled children and resilience

The concept of resilience as applied to disabled children can be problematic. It is all too easy to fall into the trap of characterising successful disabled individuals as 'plucky' children who have bravely overcome impairment – this is not only patronising to the children concerned but damaging to others if they are held up as examples of what should be achieved with the 'right' attitude. There is very little research into resilience and disabled children. On the one hand, as children they can be assumed to benefit from the factors associated with resilience in any child; on the other hand, there may be specific and different qualities needed to cope with the interaction between some types of impairment and the environment (Young, Green and Rogers 2008). This issue is explored in more detail in Chapter 7 in relation to deaf children.

The importance of secure attachments has already been highlighted. Related to this, Kennedy and Wonnacott caution against the danger of characterising parents as 'carers' if it means losing sight of all the other aspects of parenting (as set out in Chapter 3). Paying attention to the self-esteem and self-efficacy of disabled children will be an important part of nurturing resilience. Again, like all children, they require opportunities to take part in activities they enjoy, to experience successes and knock-backs and to be encouraged to master new skills. As with all children, self-efficacy is likely to be enhanced if children can contribute to decisions about their lives and are supported to communicate their feelings and wishes. A survey of all social services departments in England, coupled with more detailed case studies, found that participation 'at any level is only happening for a small number of disabled children' (Franklin and Sloper 2005 cited in Stein 2009, p.146). Effective participation occurred when social workers had been trained in the use of communication tools and senior managers championed and monitored practice with disabled children. The positive effects of participation included: 'children feeling included in what was happening around them, feeling valued, being listened to, gaining confidence, having attention and lots of fun, and learning new skills' (cited in Stein 2009, p.147).

Running throughout consideration of disabled children is the fundamental importance of supporting communication. For example, the child protection system needs accessible routes for disclosure and additional time for children with additional communication needs, and disabled children need access to practitioners with specialist knowledge and skills (Stalker *et al.* 2009). Extensive resources and guidance to support practice with disabled children can be found in *Safeguarding Disabled Children* (Department for Children, Schools and Families 2009b) and on the website of Triangle (www.triangle.org.uk).

Activity 4.3

Think of a young disabled child whose healthy developmental progress is in question.

1. What information would you need in order to distinguish between the impact of the impairment and the care-giving environment?

2. What information may be held by other professionals?

3. What information would you need to explore the extent to which the parent is able to meet the child's developmental needs?

Experiences of separation and loss: implications for resilience and vulnerability

Experiences of separation and loss are, as we know, very much part of human experience, as developmental progress involves not only gains, but also losses associated with what is known and familiar. Some losses are inevitable in the course of development in our culture, for example leaving home as a five-year-old to go to school and leaving primary school to move on to secondary school. However, those children whom we are meeting daily in our practice have often been subjected to multiple separations from, and sometimes the permanent loss of, those people who are of greatest significance in their lives. Thus their sense of a secure base, however tenuous, is threatened. Some children are, of course, more vulnerable to the effects of separation than others and it is our assessment of the potential or actual *effect* on an individual child or adolescent which informs our interventions. For example, a child who is sensitised to separations and anxiously attached to carers may need particularly thorough preparation for a move away from home.

The way in which we understand children's experience of loss will shape not only any preparation for an anticipated move, but also vital elements of reparative care they may need following planned or unpredicted separations. In reflecting on separation and loss we shall address a number of areas which may be of significance, namely:

- understanding the process of grieving in children

- considering key variables which may affect a particular child's adjustment and recovery

- an awareness of the psychological tasks which confront the child or adolescent

- reflection on the additional tasks facing children who have been placed apart from their families of origin.

Jewett (1984) explores in some detail the normal healthy process of grieving in children. In many ways this parallels the experience of adults, one obvious key difference being that children at different ages will have varying capacities to process and understand the experience of separation and loss. The three key stages of grieving explored by Jewett may be summarised broadly as follows.

First stage: early grief
SHOCK AND NUMBING
Jewett describes the typical emotional withdrawal of the child which is often accompanied by somewhat mechanical behaviour, as if the child is behaving without deliberate intention but almost on 'automatic pilot'.

ALARM
Behavioural reactions which commonly accompany this feeling in the child are numerous bodily reactions including an increased heart rate, signs of tension, sweating and other reactions associated with anxiety, including the relaxation of bowel and bladder functions leading to bed wetting and soiling on occasions.

DENIAL AND DISBELIEF
It is very common at this stage of grieving for children to feel a need to deny the loss of the loved one. Commonly this is accompanied by a refusal to acknowledge the facts of the loss. Equally the child may deny the feelings accompanying the loss, for example it's not

at all unusual for a child to say 'I don't care about him/her anyway' or 'I don't want to go home'. Frequently we may hear the child making rejecting or deprecating statements concerning the lost attachment figure and it is important for practitioners to be aware that this is very typical at this stage of grieving and there may be a significant change in the child's feelings at later stages of the grieving process.

BARGAINING

In their struggle to cope with the pain of the loss, children may well begin to construct ways of thinking which protect them from painful feelings. For example, children encountered in the care system commonly go through a process of constructing ways of thinking to defend themselves against the reality of the separation. A child might think 'If only I hadn't been naughty/difficult I would not have been separated and if I am good, I can return'. Therefore bargaining as a form of denial can lead to or reinforce existing self-blame and therefore can also impact on the self-image of the child.

SUPPORTING A CHILD IN THE EARLY STAGES OF GRIEVING A LOSS OR SEPARATION

Children and young people need a great deal of comfort at this stage of the grieving process and a real recognition by carers that something very significant has happened for them. However, some children we meet in our practice can get stuck at this stage and it may well be helpful to try to tune in to the way in which the child is beginning to make sense of the loss and any part he has played in the separation. Supporting the child by clarifying misconceptions about the reasons for the separation and teasing out a realistic picture of the child's involvement can prevent later difficulties in moving towards the acute stage of grieving.

If the denial persists over weeks and months, the child is likely to need more active support from the worker and/or parents and carers in order to help them take on the painful reality of the experience. Jewett (1984) explores a range of methods which practitioners might use to begin to talk with the child or young person about his experience.

Second stage: acute grief

This is the phase in which many of the most powerful feelings about the loss begin to come to the surface. The first part of this phase is often characterised by elements of yearning and pining in the child. We often see children also searching for the lost person and wishing for the restitution of the relationship. This stage is characterised by a conflict between the need to let go of the person and a wish to hold on to the relationship. This can be very tiring for children and they are frequently emotionally labile at this stage. These mixed feelings can cause not only exhaustion and fractiousness in the child but also in some children regression to an earlier stage of development. It is all too easy for practitioners to assume, for example, when working with a child who has been severely abused, that the ceasing of the abuse is the most important factor for the child. The child's experience may be very different, and the experience of separation may be the worst pain that the child could think of in terms of a consequence of action by social workers or other professionals. This can be very complicated in cases of abuse where a child has decided to disclose, in a purposeful fashion, and may explain why, once the separation has become apparent, he regrets and begins to retract the disclosure.

We see in the middle of this stage of grieving the emergence of strong feelings. Some of the commonest feelings that children experience when grieving a loss are sadness, anger, guilt and shame. The expression of these feelings may be direct or indirect and the child/young person may appear overwhelmed by these feelings at times. There may be no apparent trigger to outbursts of aggression or sadness and commonly it may be more acceptable in some cultures than others to express either sadness or anger. Jewett (1984) stresses that it is often the *mixed feelings* that children have about an experience of separation or loss which complicate the grieving process.

Following, or even accompanying, this expression of powerful feelings comes a sense of disorganisation in the child's emotional life. At this stage children often appear to lack energy, to be completely unfocused in their activities and to exhibit an atypical lack of concentration. They may find it very difficult, for example, to retain any information at school and may in fact experience the loss of familiar skills which they thought they had mastered. This can be extremely frightening not only to a young child but also to an adolescent, and workers and parents can help by being sensitive to the fear that this temporary loss of competence engenders in the child or young person.

DESPAIR

This can be the most frightening stage of grieving in the child and for the adult working with them. The child may exhibit complete loss of interest in everyday life and a strong pessimism about the future. This is the stage at which a child may be vulnerable to suicidal thoughts and it is important to tune in to adolescents in particular as they may be especially prone to para-suicide attempts, or indeed suicide, at this stage.

The loss of energy in the child and the feelings of hopelessness may be very difficult for adults to tolerate. This may be particularly true if the child remains in a household where other family members have very different feelings about the loss, or indeed are at a different stage in the grieving process. A child or young person is especially vulnerable to unresolved grief if their own feelings are denied by those on whom they are dependent for their care. For example, it can be very difficult for a child who has lost an adult who is perhaps significant for them while being hated or rejected by the child's parent.

REORGANISATION

Gradually the child begins to emerge from the grieving process and to experience a slight increase in self-control. The emotional energy returns which allows the child to begin to invest in relationships and to let go of the preoccupation with the loss. This then allows the child to begin to look to the future and sets the stage for the integration of the loss and grief.

Third stage: integration of loss and grief

When the child's energy returns this may be very slow but we may notice the recovery in increased physical energy or psychological robustness. Gradually the child will begin to feel better about himself and to be able to replace the pain of the extreme loss with a more reflective attitude. It then becomes possible to help the child to concentrate on regaining competence and mastery in the current setting, for example school and clubs or hobbies, and to begin to contemplate looking towards the future.

This is a crucial chance for parents or carers to offer valuable support to the child in restructuring their activities and regaining skills. If this is accompanied by an acknowledgement that grieving is important emotional work for children and they are offered support in regaining lost ground, there is every chance that the child will make a good recovery and also that the existing attachments with the supportive adults may be significantly strengthened.

Timing

The time it takes a child or young person to go through the grieving process varies greatly in individual children as it does in adults. We need to be particularly aware of children who have not had the benefit of any emotional support in their grieving. They may take much longer to move through the stages of grieving or may indeed be 'stuck' at one stage.

Lack of positive integration

Any one or more of the following signs in behaviour indicate that a child may be struggling with unresolved feelings about an important loss:

- prolonged anger and depression

- an inability to express feelings – helplessness, giving up

- unwillingness to become involved with others

- blocked development

- unusual vulnerability to new separations

- being difficult to control

- marked impairment of self-esteem

- discounting of self and others

- destructive behaviour towards self and others.

Practice point

Many of the children we work with, either in their own homes or in substitute care, have had repeated, unpredicted experiences of separation from loved ones. Some children and young people have complex feelings of loss. Frequently at the time of the loss, they have not been offered the kind of emotional support which would help them experience the grief process in a healthy way. Typically, we might find they have become stuck at one particular stage of the grieving process, unable to progress further without additional support. Further losses, in the context of existing unresolved losses, may only serve to confirm this survival strategy. However, if we are aware of significant losses in the past, new losses may represent an opportunity to support the child to reflect and express confusions and misperceptions of previous losses.

Key variables affecting recovery from loss

Particularly significant variables have been identified by Fahlberg (1994) as potentially relevant in affecting the nature and extent of difficulty in resolving an individual loss for a particular child or young person and include:

- the child's age and stage of development

- the nature and strength of the child's attachment to parents or carers

- the nature and degree of the care-giver's bonding with the child

- the child's perception of the reasons for the separation

- the degree of emotional nurturing available in the environment the child is leaving

- the parting message

- the post-separation environment and degree of emotional nurturing available

- the child's temperament

- the support available to the child in developing a coherent story

- the availability of continuity in relationships or environment.

Following a traumatic loss, practitioners often attempt to maintain as much continuity in the child's environment as possible. The availability of attachment figures in supporting the child after the separation may well be critical in facilitating healthy grieving. Rutter and Rutter (1993) argue that, in order to understand the effects of loss and to develop effective modes of intervention, it is important to examine specific features which may modify grief reactions. They argue that four particular factors would appear to make things more difficult for children:

1. an ambivalent or unduly dependent relationship with the person who is lost (i.e. where the mixed feelings experienced by the child complicate the grieving process)

2. an unexpected or untimely death

3. the coincidence of the death with other stresses or crises, for example family discord or loss of employment

4. the experience of previous losses especially when they have been incompletely resolved.

Conversely, they argue that there are four features which seem to be associated with less disturbed grief reactions:

1. the availability and effective use of social support from family, friends and others

2. the re-establishment of life patterns

3. the development of new intimate relationships

4. the provision of crisis intervention.

The psychological tasks which confront the child or adolescent

Goldman (1994) identifies four critical tasks in the child's psychological adjustment to loss:

UNDERSTANDING

This is the first psychological task of dealing with loss. Children need to make sense of the experience. This is particularly true of a death and we need to remember that children's understanding of death changes as they develop. Children perceive death differently at various childhood stages and their perception has a predictable influence on their grieving. Young children in particular are vulnerable to misunderstanding losses.

Understanding affected by magical thinking

Young children feel responsible for what happens in the world around them. Therefore when children experience a loss, not only a death or significant separation, they commonly believe that they have caused the loss themselves. If not helped to understand the circumstances they may live with overwhelming guilt for many years to come.

Understanding blocked by common clichés

Common clichés and euphemisms can interrupt the grief process. We need to give honest answers to questions about loss, not only death, using simple and direct responses. Facts need to be presented accurately.

GRIEVING

Grieving is the second psychological task for children who have experienced a significant loss. Anger as well as grief must be dealt with and many times anger is less acceptable to parents, schools and friends. Children's grieving is an ongoing process, often continued and reworked through to adolescence.

Behavioural symptoms

Symptoms include sleeplessness, loss of appetite, crying, nightmares, dreams of the lost person, sighing, listlessness, absent-mindedness, clinging, over-activity, withdrawal from friends, verbal attacks on others, fighting, extreme quietness, bed wetting, excessive touching and excessive hugging.

Thought patterns

They may show an inability to concentrate, preoccupation, difficulty in making a decision, self-destructive thoughts, low view of themselves, confusion and disbelief. There are clear links here with attribution theory, which is explored more fully below.

Feelings

Feelings include anger, guilt, sadness, mood swings, depression, hysteria, relief, helplessness, fear, loneliness, anxiety, rage, intense emotions and feeling unreal.

Physical symptoms

Physical symptoms include headaches, fatigue, shortness of breath, dry mouth, dizziness, pounding heart, hot or cold flushes, heaviness of body, sensitive skin, increased illness, empty feeling in body, tightness in chest, muscle weakness, tightness in throat and stomach aches.

COMMEMORATING

This is the third task of grieving. Children need to establish ways to remember the person they have lost. It is important to find formal and informal ways of commemorating the significant person. The child's own creative ideas are an essential part of this process. For example, photographs, videos, drawings, posters and other personal mementoes can be invaluable in keeping alive for the child his memories of the lost person.

GOING ON

The last psychological task for children experiencing significant loss is one that emphasises looking forward to the future. Children can begin to risk loving again and enjoying life. This does not mean forgetting the person who has gone; it means developing a readiness to participate once again. Sometimes it signals the release of some deep guilt that is often felt, especially by young children.

Our intervention may be more effective if we use an analysis of the degree to which these tasks have been completed to inform a focus on creating opportunities for these missed areas to be addressed, for example by creating a personal ritual within which a child can commemorate his loss of someone important.

Additional tasks facing children who have been placed apart from their birth families

Littner (1975) identifies key additional tasks facing children who are separated from their birth families.

MASTERING THE FEELINGS AROUSED BY SEPARATION FROM OWN PARENTS

These feelings may be very complex depending on the nature of the child's attachment relationship, the nature and degree of bonding from parents and the circumstances of the separation.

MASTERING FEELINGS AROUSED BY PLACEMENT WITH NEW FAMILY

The new placement may trigger painful memories of family life and arouse poignant feelings in the child. Some children are more ready and able than others to accept support with what are often complex mixed feelings, for example guilt and relief.

DEALING WITH SUBSEQUENT SEPARATION FROM NEW PARENTS

Having already experienced a highly significant separation, these children are vulnerable to difficulty in dealing with even brief subsequent separations from their new carers. For example, they may become very clingy when separation is threatened or withdraw emotionally in order to protect themselves from pain.

MASTERING THE THREAT OF CLOSENESS TO THEM

The particular pattern of attachment experienced by the child in relation to key attachment figures is likely to determine the degree to which closeness and intimacy with new carers is experienced as threatening. Downes (1992) and Hughes (1997) explore ways in which substitute carers of adolescents can promote increased feelings of trust in children who have had distorted or unhealthy early attachment experiences.

Activity 4.4

Consider a child with whom you are working who has experienced a significant loss, either recently or in the past.

1. How long ago did the loss occur and what were the child's reactions?
2. What stage of grieving has the child reached and what might be the signs in his behaviour or account of the loss?
3. How can the child be supported by parents/carers to make sense of the loss?
4. Who is available in the child's close environment who may offer support?

Childhood depression: the relevance of attribution theory for resilience and vulnerability

Zimmerman (1988) explores the significance of understanding processes at work in children who have experienced many moves and losses and who frequently manifest symptoms of childhood depression. Although her article focuses on working with foster children in a care setting, there are useful ideas in her theoretical formulation which may be adapted to work with parents as well as with substitute carers. Zimmerman explores the connection between repeated experiences of moves and separations beyond the child's control with the phenomenon of 'learned helplessness'. The learned helplessness theory was first explored by Seligman and Peterson (1986) and was derived from animal learning research in which dogs were subjected to electric shocks. When the dogs were subjected to repeated shocks, initially with no possibility of escape, they became more and more passive in the face of the shock stimulus. Thereafter, when means of escape were available, the dogs did not take advantage of them. In more recent research with human beings, the model has been developed to attribute depression to the perception of an inability to influence outcomes in one's life or the inability to avoid negative outcomes. In addition, this theory takes into account the individual person's interpretation of the causes of the uncontrollable event.

The model explores three explanatory dimensions which an individual must face when dealing with either positive or negative events in order to explain the cause of those events. The first concerns whether the cause is internal or external to the person, i.e. whether the cause is due to something about the person or their behaviour or about the situation and other people. The second dimension concerns the persistence of the cause, whether it is stable or unstable. For example, in the stable explanation, the cause is seen as continuing over time, while in the unstable explanation the cause is viewed as transient. The third dimension deals with how pervasive the effect might be; in other words, how many outcomes the cause will affect. It may be thought to affect a variety of consequences, i.e. the global explanation, or it may be thought to affect just one outcome, i.e. the specific explanation.

Where a child is thought to believe that the cause of the negative event lies with himself, i.e. is internal, this pattern of thinking is believed to lead to a loss of self-esteem. Where the explanation focuses on an external source of bad events, the individual is more likely to feel anger towards the external source. The combination of interpretations across these three dimensions which is believed to be most often associated with depression in individuals is that of an internal, stable, global explanation, i.e. 'it's my fault, it's going to last forever, and it's going to affect everything I do' (Petersen and Seligman 1985). This style of thinking associated with depression in adults has also been confirmed to exist in children. Rutter, Tizard and Reads (1986) found that depressed children aged eight and over often have an attributional style in which bad events are seen as caused by internal, stable, global reasons. Good events, however, are seen as external, caused by other people, unstable, unreliable, and specific to one event, not to be generalised to events in the future. Children in foster care often develop patterns of thinking which mirror these patterns. Zimmerman argues that depression in foster children is often an overlooked explanation for behavioural problems.

Often children may not view themselves as responsible for any positive action or feel able to produce any good effect. They may additionally hold themselves responsible for events which, in reality, could have had little to do with them. Zimmerman (1988) argues that 'these cognitive distortions in turn limit their interpersonal problem solving skills and impair their ability to learn from new experiences' (p.43).

Interventions to promote self-efficacy

- In day-to-day care children need to experience an environment which is structured consciously to permit them to experience desirable outcomes as a result of their own actions, i.e. to be in control of good results.

- It is also useful if negative outcomes are experienced in an environment that helps the child to explore how far his own actions may be linked to the specific negative outcome.

- If they are responsible for the negative outcome, support can then be offered in order to explore other ways of behaving which might produce a different outcome.

In addition to circumstances involving the trauma of repeated separations, experiences of abuse or neglect can lead to patterns of thinking or attribution in the individual child which need to be understood if help is to be geared to the very specific needs of each child. For example, the degree to which an individual child or adolescent blames himself for complying with sexually abusive experiences will vary considerably. Whereas one child may blame himself and believe 'I deserve this because I am dirty', another child may blame a non-abusing adult in preference to blaming the abuser. It is important that practitioners are aware of the pattern of *thinking* of the individual child and the way in which this is influenced by the particular unique circumstances of the abuse. What the child has taken from the experience by way of a view of himself will be vital in informing therapeutic work.

THE VERY YOUNG CHILD
Basic accomplishments like riding a bike, throwing a ball and learning to dress oneself are all fundamental competencies which can result in the child feeling effective and receiving positive feedback.

THE PRIMARY SCHOOL-AGE CHILD
Children at this stage can be encouraged to learn how to make a friend, how to protect themselves when under stress, how to please adults how to focus on learning tasks. Zimmerman puts a particular focus on managing in school, both academically and socially, as this is of powerful significance to children at this stage of development (see Chapter 7).

THE ADOLESCENT
Giving adolescent foster children appropriate involvement and control over particular aspects of their lives, and working in whatever placement, either at home or in foster care or residential care, to ensure that they develop social, occupational and self-care skills, are all means of mitigating against the helplessness they may feel. For children separated from their families the following factors seem especially significant:

- Age-appropriate understanding of the reasons for the placement need to be congruent with the child's age and stage of development so that they match cognitive changes and circumstance changes. Zimmerman argues that these explanations are a must to prevent the child blaming himself for negative life events.

- The involvement of older fostered children in pre-placement visits and allowing them an appropriate voice in determining their living arrangements can also be viewed as preventing the development of learned helplessness.

- Involving the child, particularly the older child, in negotiations over the planning of family contact can mitigate against the feelings of powerlessness occasioned by the separation.

- All areas of choice and consultation allow the young person to know that they can have a voice which will affect the people who control major aspects of their lives. This, in turn, develops self-efficacy, an important feature of later resilience.

Effective purposeful contact as an aid to healthy adaptation

In order to maximise the benefits of contact for each individual child, it is most helpful to focus on the *purposes* of the contact. Well-planned and well-managed contacts can maximise the possibility of the earliest possible successful return home for the child. As most children who are in out-of-home placements are likely to return home, maintaining effective contact is of prime significance in planning for their care and well-being. Even for those children who are unable to return home, work which actively supports their positive contact with their birth families can be of significant long-term benefit.

Exploring the purposes of contact

ASSESSMENT

Particularly at the early stages of work with a family, it may be important to structure contact in order to build a picture of the relationships which exist between parents, siblings, extended family and a child in order to assess the potential for rehabilitation. Well-managed contact can facilitate an assessment of the nature of the child's significant attachment relationships and this can shape the focus of future work.

SEPARATION WORK

It may well be that contact can be used to help a child and/or the adults to work towards an effective separation. It may also be important to facilitate the child's grieving work on previous losses or changes within the family system in order to facilitate later reintegration. This can help to build a 'coherent story' for the child which may be protective to his emotional well-being in the long term, whether or not he returns home.

PLANNED FAMILY WORK

It may well be that contact sessions can be used purposefully to involve the child with the whole or part of the family system in order to work on particular identified family difficulties.

RE-INTEGRATION INTO THE FAMILY

Contact may at a particular time be focused on preparation for the child's return to the family unit. For the child who has been away from home for any considerable period, it may be that there have been changes within the family. These can be acknowledged and explored in family contact sessions, and the family can then re-negotiate room for the separated child. If this is managed in a planned and sensible way, problems should emerge more clearly and effective intervention is then easier.

HELPING WITH IDENTITY FORMATION

For children who are living separately from their families, their developmental tasks can be particularly complicated. The key area is the formation of a secure identity: in other words, answers to the questions 'Who am I?'; 'Why am I here?'; 'Who am I like?'; and 'What will I be and what will I do?' Even for those children permanently separated from their families, contact which is clearly focused on meeting this purpose can benefit the child in the longer term. The experience of direct contact rather than a hazy idealised picture of the parents can facilitate secure identity formation, particularly in adolescence.

SHARING INFORMATION

Additionally, for those children separated permanently from their families, it may be important at particular stages of their development to reconnect with family members, even if contact has been lost, in order to clarify misperceptions about the past and reasons for separations and to reallocate responsibility for negative life events. It is possible then also for the child to be updated about changes in the family structure.

TRANSFERRING GAINS IN BEHAVIOUR

In order to maximise the possibility of a successful return home for a separated child, it may be very important to use family contact time to work at identifying, confirming and transferring established gains in behaviour from the substitute care setting. The more explicitly families are helped to understand what changes have occurred, and how these have been achieved, the more readily they may be able to take on these gains and transfer them to the home setting.

WORK ON LOYALTY ISSUES

Commonly, children who are separated from their families feel bound up in conflicts of loyalty. It may be of particular value when working with parents in direct contact with their child to release the child from these conflicts where possible. Frequently, the child is receiving covert as well as explicit messages from birth family members that he or she does not have permission to be in the placement and to do well. Releasing the child from this stress, even minimally, can maximise the child's potential in using the substitute placement, whether residential or foster care.

ATTACHMENT WORK

Underlying this purpose in the contact may be the effective maintenance of existing, significant relationships for the child and communicating the continuing concern of significant people in the child's life. The child may be building relationships with new family members or renewing a key link with previous carers. Clear, purposeful contact can be a major benefit in preparing a child to maintain and transfer attachments. Clarifying the purpose of the contact often helps to shape decisions as to where, when and how the contact should happen in order to meet the interests of the child. It is important to note however that the developing child may have a greater potential for emotional health than a parent, therefore we need to be continually aware of the child's changing needs for contact (Hess and Proch 1993).

Important aspects of putting together a plan for contact

Hess and Proch (1993) set out key elements of the visiting plan which need to be considered and reassessed as the placement unfolds. The visiting plan should reflect the purpose of contact and should specify the following:

- frequency, venue and length of scheduled visits
- if and how visits are to be supervised
- who is to participate in the visits
- tasks that are to be accomplished during visits
- agency and parental responsibilities related to visits. (p.29)

It is important to remember to brief in full any supervisor of contact. Are they to be concerned, for example, merely with the safety of the child, or primarily with the careful observation of interaction? If the latter is the case, what aspects will guide and structure the supervisor's assessment? Contact following separation as a result of domestic abuse poses a range of specific challenges and these will be considered in the next chapter given that domestic abuse constitutes such a chronic adversity for children.

Activity 4.5

Think of a child or young person separated from the family in an out-of-home placement.

1. What are the purposes of contact at this stage of care planning?
2. Does the frequency and shape of the contact reflect these purposes?
3. What is the impact of the contact on the child's behaviour, development, self-esteem and attachment security?
4. What messages are communicated to the child in contact meetings?
5. What, if any, changes are required in the contact plan in the child's best interests?

Foetal Alcohol Syndrome

The effects of heavy drinking in pregnancy were first described by Jones and Smith (1973). The term Foetal Alcohol Syndrome was coined to describe the effects of alcohol on the developing foetus and includes the following.

Pre- and post-natal growth deficiencies

Babies born with the condition were seen to be lighter and shorter and had smaller head circumferences, failing to catch up with healthy children as they matured. They are often identified at 'failure to thrive' clinics but may be misdiagnosed.

Facial features, physical anomalies

Particular facial features have been identified when a mother drinks at a particular stage of pregnancy but many children suffer significant negative effects without these signs being apparent. Heart and kidney problems may also be identified.

Central Nervous System effects

This is the most concerning problem as these effects can include significant learning difficulties and may be long-lasting, affecting maturational progress throughout later stages of development. Plant (2000) identifies two key factors of relevance:

- the frequency of high levels of alcohol use
- the stage of pregnancy when the drinking occurs.

While the first 12 weeks are critical for organ development, later stages are vital for brain growth and development. Notably, an individual child can be severely affected without demonstrating characteristic facial features.

The term Foetal Alcohol Spectrum Disorder has more recently been developed to include children who, despite not attracting the full diagnosis of Foetal Alcohol Syndrome, nevertheless may be significantly compromised in various aspects of their development. Children of heavily alcohol dependent fathers are at higher risk of heart defects. Particular effects can be seen at different stages of development and it is crucial that accurate diagnosis is pursued so as not to confuse the treatment plans.

FIRST YEAR

Babies may:

- be of light weight and short length with smaller head circumferences
- have problems eating, sleeping or settling into a routine
- be irritable
- be at higher risk of infection because of depressed immune function
- have problems and delays in socio-emotional development
- have difficulty forming attachments which renders them prone to a misdiagnosis of attachment disorder/difficulties
- be hard to soothe including distress when held.

EARLY YEARS

These problems continue into the early years and may also include:

- problems with socialisation, both with adults and other children
- difficulty in tolerating stimuli
- poor concentration.

PRIMARY SCHOOL

Problems at this stage can include:

- short attention span
- problems with cause and effect

- difficulty adapting to new experiences

- problems with the transfer of learning

- poor impulse control

- highly demanding and distractible behaviour.

SECONDARY SCHOOL

Added to the compound negative effects of earlier problems this stage can also bring:

- poor awareness of danger

- low self-esteem

- a feeling of being different from other young people

- an increased risk of mood and anxiety disorders.

As will be seen from the factors described, there is a real danger of misdiagnosis at every stage, particularly in relation to attachment issues and/or Attention Deficit Hyperactivity Disorder. Children affected by parental alcohol misuse present real challenges, not only to paediatric and other health professionals but also to those working in education and social care. The child with these problems may well have his particular needs masked or unmet and there may be a focus on the behavioural effects without an appreciation of the real problem. This can, in turn, lead to inappropriate behavioural sanctions and/or helping strategies.

Particularly effective inter-agency working, first in pursuing a successful diagnosis and second in structuring appropriate, integrated management and support strategies, will be necessary if the needs of these children are to be met and for the challenges they present to their parents to be fully understood. For example, the learning setting may well need to be adapted significantly to respond to an individual child's particular problems with concentration. If the environment can be appropriately adapted, however, the child may be supported to experience success and mastery.

Activity 4.6

Think of a child or young person with whom you are working who has experienced negative life events.

1. Focusing on how he or she thinks about him- or herself in relation to his or her responsibility for these events, does he or she see the cause of negative events as internal or external?

2. Does the child see this explanation as stable or transient?

3. Does the child believe that negative events will always happen?

4. What opportunities may be created in the child's current living situation to challenge his or her habitual way of thinking about both positive and negative events in his or her life?

5. What attempts have been made to help the child put together a coherent story about his or her life to date?

6. How might this be done and by whom is it best carried out?

Key messages
Key themes

- When formulating assessments of family functioning in relation to a child 'in need' or at risk of 'significant harm', it may be helpful to take an overview of salient factors which clarify the current *predicament* of the individual child.

- It may be helpful for practitioners to focus on eliciting strengths and capacities, problem-solving skills and coping strategies within the child, the family and family supports so as to maximise these and harness them in the way in which support may be structured and offered.

- The process of identifying vulnerabilities within children, their close family settings and their extended family and community supports can help in focusing attention on the most vulnerable children.

- Such an analysis can be used as a basis for building partnerships with the children themselves and with their families and the overall framework offered can be shared between professionals to enhance multi-agency cooperation.

- Sibling relationships have great significance for individual children, and their contribution to the development of both younger and older siblings needs to be taken seriously in work with individual children and with the sibling group as a subsystem of the family.

- An appreciation of core factors influencing the *impact* of adversity on the individual child is vital in structuring effective intervention.

- The powerful negative impact of carrying the role of scapegoat within the sibling group needs to be viewed with the utmost seriousness by professionals.

- The experience of loss in all the different forms is a common adversity and the process of grieving in children needs to be understood if helpful resources are to be offered to families and to the children themselves.

- The framework of attribution theory has much to offer the practitioner in building an understanding of the dilemma an individual child carries as a result of negative life events.

- Contact after divorce, abuse and following a child's removal from the home to local authority accommodation may reflect complex considerations and the *purposes* and *benefits to the child* should be vital determinants of the way contact is planned and supported.

Messages for practice

- When working with complex situations, practitioners may be helped by the use of the simple framework offered in this chapter to isolate key variables of resilience and vulnerability in structuring an analysis of information about a child at the assessment stage and in formulating interventions, often in partnership with other agencies.

- This framework can be used to set broad targets, for example building upon the resilience of family support systems or on key abilities and strengths in a child and to monitor progress.

- A key question here may be 'How will we know when things have improved/developed?' The framework may help practitioners to tease out, from a mass of information and description, an analysis of the *impact* and *meaning* of events or circumstances in the life of an individual child. For example, how might the loss of a key family member affect the balance of safety and well-being for a particular child?

- An emphasis on resilience can enable workers to tap into the child's skills and strengths, especially useful in, for example, focused brief therapy.

- Work which focuses on resilience-building strategies with individual children and young people can increase feelings of security, self-esteem and self-efficacy, all of which are important for later resilience.

- Friendships, schooling and experience in problem-solving and pro-social activities involving empathy may be as important as placement security in work with children unable to live in their birth families, as well as for those at home in less than ideal circumstances.

- It is the impact and meaning of experiences of separation and loss which determine the degree to which children may be interrupted in their healthy developmental progress. Age and temperament, the nurturing relationships and the emotional support available to children before, during and after key separation or loss experiences are highly influential in recovery.

- It is the sense which the child makes of the loss, through support in the emotional and cognitive working-through of the coherent story, which can be helpful in clarifying misperceptions and in reducing self-blame. Repeated losses experienced without emotional support can lead to feelings of powerlessness resulting in reduced self-efficacy and even depression.

- Strategies which focus on challenging the negative messages which the child may have taken from these losses or disruptions, and providing opportunities for assertion and involvement in decision-making, can challenge negative patterns of thinking.

- A sensitivity to these patterns of thinking, as explored in attribution theory, may be as useful when applied to the effects of abuse and/or neglect as to experiences of separation and loss.

- Clarifying the *purposes* of post-separation contact in a variety of circumstances can be helpful in structuring plans *in the child's best interest.*

- While it is generally recognised from the research that direct links with carers are of value to separated children, some circumstances may cause further distress, interrupt children's development, or even leave them open to abuse.

- The careful interpretation of distress in a child is a core skill informing key decisions about contact and placement.

- The support from parents, carers or workers to the child in developing and reworking at later stages of development a 'coherent story' of life events and circumstances is likely to be highly influential in building the child's strengths and future resilience.

- Understanding the child's coping skills and survival strategies helps workers to make sense of puzzling 'bizarre' or 'difficult' behaviour following traumatic events. This, allied with an understanding of the messages the child has taken from these events, helps to inform sensitive strategies for work with individual children, be they family, group or individually based.

CHAPTER 5

Protective Factors and Adversity

Introduction

In Chapter 1 we set out the resilience matrix and in Chapter 4 we described the intrinsic characteristics associated with resilience and vulnerability. In this chapter we move outwards to consider the factors in the child's environment that can buffer against the effects of adversity or else constitute adversity (see Figure 5.1).

Figure 5.1 Resilience matrix, showing chapter focus

To summarise the definitions:

- protective factors in the child's environment act as a buffer to the negative effects of adverse experiences

- adversity is the experience of life events and circumstances which may combine to threaten or challenge healthy development.

As cautioned in the previous chapter, intrinsic and extrinsic factors will interact, for example there is often a clear relationship between past adversity and increased future vulnerability as a consequence of that adversity.

In this chapter, we shall explore a series of adversities that are commonly experienced by the children and young people encountered in child protection and safeguarding practice. We shall set out the implications for children's development of the experience of these adverse factors and describe aspects of practice that can help protect against their negative impact upon development.

Risk

The concept of risk causes great anxiety for practitioners and organisations. Risk is strictly speaking a neutral term, but in child protection contexts it has become associated with bad outcomes: as Munro (2007) points out, we do not tend to talk about the risk of a good outcome for a child. 'Risk' has therefore become inextricably tied in with concepts of harm, both acute forms of harm such as physical injury, and more chronic forms such as compromised global development as a result of neglect. The range of different risks has been summarised by Cooper, Hetherington and Katz (2003):

> There are both explicit and implicit risks: risks of intervention (trauma for children); risks of non-intervention (continued abuse); risks to third parties (siblings, neighbours); and risks to professionals (getting it wrong, stepping over organisational boundaries, misusing scarce resources). (p.15)

Risk can be used both to denote the likelihood of abuse occurring and the likelihood of harm resulting from abuse. In practice it is used as shorthand for capturing an often ill-defined combination of issues including the chances of:

- a child experiencing a particular adverse circumstance
- a child being sexually or physically abused, or re-abused
- the parents or carers being unable (or unwilling) to ameliorate the impact of adversity
- the adverse experience having a significant negative impact upon well-being during childhood
- adversity compromising development in any domain
- longer-term negative outcomes as a result of experiencing adversity.

There has also been some concern that the assessment framework used in England (Department of Health 2000) focuses too much on children's needs and upon strengths, and not enough upon risk factors, and practitioners have reported difficulties with incorporating risk into their assessment practice (Brandon *et al.* 2006). However, such anxieties are associated with an unhelpful and unrealistic 'split' between concepts of *needs* and *risks*, which is often built into organisational referral pathways. Taking a developmental perspective it is clear that risks to children flow from the effects of unmet developmental needs, including needs for protection from harm (Aldgate and Rose 2008). Such an artificial split can be more dangerous for children if it means that unmet need is overlooked and the focus is only on 'incidents' of abuse.

In the context of the resilience matrix, 'risk' can be used to denote the chances of adversity translating into actual negative outcomes for children. It is crucial that practitioners carefully assess the extent of unmet need and gauge the likely impact of adverse factors upon development. Practitioners must also be highly alert to the specific dangers posed by adults with a propensity to physically assault or sexually abuse children. All this reinforces the importance of practitioners pooling their knowledge and assessment skills so that they can simultaneously assess:

- the dangers from acute events
- the impact of chronic factors.

The key message is that assessment of risk is complex and there are no quick shortcuts – it *should* feel challenging and it requires time and support to undertake properly.

Activity 5.1

1. Consider children on your caseload who are described as 'children in need' and re-consider the extent to which their unmet needs pose a risk of poor developmental outcomes.

2. Consider children on your caseload who are described as 'children at risk'. Re-consider the extent to which their unmet needs have been overlooked because of a focus on acute risks.

3. Looking across the children you are working with explore the extent to which you are balancing attention to all the unmet needs they have, including needs for protection.

Racism

When working with individual children, the worker must be aware that racism is endemic within British society and that it is not *if* but rather *how* this impacts upon the individual child and affects the child's sense of identity and self-esteem that must be considered. McDonald (1991) suggests that all workers need to be aware that they must:

- take care to inform themselves of the cultural and ethnic origins of the families and children with whom they work and remain sensitive to the significance in their work of their own origins

- strive actively to combat racism in their work at all levels, whether with groups of clients or with individual families or children.

The practitioner should begin from a position of building on the strengths and achievements of black children. This is entirely consistent with a resilience-based approach to work with children but, unless the worker starts from an awareness of the prevalence and pervasiveness of racism, vital skills which the child needs to combat it may be overlooked. The Children Act 1989 and the Children (Scotland) Act 1995 define a requirement for social workers to consider the multi-ethnic and multi-cultural diversity of our society when assessing and providing services to meet children's needs. However, what will be vital in making a real difference to the experience of the children and their families will be the degree to which a sensitive awareness on the part of practitioners and managers is translated into practice at all levels, from the assessment of overall need in devising children's service plans in individual authorities, to individual work with each child. Ahmed (1991) comments that 'not to take account of racial, cultural, religious and linguistic needs of a black child within his or her individual needs is tantamount to extracting the child out of his/her social reality' (p.ix).

Being a child who is black or of mixed parentage will add a dimension to the child's experience of negative life events, for example physical or sexual abuse, neglect or rejections. Once again, however, assumptions should not be made as to how an individual child will have made sense of her own experience but, rather, care needs to be taken to tune in to the *meaning* each child has put together for herself. From this the worker can assemble a picture of the dilemmas *this* child is left with and this will shape future work, whether family-focused, individual or group support. We know that children who are of mixed parentage are especially vulnerable to periods in local authority accommodation. As described in the Department of Health publication (1991) current research emphasises this high-risk factor:

> [There was] a remarkably high overall admission rate for children of mixed parentage…in all age groups but particularly among pre-schoolers… When the authorities' figures for admission of mixed parentage children are examined individually, interesting differences can be seen. In areas with large black populations…mixed parentage children accounted for less than half of black admissions to care. But in authorities where black people account for a smaller proportion of the population, the majority of black children admitted to care proved to be those of mixed parentage. (p.15)

Their readmission rate was more than twice that of young white children in the *Child Care Now* sample (Rowe, Hundleby and Garnett 1989) and the implications are that an alarmingly large proportion of youngsters who have one white parent and one parent who is black or from a different ethnic group will experience multiple admissions during their childhood. Practitioners need to be active in preventative work with parents if we are to avoid those unnecessary repeated separations for young black children in particular. Sensitive approaches to work with both black and white parents of these children is vital if we are to meet their needs for support:

> Ethnic monitoring is an essential prerequisite to the provision of services for black and minority ethnic children, families and carers. It should be carried out routinely and translated into policy, service design and practice which should in turn be monitored.
>
> Special attention should be directed toward the situation of mixed parentage children who are at present in care in disproportionate numbers and at risk of multiple admissions to care or accommodation.
>
> The cultural backgrounds of children's families and the influence of this on their family relationships need to be better understood. Cultural issues should receive more attention both in the provision of services and in direct work with children and their families. (Department of Health 1991, p.34)

McDonald (1991) urges workers to challenge their departments about the range, quality and appropriateness of services offered to black children and their families. She urges us to consider our assumptions in the assessments of black families, using two possible models, the 'deficit' and the 'empowerment' model. Whereas the deficit model emphasises problems and dysfunction, the empowerment model, by contrast, emphasises strengths, abilities and the capacity to solve problems and overcome obstacles. The latter model seeks to identify resilience within the family system which may be harnessed to manage current stresses and crises. Phillips and Dutt (1990) explore these vital differences in approach in full. In the assessment of black families, two added dimensions are stressed from the family's perspective:

- their own experiences of racism and its effect on the assessment situation and interaction

- the personal and institutional stance of the worker and agency on anti-racism. (p.7)

McDonald (1991) further argues that practitioner assumptions about families influence assessments by shaping:

- the information asked/not asked for

- who is routinely included/excluded from assessments

- perceptions about family lifestyles

- what interventions/services are necessary. (p.49)

An open-minded, curious and respectful approach is more likely to be successful in obtaining the information as to how *this* family functions than an approach based on stereotyped assumptions and a deficit model. More sensitive family support could significantly reduce the number of black children who are accommodated.

Parental mental health

Parental psychiatric illness can be one of the 'most potent' risk factors for a child because of the combination of hereditary effects and the impact upon the child of inappropriate childhood experiences (Schaffer 1998). A large-scale longitudinal study into the impact of childhood adversity upon adult personality carried out in Australia found that childhood adversity more than doubled the risk of adult neuroticism, negative affect and behavioural inhibition. The main adversity reported by subjects was maternal psychological ill health and the authors highlight the importance of recognising the long-term effects of maternal mental health during childhood. Children of depressed parents have been found to be two to five times more likely to develop behavioural problems than children of non-depressed parents (Cummings 1987; Cummings and Davies 1994).

Parental mental health problems constitute adversity for children that not only poses an elevated risk of genetic transmission but can impact in other ways. The pathways to effects on children can include these other possibilities:

- Depression can have an indirect effect on the child as it may well influence the quality of the parent–child relationship.

- Parental depression may lead to family disruption and specifically to separations for the child which in turn may lead to psychopathology.

- Marital discord, often correlated with depression of a parent, is known to lead to psychological problems in children. (Rutter and Quinton 1984, p.75)

Depressed mothers may have relatively little confidence in their care-giving abilities and low levels of perceived parental efficacy and may react to unresponsive and uncontrollable children with substantially higher levels of withdrawal, unassertiveness, negativity and physiological arousal (Cummings and Davies 1994). Depression may also interfere with the development of secure attachment relationships, therefore potentially undermining the fundamental quality of the emotional bond between parent and child. Living with a parent who is depressed may also impact on the child's relationships with others outside the home, especially if parents are unwilling or unable to encourage their children's social activities or assimilate them into social groupings and events outside the immediate family. If parents have a condition associated with psychotic episodes children may be faced with frightening behavioural and emotional swings and may be drawn into hallucinatory episodes.

Parental mental illness can be especially challenging for child safeguarding and protection practice. Cleaver, Unell and Aldgate (1999) have brought together evidence to show the extent to which parental mental illness and substantiated abuse or neglect of children are associated, with, for example, it being a factor in 25 per cent of cases at case conference stage. Cleaver and colleagues (1999, 2006) have also illustrated the extent to which mental health problems and a number of other adversities can co-exist, such as parental alcohol and drug problems and/or domestic violence. The extent of such problems may be underestimated because not all mental health problems are formally diagnosed and some mental health problems may be masked by substance misuse.

Some forms of mental illness are characterised by a lack of insight into difficulties and therefore it can be difficult to engage parents in meaningful discussion about what needs to change. Symptoms may also be episodic. Practitioners, who are all too aware of children's needs for consistency and stability, can be hampered in their planning by the episodic interruption of parental capacity. Purposeful planning for unpredictable episodes of symptoms that disrupt parenting is therefore something that practitioners may need to tackle head on and build into protection plans (Rosenman and Rodgers 2004).

It can also be a challenge to balance children's and adults' needs. Mental health workers may express concern that child care decisions will exacerbate the mental illness. On the other hand, child care workers can be concerned that mental health workers pay insufficient attention to the welfare of children (Darlington, Feeney and Rixon 2005; Rosenman and Rodgers 2004). Therefore it is important for workers from child care and community mental health services to work together closely (Stanley *et al.* 2003).

It is important to have clarity about roles and responsibilities, to respect the specialist knowledge of others and to be clear about who should take the lead as key worker for the child and for the parent. Practitioners need to take account of unpredictable episodes of symptoms and build strategies to address this into protection plans, and flexible services are required that incorporate the range of required knowledge and can engage with complexity.

Much emphasis is placed on maternal depression in the literature with a corresponding dearth of studies into the effects of paternal depression. The assumption, all too readily available, is that the woman should take responsibility for the nurturing and well-being of the child. An emphasis on individual pathology without consideration of the structural factors impacting upon maternal mental health is too narrow a perspective. It is vital, therefore, to identify the depression and help the parent to seek medical help, to aim to ameliorate the wider factors affecting parental mental health and to provide structured and clear support for parenting. Resources within the extended family or within the community may be offered with the aim of providing at least one 'warm confiding relationship' while taking care not to bombard a parent with offers of help just at the point when emotional energy is low.

Weir (2003, pp.320–321) offers a helpful framework for the assessment of parents with a wider range of mental health problems. She identifies key variables influencing the impact of parental mental health problems on the child:

- the symptoms and nature of the illness, including severity and duration of symptoms

- the degree to which the child is involved in the parent's symptoms and behaviour

- treatments and medications given to parents which may affect parenting capacity

- additional difficulties, e.g. substance misuse or learning disability and associated compound effects

- the degree to which parents' social and psychological functioning is affected, and the interaction with the child's developmental stage

- the extent to which the child remains stressed even when the parent is well

- separations and discontinuities of parenting affecting attachment security and predictability of care

- social isolation of parents combined with poverty

- the effects on children from marginalised groups, e.g. ethnic minorities, as the effects of mental health difficulties and discrimination compound one another.

Weir also identifies the following protective and vulnerability factors:

- the child's access to significant others, particularly if there is another parent with more positive mental well-being

- the child's age and stage of development – the younger the child, the more vulnerable they are likely to be

- the child's resilience and coping style

- the availability of wider social supports, extended family, friends or teachers.

Activity 5.2

Focus on a family where parental mental health issues are a problem.

1. Does each child experience emotional warmth from the parent/s?
2. Are predictable nurturing routines maintained?
3. Is there evidence of safe boundaries being placed on the children's behaviour?
4. To what degree are the children involved in any of the parent's irrational thought processes?
5. To what degree do the mental health issues interrupt predictability of care, e.g. through sudden separations?
6. What are the parental attributions towards the children?
7. Is there access to an emotionally healthy adult either in the household or close extended family?
8. What are the effects of patterns of care-giving on each child's development, behaviour, self-esteem and attachment security?
9. Is there evidence of partner conflict or domestic violence?
10. What do the children think and feel about their circumstances?
11. What supports are available in the children's extended family and community and how are these harnessed to help the children?
12. How are interventions with the children and the parents from within both adult and child services coordinated and what are the mechanisms for review of the effects on the children?
13. What strategies are in place to enhance the children's resilience and how is the impact of this work on their well-being measured?

Marital discord

Child development research abounds with references to the significance of marital conflict in contributing to children's difficulties. Cox *et al.* (1987) found that marital discord was more closely related to disturbances in mother–child interactions than maternal depression alone. Particular features of marital discord appear to be of significance.

Anger and aggression

Inter-parental aggression is linked with child maladjustment. Children from maritally violent homes are four times more likely to exhibit psychopathology than children from non-violent homes. Witnessing verbal and physical anger between parents is linked with severe internalising and externalising problems in children, i.e. this leads to children being likely either to blame themselves severely or to externalise their anger towards others in a persistent way.

Conflict resolution

Cummings and Davies (1994) reflect that the way in which conflicts end, and specifically whether or not there is a resolution to parental battles, may also be of real significance for the impact on the child. Cummings and Davis reported that unresolved quarrels, continued fighting or 'the silent treatment' elicited more anger from children than partially resolved disputes, which in turn resulted in more anger than resolved conflicts (apology, compromise). Therefore the resolution of conflict significantly reduces its impact on children's emotions and behaviour. This points to the importance for intervention of working actively with the parental conflict itself and building parental strategies for conflict resolution.

Explanation

It is highly significant that parental explanations absolving the child from blame in the conflict buffer the child from feelings of fear and responsibility. Explanations that imply or attribute blame to the child as the cause of the marital dispute only increase children's feeling of shame and distress.

Parental divorce and remarriage

Rutter and Rutter (1993), in exploring the findings of longitudinal studies of divorcing families by Hetherington (1989), pull together six main points of significance.

1. The studies confirm that long-term psychological disturbance is more likely to follow parental divorce than parental death.

2. The psychological disturbance often precedes the divorce which is suggestive of a link between marital discord and strife and the disturbance rather than the marriage break-up itself.

3. Psychological disturbance is found to be as frequent in non-divorcing families where there is marital discord, which confirms point 2.

4. The disorders themselves tend to be conduct disorders including aggression, the poor control of impulses and disturbed peer relationship rather than depression. This does suggest once again that the link is between the stresses of family discord and its effect on the child rather than the grief of the loss itself.

5. Disorders in children following divorce tend to arise more often if parental conflict continues. This is particularly relevant if the parenting following the divorce is less than adequate or if the parent who has custody is depressed or in other ways is not managing.

6. It seems clear that these effects may have an increased impact on boys who are already temperamentally difficult.

Hetherington also found that on the whole, in terms of remarriage, boys tend to benefit more from their mother's remarriage whereas girls tend to show more psychological difficulties. Also, in terms of age, younger children are more likely to benefit than adolescents. Girls who had a warm close relationship with their mother before remarriage are more likely to have a conflicted one afterwards.

Additionally, where step-fathers attempted to exert some control over children's challenging behaviour at an early stage in the relationship, this is associated markedly with poor step-father–child relationships. This parallels the finding from Dunn and Kendrick's study of siblings (1982) where they found that a girl with a close relationship with her mother before the birth of a sibling was more likely to be hostile to her young brother or sister afterwards, as if some jealousy or rivalry reaction were operating.

Domestic violence

In 1997 NCH Action for Children (now Action for Children) summarised research into the prevalence of domestic violence by men against women in Britain which showed that it constituted more than 25 per cent of crime reported to the police in Britain and that, in 90 per cent of those incidents involving domestic violence within families, children were either present when the assault was occurring, or in the next room and able to overhear the conflict. Not long afterwards Hester *et al.* (2000) produced a highly influential book, *Making an Impact*, that marshalled the evidence on the deleterious effects of domestic violence on children. Since then there have been a number of policy and practice initiatives in the UK and in other jurisdictions with similar child welfare systems with the aim of improving the professional response to children. Such initiatives have had mixed results and even some counter-productive outcomes. For example, in a number of countries the police began to routinely alert social services to cases of domestic violence where children were present. This resulted in a flooding of child protective services and near paralysis of the system (see, for example, Cleaver *et al.* 2006). Nonetheless, there is now much greater awareness of the issue of domestic violence and its relevance to child safeguarding and protection practice.

It is telling that a recent comprehensive review of the international literature on child maltreatment included 'intimate partner violence' as a category of child maltreatment, defining it as: 'any incident of threatening behaviour, violence, or abuse (psychological, physical, sexual, financial, or emotional) between adults who are, or have been, intimate partners or family members, irrespective of sex or sexuality' (Gilbert *et al.* 2009, p.69).

Reviewing various evidence they found prevalence figures of between 8 and 25 per cent. The study of violence in teenage relationships described in Chapter 8 suggests that many seeds of continued problems are still being sown (Barter *et al.* 2009). There is now, also, even greater awareness of the extent of the overlap between domestic violence and the sexual, emotional and physical abuse of children (Bentovim *et al.* 2009). The estimate in Gilbert *et al.* (2009) is that the risk of other forms of child maltreatment for children who are witnessing domestic violence is between 30 and 60 per cent.

A second edition of Hester *et al.*'s book (2007) indicates that we have developed even greater understanding of the potential impact of the adversity of domestic violence upon all domains of development. Taken together, studies have indicated a range of effects which witnessing domestic violence may have on individual children, including:

- feelings of guilt, shame, powerlessness, anger and responsibility for their mother's suffering

- feelings of fear and anxiety that may result in low self-esteem and self-confidence

- nightmares, disrupted sleep patterns, bed wetting and eating disorders

- depression, withdrawn behaviour, passivity and aggressive and disruptive behaviour

- disruptions to schooling due to a range of factors such as injury, caring for siblings and moving

- experience of suicidal and self-harm feelings

- isolation from peers – children may be violent or act out violence towards their peers and siblings

- in cases where mothers take the side of their violent partners, children may experience a sense of betrayal

- running away from home and leaving home prematurely in adolescence without having made adequate plans for the future

- low educational achievement.

Because of the extent to which domestic violence co-exists with a range of other adversities it is difficult to directly attribute specific problems to the impact of domestic violence alone, but a number of adverse and protective factors may affect children's responses to the violence (NCH Action for Children 1997):

1. the frequency and severity of violence children have witnessed being inflicted on their mother, either through overhearing or observation

2. the length of time children have been exposed to such violence

3. issues relating to race, culture, age, gender, disability, sexual orientation and socio-economic status

4. whether the child has any outside support from extended family, friends or community

5. the nature of external interventions from agencies or community

6. whether children blame anyone, including themselves, for the violence

7. whether children perceive violence as a way of getting their needs met

8. whether there is inconsistent punishment from the mother or father

9. whether the abusive man manipulates family relationships

10. the quality of the mother's relationship with her child. (pp.15–16)

In summary, domestic violence constitutes a significant adversity. In a study of practice where there was a need for both adult and children's services Cleaver *et al.* (2006)

considered cases referred to children's social care where there was domestic abuse and/ or substance misuse. The research was undertaken in six local authorities, and involved case file scrutiny for 357 cases and in-depth case studies for 17 cases. Half of the 357 cases related primarily to domestic abuse and half to substance misuse, although they overlapped in at least a fifth of cases. High levels of co-morbidity were found and in the case studies many parents in the sample had combinations of poor mental or physical health, learning disability, poor housing, debt, and involvement in prostitution. All these factors constituted high levels of adversity leading to significant effects on children:

> three quarters of children had unmet needs in at least one area of their development, 85% were living with parents who were not able to undertake all key parenting tasks, and the wider family and environment were having a negative impact on most children (87.5%). Indeed, a fifth of cases were classified by the research team as *multiple problem* (that is children had severe needs in relation to all three domains: developmental needs *and* parenting capacity *and* family and environmental factors). (p.5)

Cleaver *et al.* also described very patchy assessment practice and poor collaboration. For example, domestic abuse services were only represented at 5 per cent of case conferences even though 72.7 per cent of the conferences related to domestic abuse. There was a clear need for greater collaboration across adult and children's services and also with housing services. Messages from parents who were interviewed were that

> services to help families like their own could be improved if practitioners paid greater attention to ensuring families understood what was happening; consulted them throughout the process of assessment, planning and intervention; adopted a more honest, open and respectful approach; provided longer-term service provision; and co-ordinated better with other service providers. (p.8)

A clear pointer from this study for practitioners is that domestic violence must be taken very seriously, and that practitioners must fully assess the impact of adversity on both the children and parent (nearly always the mother) and pool their efforts with other professionals and specialists. O'Hara (1993, 1994) has delineated areas for practice consideration in the context of domestic violence in relation to consultation with children, alliances with mothers and confrontation of violent men.

Consultation with children

It is important to raise the issue with children themselves as research suggests that fewer than one-fifth of mothers discuss the violence with their children which can increase feelings of both confusion and isolation (NCH Action for Children 1994). Children have varied responses to domestic violence and it is important for practitioners to recognise that each child's experience will be unique. The fact that the violence is subjective underlines the importance of practitioners' awareness of the meaning of the violence to each child. It will then be possible to harness more effective supports and devise intervention more appropriately. While there are some children who need relatively little support, others may need not only intensive help, but over a longer period.

It is also important to understand that the individual child's particular coping and survival strategies may be critical in helping her to elicit appropriate support from other adults as well as clarifying the underlying cause of what may be perceived as difficult behaviour. Children need opportunities to communicate about a range of difficult issues in their lives but especially about domestic violence. For those children who attend day care centres or support projects, the provision of play materials, books or activities which raise the issue of violence in the family may allow the child a vehicle for communicating about their experiences. These may also provide opportunities for helping them to make sense of what has happened to them. Above all, it is vital that practitioners seek to understand the child's feelings and dilemmas and to take them seriously in their interventions.

Information about sources of help and protection for children and young people is vital in communicating an awareness that adults outside the family may be able to help them, as well as communicating information about some of the effects that living with violence may have upon them. In particular, those children who face various forms of discrimination because of a number of factors, for example race, disability or class, may need particular support in considering the impact of the violence in their lives.

The formation of alliances with non-abusing mothers

It will be helpful initially to raise the issue of the prevalence of violence in families, as many women are reluctant to disclose that they are experiencing verbal and physical abuse from their partners. They also need reassurance that they are not going to be judged to be bad mothers if they have not been able to prevent the violence. Practitioners need to be aware that many women have already developed a range of strategies for coping with the violence. Building on these strengths may well be a way of developing and strengthening a helpful alliance with an individual mother. Given that so many mothers find it difficult to discuss the violence with their children, encouraging them to do so may well be of great help to the child. Many women will also be experiencing racism or discrimination due to disability or class, which may have powerful effects on their ability to seek and make use of help. They may well feel that they have very limited alternatives to continuing to tolerate the violence so the exploration of practical alternatives of seeking help for themselves and protection for their children may well be critical.

The direct confrontation and control of the behaviour of violent men

Women are still expected to carry the responsibility for the protection of children, even though the perpetrators of domestic violence are predominantly men. Locating the responsibility for his actions with the man is, therefore, important for the network of professionals involved. Prior to engaging in work with violent men, it is crucial to make an assessment of the protection and safety needs of the women and children involved. An awareness of the effect the work with the man might have on the woman is vital in considering how to intervene. Contacts with local police domestic violence units and close working with colleagues in probation and criminal justice teams will be useful in developing an alliance for workers to develop strategies for safety and protection not only for the women and their children, but also for staff.

Contact in the context of domestic violence

The issue of post-separation contact between children and fathers is particularly challenging in the context of domestic violence. Hester and Radford (1992, 1996) and Hester and Pearson (1993) explored the impact of domestic violence on the negotiation of contact arrangements in Britain and Denmark for children after divorce or separation. Of significant concern from the study was the absence of clear linking between the safety of women and the safety of their children in the professional plans for organising contact between children and their separated parents. They sum up their views in the following three points.

1. The lack of regard for women's safety among professionals and legal personnel, and the effect of this on the welfare of women and children.

2. The misguided belief of professionals and advisors that to face visiting contact with an abusive father is *always* in the best interests of a child.

3. The difficulties which professionals and advisors have in considering the actual, rather than hypothetical, needs and views of a particular child. (p.103)

The mother may be at risk of further violence or intimidation directly from the abusive ex-partner and needs ongoing post-separation support. The availability of resources and legal advice is especially critical for black women as institutionalised racism in the provision of such services leaves these women particularly vulnerable in contact arrangements (Mama 1989). Even in cases where physical or sexual abuse of a child has been established, there is a worrying tendency on the part of those structuring contact with a father to challenge the child's reluctance to see him and structure arrangements which potentially leave the child additionally at risk. There may be significant risks to the children themselves within the contact arrangements including possible kidnapping of the child and also physical, sexual or emotional abuse during contact visits. The child may witness or be implicated in the further violence or abuse of the mother. A recent study in Ireland has also confirmed the extent of ongoing physical and emotional abuse of children by fathers post-separation and has highlighted that children are not given sufficient opportunities to give their views (Holt 2010).

Hester (2009) has developed the 'three planets' model that describes the domestic violence planet, the child protection planet and the child contact planet as having their own distinct 'histories, culture, laws, and populations'. She argues that those whose primary focus is domestic violence take a feminist perspective and have a clear focus on the gender issues involved and the responsibility of the man for his violence; those on the child protection planet are primarily focused on the protection of children and may often place considerable pressure on mothers to take responsibility for protection and for separation from the violent man; and those on the child contact planet are focused on the importance of maintaining children's relationships with absent parents. Decisions in all these arenas may be very different, with court decisions about contact appearing to downplay the impact of the violence upon children.

For practitioners working with children it is vital that they establish a relationship of trust, are aware of the position of the children in relation to any violence, and consider the age and stage of the children and hear their views. Children's views and emotions may be confused and mixed and may change over time. Not only is it important to seek and to continue to monitor children's views, but the practitioners working most closely with the child must ensure that these views are heard by the wider network of professionals. Further guidance on working with domestic violence can also be found in Humphreys and Stanley (2006).

Emotional abuse

While some children suffer emotional abuse from parents who do not deliberately intend to cause harm or distress, for example parents who are mentally ill, abuse alcohol or drugs or who are themselves immature and do not understand the child's emotional needs, it needs to be recognised that in a small number of situations we meet parents who deliberately target their children in an emotionally punitive manner. Regardless of parental intention, practitioners need to focus on the *effects* of the parenting interactions on the individual child. The following categorisation of various forms of emotional abuse has been used to examine parenting behaviour in relation to a specific child.

O'Hagan (1993) suggests that emotional and psychological abuse may be differentiated from one another and offers the following definitions:

> Emotional abuse is sustained, repetitive, inappropriate emotional response to the child's expression of emotion and its accompanying expressive behaviour. (p.28)

> Psychological abuse is the sustained, repetitive inappropriate behaviour which damages or substantially reduces the creative and developmental potential of crucially important mental faculties and mental processes of a child; these include intelligence, memory, recognition, attention, language and moral development. (p.33)

Some parents, for example, fail to respond to a child's experiences of feeling pleasure, distress or anxiety. Others ridicule or diminish children's capacity to think for themselves, to develop links between cause and effect or to practise and enlarge their ability to memorise events and facts. He argues that, while the former primarily affects the child's ability to recognise and accept her own feelings, the latter interrupts the healthy development of broader cognitive skills, affecting the child's confidence in exploration and learning and her healthy moral development.

An alternative classification of types of emotional abuse is suggested by Garbarino and Garbarino (1986) and is described as follows.

Rejecting

The adult refuses to acknowledge the child's worth and the legitimacy of the child's needs.

Isolating

The adult cuts the child off from normal social experiences, prevents the child from forming friendships and makes the child believe that they are alone in the world.

Terrorising

The adult verbally assaults the child, creates an atmosphere of fear, bullies and frightens the child and makes the child believe that the world is hostile and unpredictable.

Ignoring

The adult deprives the child of essential stimulation and responsiveness, stifling emotional growth and intellectual development.

Corrupting

The adult mis-socialises the child and stimulates the child to engage in destructive, antisocial behaviour, leading to problems in the child's social development.

The authors caution practitioners to recognise the characteristics of emotionally abusive parents, suggesting that behavioural extremes are the most significant features to note. They suggest that practitioners should be especially aware of the parent who is so over-controlled that there is no opportunity for the normal healthy ventilation of negative feelings on a day-to-day basis, and equally of the parent who is so under-controlled that the slightest distress that they experience will be projected on to the child. They note:

> children are resilient and they can handle parents' normal emotional ebb and flow; what most children typically cannot handle is a pervasive pattern of destructed emotions or extreme outbursts that threaten their world. In most cases, isolated trauma is not nearly so threatening as repeated emotional assault. (p.12)

When further defining emotional maltreatment Garbarino and Garbarino describe four ways in which parents may penalise the child for particular behaviours:

1. By punishing smiling, mobility, exploration, vocalisation and manipulation of objects. They emphasise that children have a natural drive to explore their environment and to achieve mastery. The punishing of this drive and the behaviour which accompanies it threatens the child's development of competence.

2. By the discouraging of care-giver and infant attachment. Because the development of healthy attachment relationships is central to other aspects of development, persistent efforts on the part of parents to discourage this attachment imply a direct threat to healthy development.

3. By penalising a child for showing signs of positive self-esteem.

4. By penalising the child's use of inter-personal skills which are necessary for adequate performance outside the home, for example at school and in peer groups. Not only do abusive parents commonly discourage their children from social interaction,

but they additionally do not provide the positive reinforcement necessary for the development of important key interpersonal skills. (pp.19–20)

Prior and Glaser (2006) identify particular qualitative dimensions of emotional abuse of relevance in assessment. These include:

1. persistent negative attributions toward the child

2. emotional unavailability

3. unresponsiveness or emotional neglect, sometimes described as 'the trauma of absence'

4. failure to recognise the child's individuality and personal boundaries

5. inconsistent expectations

6. mis-socialisation. (Quoted in Bentovim *et al.* 2009 p.26)

Emotional and physical neglect

For children, the experience of neglect is one of the most significant adversities. The effects are often compounded by the fact that neglect so often co-exists with a range of other adversities and structural disadvantages. As Bentovim *et al.* (2009) comment:

> physical neglect comprises a lack both of physical care taking and supervision and a failure to fulfil the developmental needs of the child in terms of cognitive stimulation. Severe neglect is associated with major retardation of cognitive functioning and growth, poor hygiene, withdrawal and, in extreme states, a pseudo-autistic state, all of which can rapidly reverse in alternative care. (p.26)

Physical and emotional factors are often intertwined. Although emotional neglect may occur in the absence of physical neglect, it is important to understand the extent to which physical neglect can impact emotionally upon children. The myth of 'unhappy but dirty' children does chronically neglected children a real disservice. Developing a clear definition of neglect is therefore complex; one can break it down into many categories such as medical neglect, educational neglect and so on. However, in keeping with the theme of this book, we suggest starting with Dubowitz *et al.*'s broader definition of 'neglect occurs when a basic need of a child is not met, regardless of the cause', because this keeps the focus on the child and avoids deflection into issues of parental culpability and intent (Dubowitz *et al.* 1993). A definition of neglect which requires that there are observable effects of an immediate nature also presents problems for the practitioner as it is apparent from the research that the true impact of neglect may only emerge at later stages of development.

Significant findings in relation to neglect have come from the Minnesota Mother–Child Project Study (Erickson, Egeland and Pianta 1989), a prospective longitudinal study designed to follow the development of more than 250 children identified as being at risk from parenting problems. Families were identified as being at risk of parenting problems due to a combination of adversities, poverty, youth of the parent, poor educational attainment, lack of support and unstable life circumstances. The study separated the children into four specific groups:

1. physically abused

2. mentally abused

3. neglected

4. those with emotionally neglectful or 'psychologically unavailable' parents.

The study showed a pattern of anxious attachment in two-thirds of the neglected children at one year of age. When seen again at two years of age, additional characteristics of low enthusiasm, low levels of frustration, considerable anger and non-compliance were also noted. When seen later at 54 months of age, these same children demonstrated poor impulse control, extreme dependence on their nursery teachers and other generalised behavioural problems in the classroom. This is underlined by the finding that there was a dramatic decline in the performance of these children on developmental tasks between the ages of 9 and 24 months. The authors distinguish between the effects of abuse and neglect, suggesting that abused children are likely to be more aggressive than their non-neglected or maltreated peers, whereas neglected children demonstrate less social interaction. Abused children are often described as having difficult temperaments, demonstrating anger when under pressure, whereas neglected children in the study were more passive, tended towards helplessness when under stress and exhibited significant delays in their development. Although abused children experience problems of language disorder or delay, these problems were found to be more severe in neglected children. They note that several studies of maltreated children, including those who are neglected, show a high incidence of attachment problems. Both abused and neglected children often demonstrate a pattern of anxious attachment. Emotional neglect, especially during the first two years of life, has a striking and long-lasting impact on the child's relationships with other children, with teachers and with family members, and also with respect to learning and problem-solving capacities. Overall, the effects of neglect are stronger than the negative impact of poverty in relation to their impact on development.

Mothers in the neglectful group did not provide appropriate health, physical care or protection for their children and, although they expressed concern and interest in their children, their care of them was seen to be inadequate to meet their needs. It is important to note the paucity of research on fathers of neglected children which underlines the extent to which the responsibility for child care is still overwhelmingly located with mothers.

Of particular note is the term *psychologically unavailable* which describes parents who overlook, for whatever reason, a child's requests for comfort and support. This more subtle form of neglect has serious long-term consequences for young children: 'whether or not the child sustains physical injury, at the core of maltreatment is lasting damage to the child's sense of self and the resulting impairment of social, emotional and cognitive functioning' (Erickson and Egeland 1996, p.5).

In the group of children with psychologically unavailable parents, the mothers appeared detached and unresponsive to their children's bids for nurturing. Their interactions were described as 'mechanical and perfunctory' and they exhibited no pleasure in the relationship with the child. Those children with psychologically unavailable parents during their infant years continued to have problems throughout their primary school years. When they were tested on the Child Behavior Checklist, they were found to be more socially withdrawn, less popular with peers, and in general demonstrated more of a tendency to internalise responsibility for negative life events. This links strongly with comments about attribution theory in Chapter 4.

Comprehensive guidance for assessment and intervention with neglect can be found in specialised texts such Horwath (2007), Moran (2009), Stevenson (2007) and Taylor and Daniel (2005). The work of Hughes (1997, 2006) provides a clear theoretical framework for practitioners, drawn from attachment theory, to help substitute carers to create an environment of close relationships for children who suffer maltreatment of various kinds. His theoretical exposition (1997) explains his therapeutic approach in full, and a later work (2006) explores specific strategies used to help a very poorly attached child who has experienced maltreatment to make new attachments. Schofield and Beek (2006) also offer detailed guidance for foster and adoptive carers in five key domains of the child's emotional life. Their very practical framework, carried through into practical suggestions, helps practitioners and carers to develop deliberate, focused strategies for promoting both attachment and linked resilience.

Assessment

Two key factors should be borne in mind when planning for neglected children:

1. the value of a developmental perspective on all aspects of the child's growth and maturation

2. the importance of partnership and cooperation, both with families and with colleagues in other professions, when making critical assessments of 'significant harm' in this area.

In bringing together issues of attachment, progress in development and parental capacity and willingness to cooperate, key areas to include in assessment are:

- the family and relationship context in which the concerns arise

- the process of development of the child in this context

- the nature of any significant harm and its effect on the child's development

- the changes which are required in order to meet the child's needs

- parental willingness and/or capacity to do this and any conditions which would be fundamental in order to achieve change

- an exploration of whether or not these changes can be achieved without compulsory measures of care

- consideration of the least detrimental alternative if necessary.

Because neglect affects all domains of a child's life it is all the more important that all the disciplines cooperate to assess the impact on development and to develop and implement a plan to ensure that all needs are met. Practitioners such as health visitors, school nurses, general practitioners, paediatricians and other medical specialists can all help in understanding the child's physical and emotional development. Cooperation with educational psychologists, clinical psychologists and psychiatrists (experienced in work with adults and with children) is vital for assessment of complex family situations. Teachers are often a source of detailed information about the child and about parent–child interaction as well as educational attainment. Educational psychologists often play a key role in identifying and interpreting the specific intellectual problems of an individual child combined with any emotional and social difficulties.

Consideration of the constellation of current and past adversities is also necessary. Brandon *et al.* (2008) caution practitioners against the 'start again syndrome', urging practitioners from all disciplines to take into account the impact of *past* history and the effects of living with domestic violence, parental mental ill health and parental substance misuse.

Intervention

Crittenden (1996) identifies issues which have major implications for agency policy.

- It is unlikely that neglectful parents can respond to interventions which require rapid change.

- Involvement of multiple helpers engaged in a number of concurrent strategies is likely to overwhelm parents because their social competency is likely to be more limited.

- The children of neglectful families require compensatory services from all agencies to safeguard their overall well-being, e.g. extra support with school, day care services.

- Only a few helpers should be involved and their relationship to the family should be long term and intensive.

- The parents' failure to link cause and effect should be central to the work and treatment should focus on the 'meaning of behaviour' and concentrate on generating positive and rewarding outcomes to interaction for the parents and the children. (p.164)

On the basis of a review of intervention literature Moran (2009) also advises that intervention should be long term, multi-faceted, be early as well as late, consider protective factors as well as risk factors, be parent/carer friendly, involve fathers as well as mothers and include a focus on attachment. Understanding the nature of the child's attachment relationships provides a useful framework, not only for understanding the impact of neglect, but also for effective intervention. Working to strengthen the child's secure base within the context of her family relationships may help her, not only at home, but also in the school setting. Emotionally neglected children may not ask for the kind of support they need from adults because they have ceased to expect a response and therefore do not even try to elicit nurturing. Work with parents focused on helping them to understand the child's needs and on locating the precise nature of any attachment difficulties is likely to be most effective. A recent systematic review identified promising indications for resilient-peer training, imaginative play training, therapeutic day training and multi-systemic therapy and video feedback to increase maternal sensitivity (MacMillan *et al.* 2009).

Neglect is complex, multi-faceted and usually chronic; therefore seeking quick solutions is misguided. Intervention should aim to tackle adversity at each ecological level and should therefore draw on the skills of the whole professional and para-professional network.

Physical abuse
Effects of physical abuse
Gibbons *et al.* (1995) reported on a follow-up study of pre-school children nine or ten years after placement on child protection registers. The aims were to assess the physical growth, cognitive ability and school achievement, emotional and behavioural problems and relationships with peers in children who were placed on child protection registers when they were under five years as a result of physical ill-treatment and compare them with children of the same age and sex who lived nearby and attended the same schools. Significant differences were found between the physically abused and comparison children after adjusting for the effects of social class and disadvantage.

- There were significant differences in behaviour as rated not only by parents but also by teachers. The abused children, both boys and girls, were more likely to display behavioural problems. These were:
  - restlessness and fidgetiness
  - looking miserable
  - appearing to be both solitary and unpopular
  - being more prone to lying, fighting, stealing and destroying property.
- The boys who had been formerly abused were additionally identified as having more emotional problems than the non-abused comparison group.
- The girls who had been formerly abused were rated by teachers as demonstrating fewer desirable behaviours and in particular pro-social behaviours than the comparison group.
- The formerly abused children had reported significantly more problems with friendships than children in the comparison group, additionally noting more bullying or lack of peer friendships and peer play.
- There were some differences in intelligence and educational attainment. The formerly abused children rated lower on a standard test of abstract reasoning.
- There were no differences in physical growth between the formerly abused and the comparison children.

An outcome profile was developed for each child. This was carried out by a statistician with no previous knowledge of the children. Three outcome clusters were identified.

Good

This group were identified by parent and teacher ratings as demonstrating few behavioural problems, good educational performance and an absence of fears and self-reported depression in the children. Whereas only 22 per cent of the formerly abused children had a good outcome, 48 per cent of the comparison children were in this grouping.

Poor

These children were defined as having many behavioural problems, low educational achievement, above-average fears and higher scores on depression. Whereas 42 per cent of the children in the formerly abused group had a poor outcome, only 19 per cent of the comparison group were found in this category.

Low performance

This was an intermediate group who demonstrated relatively poor educational achievement but both fewer behavioural problems and self-reported symptoms of fears and depression. Whereas 36 per cent of the children in the formerly abused group had a low performance outcome, 33 per cent of the comparison group were found in this category.

Overall there was no evidence that children who had suffered physical abuse automatically experienced developmental problems in the longer term. However, there were some real differences between behaviour and intellectual performance of children who suffered early abuse and those who had not, even after social status had been allowed for. An important minority of school-aged children were identified who were often in stressed and socially disadvantaged families. They were unhappy, low achievers and displayed troublesome behaviour, both in the home and in the school setting. Crittenden comments that, whether or not the child sustains physical injury, the most powerful effect of the ill-treatment is the negative impact on a healthy sense of self and the ripple effects on social, emotional and cognitive development. Crittenden and Ainsworth (1989) also found that abused children were described as having difficult temperaments, becoming angry under stress and exhibiting developmental delays.

These children also received more physical punishment at home, and were exposed to more punitive parenting styles, but they were also less warmly involved with their parents. Among those children who had been physically abused, those children with experiences of more punitive and less warm parenting, and who were living in families with significant other problems, were more likely to be more vulnerable to continuing effects following early abusive incidents. The evidence from the study points to the likelihood that physical abuse in early life is, in some cases, a 'marker' for the continuation of adverse circumstances for those children who experience parenting which is not only punitive, but also characterised by less warmth and less predictability and reliability of care. A physical assault in a family where there are no serious problems and warm, rather than punitive, parenting styles is less likely to have long-term consequences for the individual child. The study indicates that more attention needs to be paid in assessment to the prevalence of adverse factors within a particular child's relationships and circumstances. Over and above the experience of the abuse, what may be more significant is the behaviour that the child learns to adopt as a consequence of living with actual violence, or the fear of it, from adults. Poorer outcomes in the abused group would also render the children more vulnerable to all the other consequences of established behavioural problems during early to mid-primary school years. These children, we know, may be much more likely to be excluded from school and, if placed in substitute families, may experience more moves of placement and therefore fewer opportunities to receive stability of care over time, and hence more interrupted experiences of reparative care.

More recently Gilbert *et al.* (2009) have confirmed the association between childhood physical abuse and increased risk of delinquency or violence and attempted suicide in young adulthood.

Intervention

It was noticeable in the Gibbons *et al.* study that child protection registration and subsequent actions, both by professionals and parents, often led to increased instability in the children's lives and loss of significant relationships. Subsequent life experiences, including the quality of relationships available to the child in the post-abuse environment, influenced longer-term outcomes. The authors suggest that current policy and practice emphasises perhaps too strongly the protection of the child from physical danger and rather less firmly the need to find methods of intervention which act to promote children's longer-term healthy development. Social workers in the study responded, in particular, to the fears of serious or fatal injury to the child and consequently focused on surveillance and monitoring to ensure physical safety. Much less attention appeared to be paid to signs of interruptions or distortions in the child's socio-emotional development and to low achievement.

Practitioners may too readily assume that by removing physically abused children from their parents, and in particular placing them for adoption, they are automatically ensuring their well-being. As there are so many behavioural problems experienced by physically abused children consequent upon the abuse, particular strategies may need to be rehearsed and developed in the preparation and support of adoptive parents if they are not to resort to punitive methods of behaviour management.

Based on a series of systematic reviews of the literature, Montgomery *et al.* (2009) identified key messages about interventions to prevent adverse outcomes for children following physical abuse and to reduce re-abuse. They looked at child-focused interventions, parent-focused interventions and family-focused interventions. The overall study is limited by the lack of rigorous evaluation of intervention in this field but some of the key messages include:

- The most consistent and promising evidence supported the effectiveness of parenting interventions such as Webster-Stratton's Incredible Years and Parent–Child Interaction Therapy for improving parent–child interactions and child mental health outcomes. One study of Parent–Child Interaction Therapy measured recurrence of abuse, showing positive results.

- Treatment foster care was found to be effective for improving child outcomes in one rigorous study.

- A therapeutic pre-school intervention (Childhaven) that incorporated psychological services showed a reduction in antisocial behaviour in a long-term follow-up of 12 years.

- Family therapy may be effective for improving parental discipline, reducing parent–child conflict, and child abuse potential but was only compared to other types of family therapy or parent–child CBT, so the size of the effects is unclear.

- Many interventions such as family preservation services, home visiting, psychodrama, therapeutic day treatment, individual child psychotherapy, and art therapy do not have sufficient evidence to support their effectiveness due to a lack of well-conducted studies and limited outcome measures. Residential treatment and play therapy were not found to be effective, with comparison treatments showing better outcomes.

- There is evidence to support parenting and treatment for foster care interventions. Training and supervision for practitioners to be able to deliver such interventions would have positive benefits for many children and families where a child has experienced physical abuse. (pp.1–2)

Azar (1997) has brought attachment theory and attribution theory together to develop a cognitive-behavioural approach to understanding of, and intervention with, parents who physically abuse their children. She suggests that some parents have difficulty putting themselves in the position of the child and understanding her motivation and may have unrealistic expectations built around unhelpful cognitions. Abuse can occur in the context of such expectations which include:

- the *assumption of mind reading*, for example 'he knew I was tired'

- personality *attributions*, for example 'she's a brat'

- low parental *self-efficacy* and associated power struggles, for example 'she thinks she's the boss'

- negative parental *self-schema*, for example 'he thinks I'm stupid'

- problems in *discriminating* between people, for example 'he's just like his dad – bad'.

With support parents can learn to identify these thoughts and begin to change them.

There is a need for practitioners to identify those children who suffer physical abuse in the context of already poor relationships with attachment figures within an atmosphere of punitive parenting styles. These children are likely to be more vulnerable and to need skilful therapeutic support in parallel with effective parenting strategies. It is perhaps helpful to clarify first of all that, whatever the form of physical abuse, it always incorporates elements of emotional abuse. This may be experienced very differently by individual children, depending on the relationship context in which the abuse occurs. The work of McFadden (1986, 1996) is helpful here in inviting us to explore the nature of the relationship, for example, it may be relevant to consider the following:

- Is this child basically loved but over-chastised on a one-off basis? This could suggest that the child is likely to have a good enough attachment relationship with the carer but other stresses occasionally accumulate to the point where the child is over-chastised.

- Or is the child frequently physically slapped or hit because she is seen as temperamentally difficult and persistently beyond control? The relationship here may be in much more difficulty. The child's behaviour may indeed by this time be very challenging. The parent may be struggling or depressed and the relationship deteriorating to the point where the parent no longer feels willing or able to reach out to the child.

- Is physical abuse the only kind of physical contact a particular child receives in an otherwise profoundly neglectful emotional environment?

Some important factors here may be the following:

- The child may be singled out from her siblings and become the focus of parents' criticism, disapproval or rejection. When parents are feeling miserable it is very common for one child, often a daughter, to be used as a source of solace and comfort, and equally common for one child, often a son, to be the target and focus of anger and irritation.

- It is not just differential treatment among siblings that matters but also the specifics of interactions with an individual child in one-child families.

The lesson here is that attention needs to be paid both to the presence of family-wide qualities and to ways in which they impinge differently on individual children. The assessment made of the *particular emotional environment* in which the abuse is happening is vital in considering the depth of the child's needs and her vulnerability. In the latter example, we have a number of factors operating together which will be potentially much more harmful to an individual child, that is, not only physical abuse but the absence of a warm nurturing relationship would be of additional significance if this child were the scapegoated child in a group of siblings.

A second consideration is the observation of the *pattern* of abuse. How does the abuse occur? It may be extremely helpful to understand what kind of circumstances provoke the abusive incidents. Is there a particular trigger? Is this combined with alcohol abuse, or perhaps even depression, in a parent? Or does it coincide with a particularly persistent pattern of difficult behaviour in a child? Identifying the triggers will help to isolate a useful focus for intervention.

Understanding the pattern of abuse may be useful in two ways. It helps to clarify where the focus of intervention might be most necessary and effective, for example with the child, the parent, support from the community, and so forth. It also offers a clue as to what the child may be learning from the pattern of the abuse which she then may continue in her own home or transfer to a substitute care setting. For example, if a child, when behaving in a challenging way, knows that occasionally she will be slapped and that her parent will then feel guilty and buy her a treat, what has this child learned? Perhaps she has learned that, if you're prepared to tolerate some minimal discomfort, you'll later be significantly rewarded! Therefore, the treat that follows the slap is perhaps acting to reinforce the difficult behaviour. The issue here may be how parents can be supported in developing a range of management techniques for the child's behaviour which avoid physical punishment but nevertheless are effective.

The child who is completely emotionally neglected and yet somehow discovers that a certain piece of behaviour may result in at least some attention, albeit negative, has learned something very different from their experience. Perhaps it is only through the abuse that they have been touched at all, and so it is only through being hit that their existence is confirmed. This case is a much more critical scenario for intervention in that the degree of reparative care which is necessary to support this child's recovery and healthy development is much more profound than in the earlier example. This child may well suffer severely from being returned home prematurely from periods of respite in foster care. It would be important here to work very fundamentally on assessing the parent's capacity

- to meet the child's emotional needs
- to learn other disciplinary techniques and to cease punitive measures.

An additional consideration is the identification of whether or not children have transferred this learning to the degree that they have adopted a particular *role* in the family as a direct response to living in an environment of actual or threatened physical abuse. McFadden (1986) explores the particular roles which children may adopt when living in an abusive environment which they then either sustain where an abuser is removed, or take with them to substitute care environments. In either setting, the patterns of behaviour can threaten their interests, either by attracting further abuse or by perpetuating the neglect of their emotional nurturing. McFadden describes the following patterns of behaviour.

THE SCAPEGOAT
This child has learned that she will probably be the focus of punishment and so come to expect that this will happen, whatever setting she is living in. For this child, there may be no point in keeping out of trouble if she knows that she will be blamed by adults anyway.

THE PROVOKER
This child has probably suffered so much from being completely powerless in the circumstances of abuse that she begins to take control in an unhealthy way by provoking situations which result in physical ill-treatment.

THE HIDER
This child has probably learned that the safest way of making sure she is not a target in a dispute is to hide. This child may hide by removing herself physically from a situation or she may 'hide' emotionally by withdrawing.

THE CARETAKER

This child has learned to propitiate adults by caring for them and subjugating her own needs. This child may be a significant caretaker for younger or even older siblings as well as adults in the family.

Activity 5.3

Either consider a case and answer the following questions or read the case study and answer the questions.

1. When thinking of the child you know who has been physically abused, describe the emotional relationship within which the abuse occurred. How nurturing is this to the child?

2. Can you identify a clear pattern to the abuse? How might this inform your intervention?

3. Can you identify any learned patterns of behaviour or particular role in the family that the child has taken on in these circumstances?

4. What are the essential features of reparative care for this particular child?

5. How might his or her behaviour be managed effectively?

6. How might his or her particular emotional needs be met?

Case study

Julie is an immature 11-year-old girl who recently was accommodated into care after experiencing physical neglect and physical abuse by her step-father. Her step-father had hit her causing bruising and admits to finding her a 'real minx'. She has a history of poor quality care, with a number of changes and disruptions. These include an episode lasting a year when she was six and left with her grandmother while her mother moved away to start a new relationship. Recently her mother has been in and out of hospital and the main care for Julie and her younger brothers has been provided by her step-father.

Julie has difficulty with school work, relating to her peer group and managing self-care. She is unable to concentrate at school and irritates other children because of her over-intrusive behaviour. She tends to dominate the other girls and to challenge and taunt the boys.

The foster family with whom Julie has recently been placed report her to be very clinging and to be still wetting the bed. She postpones going to bed until as late as possible and frequently comes downstairs with a variety of excuses, much like a younger child. Julie does not appear to notice when the bed is wet and does not wash herself the next morning. Consequently she has a hygiene problem. Recently it emerged that Julie had been sexually abused by her step-father but Julie appeared unaware that this was inappropriate. Julie singles her foster father out for special attention and frequently attempts to tickle him, play fight with him and sit on his lap. Because of her age and because of the known sexual abuse, both foster carers are uncomfortable about allowing this, but have never cared for a sexually abused child before and don't feel confident about how to manage this behaviour. At times Julie prefers to be physically cared for by her foster mother than to do things for herself, but at other times she rejects her approaches and shows anger by swearing and storming out of the house.

Julie takes no interest in her appearance and she eats voraciously, regardless of whether she likes the food. She is very naive about the facts of life and she does not seem to understand that her step-father was at fault and that is why she is in care. She often asks if she can go home and once asked if her step-father could come and live with them. She has said little about her mother.

1. In what respects is Julie's development delayed?

2. What kinds of problems is Julie likely to encounter as she faces the developmental tasks of adolescence, given her experience of abuse and neglect?

3. What are Julie's current developmental and parenting needs and who should attempt to meet them?

4. What advice and support are the foster carers likely to need and how should this be provided?

Hints for answers

- Julie is still struggling with testing out whether she can rely on her carers to provide her with a 'secure base'.

- There are signs of a real imbalance in her ability to depend on adults and she is displaying her ambivalence in swinging between showing intense needs and demands for nurturing, and resistance to adults' offers of support.

- There are indications of poor self-care but also a lack of awareness of her physical needs consistent not only with a history of neglect but also with insecure attachments.

- Her social development is significantly delayed and she appears to have no understanding of how to pick up social graces from peers or to appreciate the reciprocality involved in making and keeping friends.

- Her inability to concentrate at school will be masking her natural cognitive potential.

- At this stage of her development she should be consolidating her friendships and her intellectual competence in advance of the less settled time of puberty and adolescence.

- In order to move with confidence into this usually more turbulent stage, Julie will need the security of trusting relationships with her female and male carers. Her ambivalent feelings about trust and healthy dependency are likely to complicate her separation from the family, even to activities with her peer group.

- Her step-father appears to have been her attachment figure as well as her abuser, which is likely to produce complications in her ability to address the complex issues around both the physical and sexual abuse.

- With the onset of puberty, even if she has shown no apparent distress about the sexual abuse, confusions and uncertainties are likely to be triggered by physical changes. There are signs of this confusion in her approaches to her male carer with a clear lack of generalised boundaries.

- Feelings of anger which are emerging may intensify with the emotional lability of adolescence and are likely to confuse or even frighten her.

- Having no friendship links will complicate her gradual separation from the family base to the identification with her peer group.

- Even though she is not identifying the sexual abuse as 'wrong' she will be becoming aware that she has had experiences different from her peers and this is likely to set her further apart.

- She is faced with a number of complex strands of her life predicament that could unravel – this is likely to be preoccupying.

- Because of the neglect, complicated by the abuse, she does not have a secure sense of self or healthy identity.

- It may be useful to consider what Julie's reply would be to questions such as: Who am I? (fuelled by the tenuous relationship with her mother and no direct link with her birth father); Why am I here? (confusions about the abuse and reasons for the separation); What happens next? (an uncertain future is preoccupying and may well consume emotional energy needed for catching up in her healthy development).

- She has learned unhelpful lessons about male abuse of power (physical and sexual abuse) and has been used for an adult's sexual gratification. These experiences are potentially damaging to moral development, self-esteem and self-efficacy, all of which are tested in the rigours of the adolescent stage.

Interventions with Julie should focus on:

- secure base and reparenting
- non-abusive care
- help with boundaries with adults and peers
- confrontation about her sexual activities in the context of supportive nurturing
- help with self-care
- activities and a living environment which builds her self-esteem
- help in expressing a range of feelings
- chances to rehearse social and friendship skills
- support with her learning
- direct support in expressing feelings about the abuse
- help to make sense of her experience of abuse, neglect and separation from the basis of a sound awareness of her current patterns of *thinking* and attributional style.

Sexual abuse

Berliner (1997) notes that it is only in recent years that mental health professionals have begun to develop a recognition that sexual abuse may have deeper and longer-lasting effects and be more strongly correlated with a variety of mental health conditions in children and adults than was previously appreciated. These issues are explored in depth by Calder *et al.* (2000). When looking at the effects on children, many researchers point out that there is a significant variability in the type and severity of children's disturbances. However, abused children are consistently found to be more distressed in their behaviour than children who have not been abused. Within groups of abused children there is a considerable range of levels of disturbance.

Some children do not appear to be behaviourally distressed. For example, Conte and Berliner (1988) found that up to 20 per cent of children could be asymptomatic while up to 60 per cent of children showed signs of acute distress requiring immediate clinical help. Berliner (1997) notes that the following features are related to a worse outcome:

- a closer relationship to the offender
- more intrusive sexual behaviour, for example intercourse
- longer duration, or more frequent abusive contact
- the use of violence
- other negative factors in family relationships, for example family violence
- family situations where there is greater conflict and less cohesion.

Bentovim *et al.* (2009), when considering outcomes for children and young people who had been sexually abused, found that long-term harmful effects were more likely when they had also received poor quality care-giving and/or had also suffered physical abuse, emotional abuse or neglect. From research into outcomes for young adult females who had been sexually abused but had received better quality care, and who had not been physically or emotionally neglected, more positive functioning was found.

Penetrative abuse, however, has been found to lead to some longer-term negative effects. Bentovim and colleagues comment that 'this is an important finding because it indicates that there may be a need for specific therapeutic work focussed on particular experiences of abuse, which may not be processed by the normal protective processes of good quality emotional support and positive parenting' (p.28).

Links with sexually harmful behaviour

Whereas having experienced sexual abuse has been found to be a risk factor for adolescent boys engaging in subsequent sexually harmful behaviour, it was 'exposure to a set of interlinked, highly stressful, abusive life experiences, not balanced by sufficient protective factors, which resulted in a negative outcome' (Bentovim *et al.* 2009 p.31).

This emphasises the compound negative effects of experiencing sexual abuse and emotional abuse, rejection and neglect, as these clusters of adversity predispose sexually abused children and young people to be most at risk of abusing others sexually and physically. 'Experiencing physical abuse in addition to being sexually abused increased the likelihood of abusing sexually eighteen times. Witnessing violence between parents, being emotionally rejected or experiencing family breakdown increased the likelihood seven to eight times' (p.31). The type of effects which are most consistent are as follows.

SEXUALISED RESPONSES

Differences between victims of sexual abuse and other children in terms of sexual behaviour have been found consistently in assessments using standardised behaviour checklists. These sexualised responses appear to be most pronounced in younger children. A similar emphasis on sexual responses to abuse have been found in studies into adolescent victims.

SYMPTOMS OF ANXIETY

Many clinical studies describe reactions to the abuse which may be subsumed under the heading of fear and anxiety. These include various kinds of sleep disturbances, flashbacks, hyper-vigilance, regression, nervousness, clingy behaviour and withdrawal from usual activities.

While many children seen shortly after the disclosure of the abuse do not exhibit severe symptoms, nevertheless, a history of abuse is highly correlated with several serious disturbances. Berliner (1997) emphasises that the full impact of the abuse on an individual child cannot really be known until adulthood (see also Berliner 1990). She explores some of the reasons why children may appear to be without symptoms of distress at the time of the abuse and considers the following possibilities:

- Some children are particularly resilient to unpleasant experiences and the experience of the abuse may not be experienced as sufficiently negative to appear dramatic to the child. The child may have coping skills which are unusually well developed and come from environments which are supportive, helping them to deal with the experience of abuse without extreme distress.

- Coping strategies developed in response to these experiences may, however, involve the avoidance or the shutting out of memories or feelings about the experience. These may be seen as psychological defences which allow a child to reduce or avoid the anxiety associated with remembering the abuse which include repression of the experience, denial, splitting, dissociation and the development of physical ailments.

We must guard against assuming that children who lack an emotional response to the abuse at the time of disclosure are necessarily unaffected by what they have experienced. They may merely be using personal strategies which are focused on allowing them to escape from unpleasant memories. The experience of abuse alters beliefs or assumptions about oneself and shapes the attributional style of a child's thinking. For example, a child may take on all the blame of what has happened or may, alternatively, place the blame elsewhere. The way in which children make sense of what has happened to them may, therefore, have effects on many other aspects of functioning as it touches on the central areas of self-belief and self-concept. For example, victims of abuse who have an internal, stable and global attributional style are found to be less well adjusted.

Some effects of the abuse may not become apparent until particular stages of development or the occurrence of critical life events. For example, it may not be possible to ascertain the longer-term effects on a particular child until she has reached adolescence when sexual development and the development of the psychosexual identity are central to her maturational tasks. Practitioners may therefore see certain children demonstrating very distressed behaviour shortly after the abuse and others who show few signs of distress. Some children appear to have no symptoms or only early or late symptoms. Particular stages of development herald the need for additional support for children and young people, whether or not they have displayed overt signs of distress. See Chapter 8 for further exploration of the effects of sexual abuse.

Factors which mediate the effects of sexual abuse

THE CHILD'S AGE AT THE ONSET OF THE ABUSE

In general terms, the younger the child, the more likely it is that the experience of extensive abuse may distort the child's development.

THE CHILD'S RELATIONSHIP TO THE ABUSER

The nature of the relationship may determine particular sorts of effects on the child: for example, the child may be attached to the abuser and therefore very confused by other adults' reactions to the abuse. Alternatively, the child might have been terrified and this may also have necessitated the child taking on a very unhealthy degree of self-blame.

THE DEGREE OF INTRUSIVENESS OF THE ABUSE

The more invasive the abuse, the greater the impact.

THE DURATION OF THE ABUSE

The longer the abuse has lasted, the more pervasive and long-lasting the likely developmental effects.

THE RELATIONSHIP WITH NON-ABUSING MEMBERS OF THE FAMILY

It is helpful to consider what level of emotional support might be available to the child and what role the child takes in the family system.

THE NURTURING ENVIRONMENT

The degree of nurturing available to the child within the family before the abuse and also the characteristics (especially in terms of nurturing) of the post-abuse environment are of major importance in reducing negative effects. A key theoretical influence on understanding children's adaptation to sexually abusive experiences can be found in Summit (1983) which describes what is known as child sexual abuse accommodation syndrome. The article explores the stages an abuser will move through in obtaining the child's compliance to sexually abusive treatment. This process has a significant influence on the child's reaction to the abuse at the time, and also important implications for the way the child feels about the abuser, the abuse and herself (for more detailed discussion see Chapter 8).

Some additional effects of sexual abuse on development

Smith (1992) has written from extensive practice experience of working with children and young people who have experienced sexual abuse, and notes key effects on areas of development.

SENSE OF SELF

This is often poor, fragmented or non-existent in an individual child. If the child was first abused at an early stage in her development, it is more likely that she will not have any sense of personal boundary or personal space. She is more likely then to encroach upon the personal body space of other people. She needs particular help with healthy boundaries of intimacy. Alternatively, the child who was abused at a stage of development when she already had a sense of her own body integrity and sense of self would be more likely to feel a sense of outrage and may be highly sensitive even to minor perceived encroachments on her privacy and personal space. Support in these circumstances needs to be respectful of this sensitivity, otherwise the child may be re-traumatised.

SELF-ESTEEM

Self-esteem may be very low in children and young people who have experienced sexual abuse. This is particularly relevant as their sense of worth may be linked inextricably with their sexuality. They have been used as objects of adult sexual gratification and in any intervention will need reassurance about their sexuality but also significant active work on building self-esteem.

AFFECTIVE RANGE AND EXPRESSION

This is often very limited in children who have been abused over a significant period of time. It is common to find the existence of sadness or even depression, emotional flatness, or angry, aggressive outbursts. The child's range of awareness and expression of feelings may be very limited and indeed many children and young people who have experienced long-standing abuse at times have no clear language for their feelings.

CAPACITY TO JUDGE PEOPLE AND SITUATIONS

The betrayal of adult trust implied by sexual abuse within the extended family setting may impair the development of this capacity. The child may trust anyone equally or may trust no one at all. Healthy survivors of sexually abusive experiences have often developed a healthy scepticism and wariness which alerts them to the need to monitor the behaviour of the other person in order to make a healthy judgement as to their trustworthiness.

SENSE OF RESPONSIBILITY

This may well be significantly under- or over-developed. We need to be alert for signs of self-blame in children or, alternatively, for a complete abdication of any responsibility for their own actions. It is common also to observe the 'learned helplessness' explored in the section on childhood depression (see Chapter 4). The introduction of healthy choices to children and active support with making sense of cause and effect in a more realistic way may also be useful. This should help them establish, over time, a healthier sense of appropriate responsibility for their own actions.

MORALITY

Young people who have been sexually abused have a distorted experience of adult morality. They may come to believe that as long as you are strong enough it is legitimate to abuse younger, weaker people, as this is their own experience. However, in healthy survivors we find a particular sensitivity to the feelings of others and this is what we would wish to model and promote in the direct care and nurturing of the child or young person.

MAKING AND SUSTAINING RELATIONSHIPS

Pseudo-maturity is common, allied with a failure to accomplish developmental tasks. This pseudo-maturity can lead to relationships developing prematurely to the stage of sexual intimacy for which the child is emotionally equipped. The child or young person needs help in developing other ways of relating, in evolving an awareness of her own feelings, alongside a capacity to communicate feelings and to negotiate within relationships.

COMMUNICATION SKILLS

Many children or young people who have been sexually abused have learned that the real meaning of adult communications is hidden and/or contradictory. Commonly, they misread social cues and are not in touch with the signals they give out to other people.

SEXUAL DEVELOPMENT

Many children and young people have been sexualised by the abusive experiences. This may make them feel different, isolated, marked out. Their emotional needs have been met in exchange for sexual activity. It is also common for the child or young person to have a distorted body image, or to fear that she has been physically damaged.

AUTHORITY ISSUES

Frequently, children have not seen adults who exercise authority in a responsible way; therefore, authority is not only unknown to them but also unrecognisable. They have experienced the misuse of power and may have learned the very unhelpful lesson that this is acceptable behaviour or even necessary for survival in an adult world. These aspects of development are complex and interrelated, but it may be helpful in planning work with individual children or young people to focus on a particular area and to clarify plans for how they may be nurtured in their current living environment in a way which challenges the messages they have received from the abuser.

Protective factors

Children and adolescents may be sexually abused in many ways. There are a number of factors that can support children and protect them against some of the negative effects of sexual abuse:

- belief in the child

- removal of self-blame

- placing of the blame clearly with the abuser

- intervention which does not further traumatise the child or young person

- non-abusive ongoing care where the child can feel protected and secure

- an environment which nurtures the whole child/young person

- therapeutic help as needed at the different developmental stages (recognising that issues of sexual abuse need to be re-addressed as children grow and change)

- links with other children or young people who have had similar experiences; particularly the availability of group support within a therapeutic setting for primary school age children or adolescents

- the identification of trigger situations which may frighten the child

- the identification of coping strategies which may have been effective in the abusive situation but later do not help the child to seek and use the support she needs

- help in managing complex contact issues if the family is split, particularly if the child or young person is scapegoated for disclosing the abuse, or was the favourite child

- strategies for self-protection from further victimisation, or the securing of the protective net around the young child

- help with communication skills

- support in catching up on developmental interruptions.

From a longitudinal study of boys who had been sexually abused in early life, a number of protective factors were identified which characterised more resilient pathways:

- a positive relationship with one parent

- a reasonable friendship network

- a period of satisfactory alternative care

- appropriate therapeutic help. (Bentovim *et al.* 2009, p.32)

Berliner (1997) emphasises two therapeutic aims in helping children to recover from sexually abusive experiences. These are the *emotional* and *cognitive* processing of the experience. She underlines the importance of assessment of the child because, as she makes clear in her exploration of the impact of abuse, children may internalise their reactions, either by way of avoidant responses or distorted beliefs about themselves or of the abusive experience. She suggests that it is important to assess the level of intrusiveness of thoughts about the abuse and also the level of psychological effort the child is spending on avoidance.

The importance of assessing the family's capacity to offer support to the child needs to be evaluated, in particular the degree of belief of the child. Because disclosures of abuse generate crises within families, attention can be taken away from the child's distress about the abuse itself and her reactions to it. Practitioners are urged to take seriously carers' responses to the meaning of the child's victimisation in terms of feelings of guilt and blame, and to be ready to protect the child, but should also ensure that focus on the support for the child is that of victimisation therapy. Two key areas are identified for therapeutic focus.

EMOTIONAL PROCESSING

This involves repeated exposure of the child to the memories of the abuse within the context of a therapeutic environment and is designed to reduce some of the fears and distress. Teaching the child some strategies for managing fear and anxiety are helpful in increasing the child's sense of self-efficacy.

COGNITIVE PROCESSING

This focuses on the way in which the particular child *understands* the experience of abuse. The child may be very confused about the experience but the greatest concern is the tendency of children to attribute blame falsely, either to themselves or other adults, rather than to the abuser. Feelings of attachment towards the abuser are significant here as some children may prefer to believe that there is something about them which caused the abuse rather than to accept that their attachment figure was responsible for taking advantage of them.

It is emphasised here that it is important for the worker to ascertain what the individual child believes, how she comes to have this belief and to understand the purpose the belief serves in the child's rationalisation of the abuse. Rushing to reassure the child that they are not to blame may be counter-productive in obscuring the particular child's adaptation to the abuse; in other words, the way she has explained and made sense of it herself. It is this process of thinking and adaptation which is invaluable in helping to articulate the therapeutic task with a particular child. Berliner summarises:

> Eventually, the child should be able to give, at an age appropriate level of comprehension, an explanation for both the offender and the child's behaviour which is accurate and meaningful. In addition, the victim should be able to identify what is different now in terms of knowledge and resources which would enable them to avoid victimisation in the future. (p.220)

In our work with individual children and young people it is important that we make no assumptions about which stresses or negative life events will have had the most powerful effect. Individual children and young people vary in a number of respects. The more that is known about the circumstances of the abuse, the child's relationship to the abuser and other key unique features of the experience for an individual child, the more readily the worker can tune in to the central dilemmas or messages the child is left to manage and live with. It is the combination of circumstances which affect the impact of the abuse. Caution is needed in tuning into what may have been the most significant events and circumstances as far as the child is concerned. For example, we may be appalled at the nature and degree of abuse experienced by a child but she may be more preoccupied with threatened or actual separation.

Activity 5.4

1. What elements of support might be helpful to a particular child or young person on your caseload whom you know to have been sexually abused (a) from family members and (b) from support services, including group work support?

2. How might additional vulnerabilities arise from, for example, a disability or communication problems, or an adversity such as living with racial abuse and discrimination?

3. What can you identify as any effects of these experiences on healthy development, behaviour and self-esteem?

4. What supportive work may be undertaken with the child and by whom?

Sibling abuse

There appears to be a need for an increased awareness of sibling abuse and the particular ways in which it can occur. It could be argued that high levels of parental tolerance of sibling rivalry help to legitimise children's negative behaviours towards their siblings. Negative sibling interactions are considered to be so commonplace that they have become accepted by parents and other adults. Much of the abuse is hidden from parents. Consequently, the impact of negative sibling behaviour on children is easily dismissed and ignored. Yet similar behaviours are considered as bullying in the context of the peer group. Kosonen (1997) argues that the issue for parents and carers is one of determining strategies for encouraging and building positive sibling interaction and fostering a longer-term aim of building supportive relationships between siblings. She considers that sibling abuse can have a lifelong consequence on the child's development and well-being.

> Inadequate supervision of children is likely to allow sibling abuse to occur more readily. This implies that the professionals need to be alert to situations where children are left together for long periods of time with inadequate supervision. The usual warning signs applying to the detection of child abuse should also be responded to when considering potential abuse by siblings. (p.15)

A further suggestion is that children who may be at risk of abuse by their siblings may explicitly be offered the opportunity to alert adults to their predicament in various ways. Parents, professionals and carers working with children in families should be aware of the general power relationships within the family in terms of gender relationships and relationships between generations and how these are negotiated in the course of family life. Children take their cues from the adults around them by observing power negotiations between adults in the family. If such negotiations are hostile and aggressive as opposed to being cooperative, children are presented with an unhelpful pattern to follow.

This alerts us to the idea that, particularly in families where abuse of power by the adults is an evident feature of the relationships, the possibility that sibling abuse is occurring needs to be considered in the assessment and also in focusing helpful interventions for vulnerable children, particularly younger siblings. It may now be helpful to return to the framework offered at the beginning of Chapter 4 and to plot the predicament of an individual child or young person with whom you are working so as to reflect upon your view of the critical elements in the case. It may be, for example, that the child is so vulnerable and the adversity so severe that separation from the family becomes necessary. Alternatively, it may well be that some protective factors could be harnessed or introduced into the child's environment which may build resilience and act as a buffer against the effects of stress.

Key messages

- No assessment of a child is complete without full consideration of the impact of the wider factors that may be impacting upon her development in either a positive or negative way.

- The experience of racism for children and their families adds a dimension to the impact of other adversities such as marital violence, abuse and neglect and disability. A keen awareness of the ethnic, cultural and linguistic background of families will be vital to sensitive anti-racist practice. The sensitivity of the helping systems to the experience of racism is vital in structuring effective, accessible support systems and in informing active work with individual children.

- Practitioners who are not experts in mental health must seek specialist advice and support from those who are, about the likely effects of a particular condition upon parenting capacity. Ensuring a proper diagnosis for a parent is a priority, followed by clear plans for treatment. Close liaison between adult and children's services is important, especially when symptoms may be episodic.

- Although some children appear to be resilient to living with parental mental health problems, there is an increased likelihood of behavioural problems. It may be critical to support depressed parents in helping children to engage in age-appropriate tasks, i.e. the maturational tasks appropriate to their stage of development. The development of positive self-concept and healthy peer relationships may well be protective in buffering children from the effects of parental mental health problems.

- Marital discord is a significant stressor for many children and is often linked with maternal depression. Marital discord must be addressed and must not be confused with domestic violence. Couples may benefit from relationship support and should also be offered help to shield their children from the effects of their conflict.

- In re-constituted families step-fathers often need to build a positive emotional relationship with the child before being able to act as an effective disciplinarian.

- Domestic violence may have many negative effects, the precise nature of these depending not only on the child's resilience and temperamental style, but also on the circumstances surrounding the child's involvement with or knowledge of violent incidents.

- Some women, having been in a powerless position in a very violent relationship, may need help and time to see the risks for the children. They should be listened to about their wishes and asked about their experience of violence. Black women, or those from other minority groups, are especially vulnerable where there is ignorance of their particular predicament and where resources available to them are likely to be meagre.

- Children's service practitioners must link with specialist domestic violence services, both in support of women and intervention with men, in order to provide a multi-faceted response to what is a complex and often dangerous practice context.

- Practitioners need to bear in mind the association between domestic abuse and child abuse as well as considering the direct and indirect effects on the child of living with domestic violence.

- Following separation of the parents it is vital to note that the woman can be at increased risk of violence. It is also important to involve the 'three planets' when considering the positive and negative aspects of ongoing contact with a violent father. Children may not initially be able to speak about what they want and need time to develop a relationship with an adult with regard to their wishes. As in other circumstances, clarifying the *purposes* of contact will be important and considering whether it can be both safe and beneficial for the child. Concerns about safety in the short and long term *must* inform the careful planning of effective supervision of contact where this is thought necessary.

- Emotional abuse is often overlooked, but may be picked up by health visitors who identify concerning patterns of parental behaviour, or by teachers who recognise the signs of distress in children. Psychological unavailability in parents is a key factor in interrupted development.

- Neglect is a complex area for assessment and requires effective multi-disciplinary cooperation on a long-term basis with regular developmental monitoring. Because neglect affects all domains of a child's life it requires attention to the full range of needs and the input of a full range of professionals. It is important to develop relationships of trust with parents and children. Issues of parental intent are key when considering the extent to which parents are able or willing to change within a timescale that fits the child's developmental trajectory.

- Children who have been physically abused have learned unhelpful lessons about the abuse of physical power and may seek to identify with their abusers and even replicate their behaviour or hide and subjugate their own needs. One of the most powerful factors which influences the likely negative effects of physical abuse is a lack of warmth in close relationships available to the child. Predictability of care is an important component of recovery for abused and neglected children and young people.

- When considering the effects of physical abuse beyond any injury it is helpful to assess the level of warmth and nurturing in the attachment relationship, the pattern of abuse and the messages it conveys to the child, any learned patterns of behaviour as a consequence of the abuse and the role the child holds within the family.

- Children who experience sexual abuse may exhibit early and/or late symptoms of distress, or show no apparent immediate signs of trauma. What helps is an appreciation of the messages the individual child has taken from the abusive treatment so as to tune in to his or her particular dilemmas, e.g. 'I'm to blame'. Challenging negative, internal, global and stable attributional styles of thinking, through the provision of good experiences which challenge these set patterns, is of value in developing a more positive self-concept and a coherent story.

- Strategies of care and work with these children which focus on the building of resilience send messages about the adult's belief in the children, in their potential and their future.

- Severe tension and violence between siblings should be taken seriously and the viewpoint of all children should be considered. This adverse factor is often overlooked or minimised.

CHAPTER 6

Early Years

Introduction

This chapter focuses on the maturational tasks of the early years and reflects on the contribution of recent research to our understanding of key aspects of healthy development. Core developmental problems will be explored which concentrate on particular stages of development, and a summary will be offered at the end emphasising key factors which may be particularly relevant for workers to hold in their minds when assessing and working with individual children.

The aim is to facilitate the clarification of the key features of a young child's development, focusing on the *impact* and *meaning* of relationships, care-giving environments and significant life events, for example separation. This, like other chapters, is based on the view that it is the *impact* of relationship support available to a young child as well as the *effects* of life events which shape the practitioner's understanding of an individual child's needs.

The core theme of the central importance of the availability of at least one 'good enough' attachment relationship for promoting healthy maturation is continued from earlier chapters and the contribution of the child's own initiatives, responses and temperamental style is emphasised. Fahlberg (1994) observes that 'a child's developmental progress is the result of the individual's unique inter-mix of genetic endowment, temperament, and life experiences' (p.61).

Although it is clear that not every child demonstrates the same behaviours or reactions to different challenges of development, there are, however, some universal themes attributable to different stages of development. The *sequencing* of developmental milestones is much more consistent than is the actual *age* at which they are attained. We see great variation between different children of the same age.

As stated in Chapter 2, relationships with family and others are the primary forces in shaping an environment that encourages children to achieve their full potential in different domains of development, that is, physical, intellectual, social, moral and emotional growth. Successful mastery of the different developmental stages is completed only within the context of relationships. Ideally, if all is going well, families help children to accomplish these developmental tasks. Children learn much earlier than was supposed about the emotions of others, and through establishing a secure base, they learn to trust others and to value themselves. They also learn to use language and how to think. Because children need emotional support and structure if they are to meet these maturational tasks with confidence, we are well reminded of the parallel importance of safety and security, stimulation, encouragement, reasonable expectations and safe limits.

In our work with families with young children, it is crucial that we are able to distinguish between normal, healthy behaviour for a particular stage of development and those aspects of behaviour which may indicate unmet developmental needs.

Maturational tasks for the first year of life

The development of feelings of safety, trust and security in other human beings

Trust is established as a result of day-to-day experiences and it is the *quality* of the frequent interaction between the parent and the young child which promotes all aspects of healthy development. These exchanges not only help the child to feel safe and secure in an otherwise bewildering world, but also facilitate the organisation of the child's nervous system and set the stage for the establishment of patterns of learning and other primary tasks for the first year.

When very small, infants do not differentiate between different kinds of discomfort. They often react in a similar way, whether or not their discomfort is physical or emotional. They are entirely reliant on the adult's capacity to 'tune in' to their discomfort, discover the source and alleviate the distress. The parent's *attunement* to the child's discomfort, when in a state of high arousal, is critical for the development of a secure attachment. Hughes (2009) defines the key process of *inter-subjectivity* as

> joining a child (or another adult) in his [sic] experience, experiencing it with him, matching his affective state, and exploring the experience with him to make better sense of it…the inner worlds of both are creating an experience together. This inter-subjectivity will impact his behaviour long into the future. (p.37)

The importance to this communication is emphasised also by Trevarthen and Aitken (2001) of its reciprocal nature, involving facial expressions, voice tones and rhythms and gestures. This is crucial, too, for communicating emotions and facilitating social interaction and language acquisition. Therefore, it is important as a foundation of healthy emotional and social development of the young child.

Sharing an affective state with another is known as *attunement* and is achieved through the capacity of the care-giver to share the young child's affective state and feed it back to the child which then helps the child to begin to organise his own experience and render it coherent.

Young children's capacity for early interaction

There has been much research into very early development and Trevarthen (1991) makes observations of his own and other studies. From three months of age babies show clear signs of pleasure in response to games which their mothers initiate. He asserts that mothers intuitively structure simple interactions to promote synchronised interactions.

Infants of five months old can take part in the familiar pattern of a nursery rhyme. From six months onwards, however, the infant plays an increasingly *active* part, often taking the initiative in repeating an action designed to elicit play or laughter from the mother. Between six and twelve months Reder and Lucey (1995) notes that infants show 'an increasing awareness of their capacity to link and reciprocate their feelings and actions with a partner' (pp.143–158). Trevarthen believes infants to be innate companions and cooperators, illustrating the centrality of the communication of emotions in the development of cognitive abilities. This underlines:

- the importance of these early interactions for the development of language and the beginnings of social understanding

- their importance in introducing humour and shared pleasure and connectedness in the parent–child relationship

- the contribution of the child's *initiatives* as well as responses in the development of the relationship.

The impact of early relationships on the development of the brain

In recent years, significant research has been undertaken into the way in which early attachment relationships impact, not only on the child's sense of security, but on the healthy development of the brain. Balbernie (2007) makes a number of key points about the impact of early close relationships upon healthy neuro-biological development which, in turn, supports the later healthy development of the child. He comments that 'positive, predictable interactions with responsive, nurturing care-givers profoundly stimulate and organise young brains' (p.1). The quality of early care-giving has a long-lasting impact on how people develop, their ability to learn, and their capacity to both regulate their own emotions and form satisfying relationships. He outlines the crucial process and evolutionary significance of the 'plasticity' of the brain. He describes the way in which the brain is responsive to its environment and how the experience of close relationships in the environment shapes the baby's brain. He comments:

> brain development is exquisitely attuned to environmental inputs that, in turn, shape its emerging architecture. The environment provided by the child's first care-givers has profound effects on virtually every facet of early development, ranging from the health and integrity of the baby at birth, to the child's readiness to start school at age five. (p.2)

The brain grows 'from the bottom up and from the inside out'. Balbernie comments that any early profound disruption of the child's emotional environment can have later effects. 'Any developmental insult may have a cascade effect on the growth of all *downstream*, later maturing brain areas that will receive input from the affective neural system' (p.2). Brain development depends on stimulation and, as the brain develops, the higher and more complex areas of functioning begin to control and modulate the more reactive, primitive functioning of its lower parts.

As the brain grows and adapts to the care-giving environment, the child gradually becomes less reactive, less impulsive and more thoughtful, mediated by the support of the carer. Balbernie notes also that the 'capacity for aggression will be increased by any factors that increase the activity or reactivity of the brain stem or decrease the moderating capacity of the limbic or cortical areas' (p.2). Here we can begin to see some of the potential negative effects of experiences of abuse and neglect in the context of frightening and unpredictable care-giving.

The key influences on brain development are divided into two categories. *Positive influences* are:

- the impact of sensitive care-giving

- sensory stimulation

- the opportunity for activity

- social interaction.

Detrimental influences include:

- alcohol

- tobacco

- drugs

- chronic stress (abuse)

- neglect.

Balbernie additionally emphasises that the young child is particularly vulnerable during the first year, not only to positive influences, but also to non-optimal and growth-inhibiting environments, for example experiences which create high levels of arousal, particularly when there is no soothing care-giver, and also the absence of a soothing adult presence represented by neglectful care-giving. He adds that 'the organising brain *requires* patterns of sensory and emotional experience to create the patterns of neural activity that will guide the neuro-biological processes involved in development' (p.6).

In the face of interpersonal trauma, all systems of the social brain become shaped for offensive and defensive purposes. The child growing up with trauma and unpredictability will only be able to develop neural systems and functional compatibilities that reflect disorganisation.

This emphasises the profound impact of experiences of early trauma, whether it be abuse or neglect and particularly exposure to disorganising environments. Balbernie concludes:

> the experience of severe traumatic attachments in the first two years of life result in structural limitations of the early developing right brain. This is the hemisphere that is dominant for the unconscious processing of social and emotional information, the regulation of bodily states, the capacity to cope with emotional stress, the ability to understand the emotional states of others (empathy) and the sense of a bodily and emotional self. (p.7)

Balbernie's work emphasises the protective value of a secure attachment relationship with a primary care-giver. This core relationship (whoever the attachment figure) is vital for:

- developing an emotional connection to others

- learning about the feelings of others and about empathy

- an opportunity to control and balance one's feelings

- a chance to develop capacities for higher levels of cognitive processing.

Finally, he notes two opposite chemical reactions in the brain to threat:

- the hyper-arousal continuum or 'flight or fight' response, noting that cortisol is also released when a baby is neglected

- the dissociative continuum or 'freeze or surrender' response.

It will be noted, however, that children under two years of age are particularly vulnerable to both the positive effects of secure care-giving environments and, by contrast, the negative impacts of abusive or neglectful care-giving. The key developmental task between 18 months and four to five years is for the child to move from behavioural expression of emotion to language and mental processing.

Autonomy, exploration and play

There is much evidence to suggest that secure children:

- explore more confidently

- are aware of their parents' availability so are free to explore

- play more harmoniously with peers

- share their own feelings and thoughts

- involve themselves in joint planning and negotiation in nursery settings

- cope better with frustration

- develop empathy towards others.

During the latter part of this pre-school stage, the child with a healthy attachment relationship is able to:

- recognise and make sense of his own and other people's feelings

- regulate his own affect

- assume other people's emotional availability

- develop positive self-esteem

- feel autonomous, socially effective and competent.

Therefore we can see the ways in which the secure attachment relationship is linked with healthy development of the young child, not only in the emotional sphere, but in social development, healthy exploration and cognitive development, providing the foundations for positive, cooperative relationships with others and the growth of empathy. The ability of a parent to 'keep in mind' the needs of a very young child is therefore an important consideration as young children's dependency needs are at their height at this stage of development.

Activity 6.1

Thinking of a young child in interaction with an attachment figure, ask yourself the following questions:

1. Does the parent anticipate what will cause confusion or distress to their infant or toddler?

2. Do they have a sufficiently clear picture of what might constitute a hazard for a mobile toddler in the home or community, e.g. fires, open windows?

3. Do they show signs of being able to read their child's cues for comfort and support?

4. Do they offer the child pleasurable experiences, e.g. playful activity?

5. Do they show an awareness of the child's need for age-appropriate stimulation, e.g. activities which promote safe physical exploration?

Making a clear analysis of the child's pattern or style of attachment behaviour (see Chapter 2) will not only clarify the child's current level of security in trusting key adults, but also inform the focus of work whether it be with the adult, the child and/or the relationship between them.

Particular positive features of attachment relationships

Ainsworth and Bowlby (1991) focus on crucial features of attachment for healthy development. Ainsworth and Bowlby explore three key themes:

1. An emphasis on the security dimension, as differentiated from other aspects of the relationship: the idea that the feeling of safety is of paramount importance and, by implication, more crucial than other features of attachment relationships.

2. A stress on selective attachments is key to security in later optimal socio-emotional development; the child's capacity to recognise particular attachment figures and to prefer their company is of critical importance here. This implies a recognition of strangers and noticeable experiences of distress or discomfort in their company, that is, what is commonly called 'stranger anxiety'.

3. The idea that later close relationships are built on the basis of initial attachment relationships.

Shared feelings and experiences

Dunn (1993) explores other elements of attachment relationships apart from the security dimension. She observes that humour and warmth are equally important in creating a bond between the child and another human being. She argues that, within Ainsworth and Bowlby's framework of attachment, several important elements concerning the significance of these central relationships remain unexplored. She outlines these as follows.

SHARING FEELINGS WITH ANOTHER

Even young children have the capacity to share feelings and experiences with another. This is an aspect of intimacy that is thought to be important in adolescents and adult relationships. However, Dunn asserts that, even when very young, some children show considerable curiosity about their parent's feelings, intentions and worries, although in such curiosity there are marked individual differences.

SHARED HUMOUR

Humour is important in the relationships of young children as well as those of adults. Dunn asserts that 'its significance lies both in the shared warm emotions enjoyed together and in the intimacy that is reflected when two individuals know each other and what the other one will find funny' (Dunn *et al.* 1991, p.23).

CONNECTEDNESS

Dunn defines connectedness as 'the degree to which two individuals sustain a connected thread of communication when they interact' (p.24). She argues that this dimension has not been explored as a significant feature of young children's relationships with their parents, even though there are marked differences in the degree and nature of connectedness in the communication between different mother/child pairs. She found from her own research that the frequency of mother/child conversations about feelings, for example, was related to differences in children's understanding of emotions.

Pro-social development and empathy

Since Piaget's assertions that children could not be aware of other people's feelings and perspectives until they reach the age of six, much has been learned about the far earlier development of empathy and pro-social awareness and behaviour, in even very young children. Schaffer (1996) reviews the literature and notes that pro-social behaviour can be observed in children as young as two years of age.

'Pro-social' has come to represent all aspects of helping, cooperation, caring and sympathetic behaviour towards another person (see also Chapter 7). In particular, where this behaviour does not involve any personal gain, it has been defined as *empathic*. When children are confronted with distress in another person, these behaviours are most dominantly apparent. This has been found to increase markedly in the second year of life. Notably, this behaviour occurs and persists, even in the absence of explicit parental reinforcement. However, some types of parental behaviour are more closely linked with the development of pro-social tendencies. These include the following:

- *The provision of clear rules and principles.* Where the parent makes these expectations clear, 'don't hit your brother', and links this with consequences, 'you will hurt him', this is more effective.

- *Emotional conviction on the part of the parent.* The more forceful the parental message, the more likely the young child is to take it seriously and the more it will affect behaviour.

- *Attributing pro-social qualities to the child.* Labelling the child as 'kind' or 'generous' is more likely to reinforce positive generous and kind behaviour.

- *Modelling by the parent.* If the parent acts in an empathic manner towards others, particularly towards the child, this is likely to have a positive effect in reinforcing pro-social acts.

- *Empathic care-giving for the child.* Warmth in the relationship with parent figures is highly influential – secure attachments in the early years are strongly related to the development of empathy and pro-social skills.

Gender development in pre-school children

During the pre-school years children learn about gender and their knowledge through the primary years becomes more complex (Golombok and Fivush 1994). Gender stereotyping may reach its peak during pre-school years and, later, somewhere during middle childhood. An awareness of gender is not merely imposed on children; rather, they actively seek to make sense of the significance and meaning of being male or female.

By the time children have reached three years of age they will have developed preferences, not only for toys, but also play involved with the use of those toys, based on their earlier experience (Unger and Crawford 1992). If we see play as to some degree a rehearsal for the adult world, it is clear that these very early influences, as reinforced by parents, by advertising in the media and later by peers, are likely to have significant effects on later life choices.

Parental beliefs, combined with biological differences, produce differences in the interaction between parents and their sons and daughters. An interesting influence at three years of age is that of peers who become important agents of gender socialisation. They too are gender-typed in their beliefs and strongly reinforce gender-type behaviours of other children. Parents talk more about anger with their boy children than with their daughters and more about emotions in general with girls than with boys. Hence we see that, by the time children are three years old, numerous influences, some more subtle than others, have combined to establish clear ideas about gender difference. Feelings, activities and personal attributes have become associated with gender.

We meet children in our practice who do not conform to their parents' stereotyped gender role expectations. These children are likely to be under particular emotional pressure and it can be seen that there are numerous additional, powerful sources of influence outside the immediate family environment, for example peers and the media. These influences are so powerful that, by the time the child reaches pre-school years, some vulnerable children may be particularly inhibited and may require particular encouragement to express feelings which have been defined as unacceptable because of adults' expectations of gender-appropriate expressions of feelings. This may be especially relevant in circumstances where a child is separated and experiences powerful feelings which are prohibited by adults close to him.

Cognitive development in young children
The work of Piaget

Although there have been criticisms of Piaget (1932, 1952), the contribution that he has made to our understanding of children's intellectual development is still significant. He suggested that children progress through a series of stages in their thinking, each of which corresponds to broad changes in the structure and logic of their intelligence. He suggested, moreover, that these stages occur in a fixed order, those stages being sensory motor, pre-operational, concrete operational and formal operational.

SENSORY MOTOR STAGE: BIRTH TO TWO YEARS

During this stage the baby knows about the world through actions and sensory information. He learns to differentiate him- or herself from the environment and begins to understand causality in time and space. Through imaginative play and symbolic thought, the child demonstrates his earliest internal mental representations of the outside world. During the sensory motor stage, the child changes from a newborn, focusing almost entirely on sensory and motor experiences, to the toddler stage, characterised by a rudimentary capacity for symbolic thought. At the end of the sensory motor stage we observe the emergence of the capacity for symbolic thought. One example is the rapid increase in language which, in Piaget's view, results from the growth of symbolic thought.

PRE-OPERATIONAL STAGE: TWO TO SEVEN YEARS

During this stage, for example, through the use of language and intuitive problem-solving, the child is beginning to understand how to classify objects, but is still characterised by egocentrism, that is, a view of himself as central. However, by the end of this stage social perspective-taking skills are emerging and the child is beginning to grasp conservation and number. Piaget divided this stage into the pre-conceptual period at two to four years; and the intuitive period at four to seven years. For the purposes of this section we will focus on the pre-conceptual period.

Piaget's observation of development at this stage has been largely confirmed by more recent research but, in some areas, it would appear that he significantly under-estimated the young child's mental capacity to organise the sensory and motor information he takes in. For example, Trevarthen (1991) demonstrated that young babies showed an ability to imitate much earlier than Piaget would suggest.

The clearest criticism of Piaget's idea about object permanence (occurring when a child actively looks for an object which has been removed from view) has come from the work of Bower (1977). Piaget postulated the baby only gradually acquires what he calls 'the object concept'. The active searching for objects out of sight is viewed as a significant intellectual milestone since it provides evidence that the child has developed an internal representation of objects, even when they are not present.

Piaget's experiments suggest that a baby is not totally confident that an object which has been removed still exists until he is about 18 months old. Bower, however, describes experiments involving infants aged five to six months old presented with an object which is then made to vanish by dropping a screen over it. When the screen is removed the object has gone. If the baby thinks that the object has disappeared when shielded by the screen, then he should logically show no surprise at seeing nothing when the screen is removed. If, however, babies think that the object still exists behind the screen, they should be surprised if it does not reappear when the screen is removed. In Bower's experiments, babies showed much more surprise at the non-reappearance of the object than by its reappearance. This, therefore, suggests much earlier development of this capacity than Piaget supposed.

Egocentrism

At the pre-operational stage, according to Piaget, thinking is still very centred on the child's own perspective and he finds it difficult to understand that other people can see things differently. Piaget called this 'self-centred' stance 'egocentrism', that is, the inability to understand that another person's thoughts, feelings or perceptions are different from one's own. He argued that egocentric thinking relies upon the child's view that the universe is centred on him. The child therefore finds it hard to 'de-centre', that is, to take the perspective of another person. Several researchers, principally Donaldson (1978), concluded from later studies that the nature of the task can greatly affect the child's ability to demonstrate his capacity to adopt the perspective of another person. Recent findings also indicate there are different kinds of skills in perspective taking, some which involve empathy with other people's *feelings* and some which involve the ability to know what other people are *thinking*. Children as young as three and four years are aware of other people's feelings and can take the perspective of others. Using a series of short stories, children were asked to indicate how the child in each story felt by selecting a picture of sad, happy, angry or afraid faces. Even the youngest children (three years old) showed that they could empathise with the feelings of another child in some situations. These results significantly challenge Piaget's argument that children between the ages of two and seven years are primarily egocentric.

The influence of the work of Vygotsky

Lev Vygotsky, a Russian psychologist, recognised that children's cognitive development occurs in a particular social context. His early theories are increasingly receiving attention. One of his most important ideas was that of the *zone of proximal development* (Vygotsky 1933c/1935, cited by van der Veer and Valsiner 1991; see also Chapter 7). Toddlers have to be motivated and must be involved in activities requiring skills at a reasonably high level of difficulty that is towards the upper end of their ability. The teacher and the child also must adapt to each other's requirements. The adult structures a task beyond the child's current level of achievement and offers support. This has been found to be effective in extending skills even in young children. This has clear implications for the kind of skill support which may be offered in day care or nursery settings to develop and extend very young children's cognitive development.

Rogoff (1990) argues that children's cognitive development is an apprenticeship which occurs through participation and social activity, guided by companions who *stretch and support* children's understanding of and skill in using the tools of the culture. She draws heavily on Vygotsky's theory in arguing that *guided participation* is widely used around the world, that is, the support of care-givers in arranging children's activities and revising their responsibilities as they gain skill or knowledge. The main idea is that, with guidance, children participate in cultural activities that socialise them into skilled activities.

This emphasises the need for practitioners to be sensitive to different cultures represented within our own community, to systems of guided participation traditional to these cultures and their likely significance in building even young children's competence and skill in learning and problem-solving.

The development of memory in young children

There are several reasons why practitioners may be interested in the memory capacity of young children. Two of the commonest reasons are the following:

- To facilitate the recall of events and circumstances in order to help a young child to clarify the past so as to contribute to his 'coherent story' over time. Additionally, the child's capacity to make use of his ability to remember external features of his environment helps him to prepare for new situations. For example, we may use many tools like photographs, videos, DVDs or drawings in order to familiarise a child with the new setting when preparing him for a significant move. This is developmentally appropriate in that young children are more significantly reassured by concrete images.

- When young children are involved in forensic interviews, we may be dependent on a young child's memory of events in order to explore the detail of circumstances surrounding possible abuse.

What is known about young children's memories suggests that they may be able to remember a great deal and that it is possible to trigger these memories by the use of visual cues, for example pictures and objects. Indeed, depending on the type of event, a very young child may have a visual and sensory memory of places and events before he has the capacity for speech.

Many adults assume that young children remember very little of what happens to them, but often the reverse is true, particularly if the events have salience and meaning for the child, for example circumstances surrounding a separation or other trauma.

It is common for separated children to be able to recall the visual details of their removal from home, especially if this was sudden and accompanied by strong reactions from the important figures in the young child's life. For example, Tammy (6) recalled recently: 'I was very little and you came in a red car and it was very cold outside and you wrapped me in a blue blanket. Mummy was crying and Daddy was very angry and shouting.' Tammy was three years old when taken from home late at night.

Hence the memories are very often a combination of visual pictures and other sensory details connected with the child's direct experience of the event through his other senses, for example smell, sense of hot and cold. When practitioners are working with young children they can use these visual cues to remind the child and hence to tune in and support him, with the remembered feelings surrounding the events. These memories can then be incorporated into a visual record of events which is built upon the child's own particular strands of memory and then used to:

- build a bridge between the child and the helping adult

- help avoid mis-perceptions of the past and any unhealthy feelings of self-blame in a very young child

- begin to build the basis of a coherent story of the past, which can be re-worked during subsequent developmental stages.

Forensic examination in young children's memory

Whereas one can be more relaxed in exploring young children's memories of events in direct work with them which has a therapeutic focus, the forensic interview imposes more restrictions. Saywitz and Goodman (1996) offer a very useful summary of what is known from current studies of children's memory and suggestibility at different stages of development.

The ability to provide accurate testimony depends on being able to remember and communicate memories to others. Therefore, the amount of information a witness reports about an event generally increases with age, as the child's cognitive capacities develop. It is often assumed that young children, for example pre-schoolers, are more suggestible than older children and adults. Nevertheless, even young children do not necessarily have full memory and they are not necessarily highly suggestible – they may merely be more compliant. Memory abilities and the ability to resist suggestion vary at any age, be it in childhood or adulthood, depending on the situation and on personality factors. Variables include:

- the type of event experienced

- the type of information to be recounted

- the conditions surrounding an interview

- the strength and salience of the memory

- the language used

- post-event influences.

Researchers consistently emphasise the importance of the context in which the child is questioned, for example the context can provide physical reminders of an incident, and it can also provide the socio-emotional atmosphere which can either support or interfere with the accurate and complete reporting of the child's memory. Much of the research suggests that other factors apart from age can play a large role in influencing eye witness accuracy.

Free recall and open-ended questions

Research literature (Dent and Stephenson 1979) suggests that free recall is typically the most accurate form of memory record, for example a response to an open-ended question like 'What happened?' One problem, however, is that such reports predictably are more limited in detail when young children are questioned. Young children, when asked more specifically about the details of an event, commonly demonstrate that they can provide more details than when offered an open-ended question.

A problem for the interviewer is that it can be hard to determine, based on a young child's free recall, whether or not something of significance happened to him. The atmosphere of the questioning is very important; for example, if the interviewer implies accusation in a question about an adult, this may lead to false reports about events, especially from the accounts of pre-school children.

Specific leading questions and suggestibility

Despite the fact that young children's free recall can be inaccurate at times, young children who are responsive to open-ended questions provide accurate but abbreviated information, rather than false information. The amount of information one can obtain is increased if children are asked specifically about information of interest or when their memory is triggered by physical cues, for example a picture of the child's home or pre-school.

The cost of more detailed questioning and 'cueing', however, is that inaccuracies in the account may then increase. A balance here needs to be found between free recall and specific questions. It may be very helpful for the joint interviewers to have some discussions prior to an interview about their own definition of what constitutes a *specific* question as opposed to a *leading* question in a particular set of circumstances. A supportive context is especially important in bolstering young children's resilience to suggestive mis-information about abuse.

There should be interviewing protocols for children at different stages of development. These must be sensitive to:

- developmental differences in free recall
- suggestibility
- communicative competence
- socio-emotional cues, that is, the variability in children's emotional state depending on their circumstances when they are interviewed.

The effects of separation and loss on young children

It is important for practitioners to remember that, even though the young child is not at the stage of cognitive development to think through his experiences in a rational manner, nevertheless negative life events, including losses, will have an impact, not only on the young child's feelings about his experiences, but also his thoughts about causation (see also Chapter 4).

Because of the prominence of magical thinking and continued egocentricity, children between the ages of two and five are particularly vulnerable to mis-perceiving the reasons for any move. The pre-school child tends to act out worries through play and significant adults need to pay close attention to the child's pattern of play as often what the child says and what he does may give clues as to the mis-perceptions which may fuel distortions of thinking. Additionally, many pre-school children who have been abused or neglected frequently show delays in their language development.

Activity 6.2

Think of a child known to you between the ages of two and five who has experienced at least one significant separation.

1. Consider the negative messages the child may have taken from such events.

2. What might be said and done to reassure this child as to the continuity of his or her secure base?

3. How, in particular, might significant adults contribute to the child's understanding of the 'coherent story' of his or her life to date?

The importance of play and exploration for promoting social and cognitive development in under fives

Observation of young children's play is often of great importance, not only because it provides clues as to the child's developmental progress, but also because it may offer an indication of the child's pattern of *thinking* about events. Play is also a key medium through which it is possible to support the child in giving him an opportunity to play out, and begin to make sense of his life experiences. It is therefore potentially a powerful therapeutic tool in direct work with very young children. As Santrok (1994) observes, 'play therapy allows children to work off frustrations and is a medium through which the therapist can analyse children's conflicts and ways of coping with them. Children may feel less threatened and be more likely to express their true feelings in the context of play' (p.480).

Play can be used as a medium for deliberate strategies of reparative work with young children:

*   It can be used as an opportunity to explore their senses.

*   Young children who are allowed to explore their senses of hearing, touch, sight and smell are more securely based in the world and this is a sound building block for later healthy development.

Play as a medium for making sense of the world

Opportunities for young children not only to explore in a physical sense and develop physical coordination, but also to investigate how things work, help significantly in their learning about cause and effect. In play, children can explore their own potential, their skills and limitations and, with support, can gain enjoyment in extending themselves. Play is also a key medium through which children can begin to make contact with peers, and to learn about cooperation and negotiation from the basis of a secure attachment with at least one sensitive and attuned care-giver.

An opportunity to express a range of feelings

This is particularly helpful in any direct or reparative work with children in distress. Play, especially social play, enhances the making of sustaining relationships. In a setting where creative play is encouraged, the child's capacity for imagination can be developed. The play experience can help the child to handle fear and worry. Young children are also able to re-enact in play particularly worrying or frightening experiences. This can help them move towards coherence about the experience, particularly when supported by an attachment figure.

Play in the management of specific life stresses

Examples of such specific stressful experiences may include hospital visits, separations and other anxiety-promoting experiences. In reflecting on how we can integrate the child's own experiences and his feelings about them, it is common to incorporate young children's drawings, stories and photographs into a life story book. Fahlberg (1988) suggests that a life story book, when it is a record of the child's view of events, can:

- provide a chronology of the child's life
- enhance self-esteem and identity formation
- help a child to share his history with others
- assist in resolving separation issues
- identify connections between past, present and future
- facilitate attachments.

Lacher, Nichols and May (2005) explore the use of stories in building attachments; for example:

- increasing trust in adults
- helping the child to recognise and resolve strong emotions relating to past events
- separating reality from fantasy or magical thinking
- identifying positives as well as negatives about his family of origin.

As young children, in particular, often express their feelings and perceptions through play, frequently concrete play, the harnessing of their chosen mode of communication in our own direct work can be a powerful reparative tool. It is common even for young children to develop a preferred mode of expression which may focus on any one, or even all, of the senses. For example, some children like to draw while others prefer to explore their experiences through stories. Useful strategies for direct work with young children can be found in the recent work of Luckock and Lefevre (2008).

The young child's physical development

Bee (1995) explores three factors which act as determinants to growth and early physical development. These are:

- maturation

- heredity

- environmental factors, including diet and practice.

Maturation

Maturational sequences are critical in the early physical development of young children. These apply, in particular, to changes in bones and muscles and neuronal and neuro-biological development. Whereas the *rate* in development varies between children, the *sequence* is virtually the same for all children, even those who have marked disabilities. The key idea of developmental milestones is very useful for the practitioner since familiarity with those markers of development achieved by most children at a particular age and stage can be very helpful in identifying crucial issues of developmental delay, interruption or distortion.

Heredity

Because of our genetic heritage Bee argues that each of us receives instructions for unique growth tendencies (1995). Both size and body shape seem to be heavily influenced by specific inheritance. For example, if parents are tall, then they will tend to have tall children. The rate of growth, in addition to a final size, also seems to unfold in any inherited pattern. Therefore, for example, parents who are early developers will tend to have early-developing children.

When working with children living in disadvantaged circumstances, it is very important that we do not make too many assumptions about their restrictive potential for physical growth. Parents themselves may never have reached their own growth potential because of adverse environmental experiences in their developing years, for example poor nutrition. It is, thus, crucially important to measure the child's 'catch-up' growth in any different care-giving settings since it often reveals for the first time the child's true potential for physical maturation.

Environmental effects: diet and practice

There are two obvious explanatory features of environmental effects which are significant – diet and practice. Serious malnutrition during pregnancy can have a permanently negative effect on the developing foetus, retarding growth. This is very difficult to determine because most malnourished babies also grow up in environments that are deficient in other aspects. What is known is that poorly nourished children tend to grow more slowly. If their diet later improves, such children may well show some increase in the *rate* of growth but they are often still typically shorter and grow more slowly than their peers.

One particular significant effect may be that malnourished or under-nourished infants and children often have less energy which can then negatively affect the nature of interaction they have, both with people and objects around them and their level of exploration of the world.

The practice of various physical activities also has some significance for the child's physical development. For example, the opportunities the individual child has for practice in walking, climbing stairs and other basic physical activities have an effect on the rate at which he acquires these skills. The results of most studies suggest that, for the development of such universal basic skills as crawling or walking, babies do need some amount of practice just to keep their physical system working. Therefore, while maturation can help to determine when a child is able to learn a particular skill, practice is clearly necessary for effective performance.

Again, any opportunity to observe the very young child in different situations, for example in nursery, will be instructive in reflecting upon the degree to which the child's healthy physical exploration may be affected by patterns of care-giving.

A common problem encountered in our work with young children who have been neglected or abused is the anxiety they suffer, either from fearfulness of an abusive parent or care-giver or from the chronic lack of engagement, commonly known as 'the trauma of absence' in neglectful situations. Lack of support from an attachment figure to explore safely and securely can often result in delays in the young child's capacity to explore with confidence.

Individual differences in early physical development
Alongside the factors already mentioned, there are two further considerations:

- whether or not pre-term babies develop more slowly
- whether gender has some influence on early physical development.

Pre-term or low birth rate babies move at a delayed rate through all the developmental sequences of the early years. This is what we might expect, as the pre-term baby is in fact maturationally younger than the full-term baby. Parents of pre-term babies may need help to keep this difference in mind as they may become overly concerned when they compare their baby's progress with that of a full-term baby. By the age of two or three years, the physically normal pre-term baby will catch up with his peers but, in the early months, the baby's physical development is likely to be slower and may cause parents significant anxiety.

Bee (1995) asserts that there are remarkably few gender differences in the physical development of many infants. Ethnic differences, however, do exist. Black African infants develop somewhat more rapidly than their white peers and Asian infants rather more slowly. The key point to remember is that our own cultural patterns and assumptions may strongly influence what we consider normal growth for an infant. We must therefore be extremely cautious as practitioners in our interpretation of patterns of physical growth in babies from different cultures.

A general guide to the practitioner is that babies triple their body weight in the first year of life and add between 12 and 15 inches to their length before they are aged two.

Some particular problems
Language delay

Language development is a critical component of learning because it promotes the development of cognitive processes and allows the young child to begin to attain self-control and gradually to delay the gratification of impulses. It gives the child a way of expressing his feelings other than acting them out behaviourally.

Early identification of any particular reason for the language delay including health problems, for example, intermittent hearing loss, is important in clarifying the appropriate focus for intervention. Douglas (1989) notes that

> the frustration in communication that these children experience is evident in their behaviour. Toys are frequently thrown when children cannot make themselves understood, social skills develop slowly as they snatch instead of asking for what they want. Poor social relationships with other children, as well as adults, are common. (p.7)

Particularly because of the link between at least one healthy attachment relationship in infancy and the development of the acquisition of language, practitioners should be attentive to any delay in the child's language. It may be that a young child who has experienced profoundly neglectful care-giving will fail to develop language, despite having the innate capacity to do so. However, there may be other problems, for example a hidden learning difficulty, or a specific problem with the processing of information.

Where there are concerns about language delay, it is therefore vital that practitioners from all disciplines seek to clarify the possible reasons for this so that appropriate interventions can be initiated. This underlines the importance of an open-minded exploration of distortions or delays in development and the particular value of a well-coordinated multi-disciplinary team being readily available to support the family. This kind of concern also illustrates the vital importance of a sound knowledge of basic child development and maturational tasks for all practitioners working with families with young children. Experiences of neglectful care-giving can profoundly affect language development.

Development delay or disability

Practitioners meet many children in the course of their work with families who exhibit mild developmental difficulties which, nevertheless, may be highly significant, particularly where they are associated with behavioural difficulties which attract negative attention from their parents or care-givers. A child may, for example, be struggling with his developmental milestones because of unidentified learning difficulties and the parents may interpret the behaviour as a problem rather than being able to see it as appropriate behaviour for the child's actual developmental stage. Early multi-disciplinary assessments again help here in that they may clarify appropriate expectations which are at one with the child's abilities. Early counselling and support from family support services may well help parents to develop appropriate strategies of supporting the development of their child to his fullest potential. Stopford (1993) emphasises a number of factors that affect young children with disabilities and their families.

- The stage at which the child is diagnosed as having a disability is a critical point at which to offer follow-up and necessary support to families. Lack of support may affect the development of healthy parent–child bonding. Lack of information about the disability at birth is seen by many parents to be very frustrating as they may recognise for themselves at a very early stage, often before the diagnosis is reached, that all is not well.

- Feelings which are very similar to those in bereavement, whether in relation to a child's physical or cognitive impairment, may result in additional stress on the family, increasing the trauma of adjustment to the disability, and at times resulting in only partial acceptance. This process of adjustment for parents may affect the child's view of himself as a family member.

- Families may have an understandable desire to protect the child and may be reluctant to allow the child with a disability the degree of independence offered to other children of the same age. This may lead to difficult behaviour at a later stage or to a failure to reach the child's full potential.

- It is common for children with disabilities to have less opportunity for social and interpersonal interaction. They may well be expected to take less responsibility and they may have lower self-esteem and feelings of self-efficacy than their non-disabled contemporaries. This may actually encourage increased dependency and loss of autonomy and reinforce poor self-esteem.

- It is important to remember that young children's sense of identity within society, alongside the psychological and emotional progress and developmental tasks, is related to the degree of physical autonomy and independence they are able to experience.

- The involvement of medical professionals and others concerned with physical or cognitive problems arising from the disability may distract attention from the crucial emotional needs of the child or young person with a disability.

Stopford makes a number of suggestions about factors which may be helpful for professionals to bear in mind when working with families with a young child with a disability.

- Practitioners from all disciplines should be aware of the professional support systems which need to be readily available at critical points in the life cycle of the child or young person with a disability. This may be vital in ensuring that support is available to the child and to the family at times when future difficulties may be mediated or even prevented, for example birth/diagnosis, entry into education. The education system will be particularly important for effective multi-agency working.

- Clear information about the availability of services, including social and emotional supports for the child and parents, as well as medical advice, may be extremely important in building the family's understanding of the child's needs and dispelling myths and misunderstandings about the disability.

- Support at all stages for parents who are coming to terms with the reality of disability, and its meaning for the child and for themselves, may be extremely helpful in preventing family difficulties, as well as encouraging independence and fulfilment of potential in the child himself.

- Working with children with disabilities in a way which encompasses an awareness of the whole child is likely to facilitate the focus on the development on a positive self-image and likely also to promote a more resourceful approach to life.

Chapter 4 explores issues of disability more fully.

Over-activity

Over-activity is a frequent complaint from parents and is a crucial feature of a child's behaviour in so far as it may disrupt the development of confident nurturing patterns of care-giving. Children who are temperamentally very active need much more supervision than their peers and often have greater difficulty entertaining themselves. This is exhausting for parents. Even babies can show a significant tendency in this regard and, as Douglas (1989) notes, 'matching in the level of stimulation to the needs of the baby is a very fine art and takes skill, patience and good observation' (p.8). The support of a well-attuned health visitor and sensitive day care services is clearly of great benefit in these circumstances.

However, it may be that patterns of high levels of activity develop in a particular young child because of the lack of parental responsiveness to his needs. As was explained in Chapter 2, some children who receive highly variable responses from their attachment figures, for example sometimes being responded to and sometimes ignored, may develop a 'survival strategy' of highly demanding, active behaviours in order to obtain and retain their care-giver's maximum attention. The unique situation of an over-active child can be difficult to assess by single observation and the value of a close working multi-disciplinary team can be especially helpful in elucidating the factors at work in each family. Issues of emotional neglect and effects on development are explored more fully in Chapter 5.

Parenting and social problems
The parent or care-giver's own attachment history

In Chapter 3 the significance of assessing the parent's own early attachment relationships was emphasised; for example, the parent who experienced abuse and neglect in his or her own early years can be helped by opportunities to reflect on these experiences, potentially promoting an enhancement of their care-giving capacity. This is described in the literature as an 'earned secure' attachment status.

Alternatively, parents who are out of touch with the effects of these abusive and neglectful experiences demonstrated by the quality of their account of their own childhood may be more at risk of promoting patterns of insecure or even disorganised attachment in their own children. The importance of identifying at an early stage those parents who may benefit from the type of parenting programmes which include opportunities to reflect on their own history will be important to the well-being of the young child. This may well be a critical area for preventing a cycle of unhelpful attachment patterns within particular families from being repeated in the next generation.

Environmental stresses

The stressors arising from poor housing and poverty are specific factors which add very significantly to the problems of parents in caring for young children. Clearly, the broadest political perspective is of core relevance here in terms of ensuring that people have access to a job, sufficient income and appropriate adequate housing in well-resourced neighbourhoods. However, the existence of a local health group, community support or individual professional, focusing on developing parents' self-reliance and working collaboratively with them, rather than imposing solutions, would appear to be helpful.

The opportunity for isolated parents to develop a warm, confiding relationship has been found to mediate, to some degree, the stress arising from the challenges of caring for a young child in adverse circumstances. The multiple initiatives in recent years to support the parent's care of his young children, for example the Sure Start programme, has led to many useful opportunities, both based on individual support and group work programmes.

Thompson (1995) encourages practitioners to consider the careful assessment of a parent's need for social support in order to identify the areas of greatest difficulty in which he needs help. For example:

- the parent may be isolated and need help to connect with effective local supports

- the parent may need specific education to learn about realistic developmental expectations of his or her children

- health, nutrition and hygiene may be a particular problem and focusing support as accurately as possible is likely to be most successful in enhancing the outcomes for the child.

We need to be cautious in assuming that informal supports to parents in their management of young children are automatically helpful as some informal supports merely confirm parents in punitive or abusive care-giving. Moreover, parents are not necessarily appropriately supported by extended family members as, depending on the nature of the relationship, parents may be undermined by their own parents' criticism. Therefore, careful assessment of a child, parent–child relationship, the parent's circumstances and relationship with partners and extended family, alongside an awareness of the links with local community support, is especially valuable in helping parents with very young children. For example, sometimes it is possible to help parents by offering direct information that they require about how to cope with a particular problem. In other circumstances, especially when parents are depressed, a wider approach of providing emotional support to parents within a consistent relationship with a professional, before even considering intervening in management techniques, may be required.

When considering the individual child's circumstances clearly issues of risk are vitally important and, as described in Chapter 4, Rutter and Rutter (1993) highlight protective factors for the child in professional interventions. These are:

- the reduction of the impact of negative effects of parental stress

- the reduction of negative chain reactions

- the establishment and maintenance of self-esteem and self-efficacy with opportunities for success and mastery

- opening up of wider opportunities for interaction and support.

The developmental importance of sibling relationships in the early years

First, it is important for the practitioner to proceed with care when defining what constitutes a sibling relationship for an individual child. Kosonen (1999) urges practitioners to consider the meaningful relationships for fostered and separated children in particular and to assess the strength of children's attachment relationships with one another. Children's own definitions of who they see emotionally as siblings may differ from assumptions based on the ties of the blood link.

Elgar and Head (1999) comment that 'siblings can also offer life support to each other and provide a sense of belonging in long term attachment' (p.19). Owusu-Bempah and Howitt (1997) emphasise the importance of siblings as providing 'socio-genealogical connectedness', in other words ensuring that children remain in touch with their background, enhancing their sense of connectedness to their roots, promoting a sense of belonging and increasing their sense of well-being. Even when they do not live together, this can be offered through contact with siblings.

As noted in Chapter 2, the Sibling Relationship Checklist (Department of Health 1991) is a useful tool for exploring the particular dynamics of an individual sibling relationship. Dunn and Kendrick (1982) have noted that infants under one year of age can demonstrate attachment behaviour towards their older siblings. This has real significance for separation effects when placing siblings in local authority accommodation. When placed together, siblings can provide comfort in an unfamiliar setting. Older siblings have been observed to calm younger children in strange situations and may be seen as the secure base from which the younger child can obtain security.

When considering the dilemmas posed by the placement of siblings in substitute care, it is important to assess the attachment relationships between each sibling pair as soon as possible. This can help practitioners to:

- place attached siblings together where resources are limited and the whole sibling group may not be placed with the same carers *and/or*

- attune to particularly tender supportive relationships which will need to be safeguarded.

If it is not possible to place closely attached siblings together, careful planning of contact arrangements may be protective of the relationships to a degree. A useful guide to considerations of sibling placement can be found in Argent (2008).

Promoting a sense of healthy racial identity in the young child

Katz (1982) examined the development of racial awareness in young children from the age of two to six years. There appears to be no doubt that young children make early observations of racial difference and these evaluative judgements begin to influence their growing awareness at an early stage. The stages described are:

- the early observations of racial cues

- the formation of rudimentary concepts of racial difference

- moving towards conceptual differentiation

- recognition that these cues, for example skin colour, remain constant

- the development of group concepts

- the elaboration of these group concepts.

Alejandro-Wright (1985) confirms the observation that racial awareness begins at the pre-school stage but elaborates upon this to suggest that a full understanding emerges at a later stage of development at around 10 or 11 years. She delineates the process from 'a vague, and undifferentiated awareness of skin colour differences to knowledge of the cluster of physical-biological attributes associated with racial membership and eventually to a social understanding of racial categorisation' (p.186).

By the age of two years, children are learning about gender differences and, linked with their learning about colour, begin to apply these to skin colour. By three years of age, children demonstrate signs of being influenced by the broader societal biases and prejudices and may exhibit an early prejudicial attitude towards others on the basis of race.

Between the ages of three and five years of age, children are struggling to make sense of the permanence of their personal attributes and are curious as to which of these attributes will remain constant. It is helpful at this stage to support children in sorting out the many experiences and variables of identity both in relation to themselves and in relation to peers who may exhibit particular differences. By the age of five, a child may begin to use racial reasons for avoiding other children who are different from themselves.

Derman-Sparks (1991) emphasises the need for what she calls anti-bias education with young children in relation to racial difference as well as gender and other differences. As a child grows he needs a care environment which reverses any negative picture associated with the child's colour. The child needs encouragement in developing a positive view of himself in relation to the difference signalled by their skin colour.

The growing black child will need active support in developing strategies for combating racism in daily life, at school and in the community. There is a need for careful consideration of the attitudes of those adults caring for, and working with, young children and an awareness of the images and play materials which are made available to them at this stage. Maxime (1986) suggests some particular ideas for encouraging a healthy self-concept in a young child.

- When bathing a young child, even though the child may be at the pre-verbal stage of development, it is helpful to make comment about the child's skin colour, linking this with positive attributes.

- The photographs, posters and so on which may be in the home or family centre need to contain black images.

- It is important to refrain, in a deliberate way, from any comment which may link the child's skin colour with lack of cleanliness, or any negative connotation.

- There has to be a preparedness to acknowledge the reality of the child's skin colour difference and to link this wherever possible with black adults in the child's life.

Maxime's series of workbooks include many ideas for direct work offering ideas for practitioners supporting carers of black children and those of mixed ethnic origin (1994).

As noted in Chapter 2, there has been considerable criticism of attachment theory because of a perceived over-emphasis on the exclusivity of importance of the mother–child bond. We need to be open in all substitute care settings to the range of patterns of family composition and a range of child-rearing practices. It is helpful to remind ourselves of the importance of the 'hierarchy of attachment relationships' so that we can be open to accepting that a particular child may be cared for by a number of adults without their security being compromised.

This is not to imply that, if the child is disturbed by the lack of predictability in any aspects of his care, it is not an issue of concern. However, it is important to guard against assumptions that role allocation in terms of caring for children will fit a Eurocentric pattern.

Equally, in our assessments of attachment relationships, we must take care to take into account the fact that the *signs* practitioners may look for as indicators of positive bonds may have different significance in other cultures. For example, Rashid (1996) cites the Eurocentric emphasis on the positive considerations of direct eye contact when assessing parent–child interactions. He sees this as merely one culturally specific notion of the strength of a relationship and adds:

> This becomes particularly important when the professionals' own cultural norms are markedly different from those of the children and care givers. Practitioners need to be aware of their own cultural norms, and those that underpin their professional judgements, as well as the cultural norms of their clients. (p.61)

We need to be curious as to the particular ways in which different cultural ideas and beliefs shape the operation of the attachment dynamics in different cultures.

Activity 6.3

Considering any child under five in a day care or nursery setting who is black or of mixed parentage, how far do you think the issues explored are being addressed within the care setting?

Key messages

- During the early years, development is specific to the individual, but occurs within the context of sequential developmental stages.

- The experience of a secure attachment is pivotal in promoting healthy development in the early years.

- The attunement and sensitive, timely responsiveness of a 'mind minded' care-giver helps the young child to:
  - regulate his emotions
  - relax and explore
  - become aware of his own feelings and those of others
  - learn to cooperate
  - feel lovable
  - develop empathy towards others in distress.

- Even though young children are *active participants* in interactions, different temperamental styles can render individual infants or toddlers more or less easy for parents to manage and nurture.

- If the attachment figure soothes and calms, the child's arousal is reduced.

- These positive experiences impact significantly on the organisation of key areas of the brain (including the limbic system responsible for the processing of emotional and social interaction).

- Conversely, experiences of abuse or neglect pre-dispose the young child to sustain either states of high arousal or dissociation.

- These experiences and adaptations may have powerful long-term effects on the child.

- Young children not only learn to trust in early attachment relationships, but also learn about shared humour, playfulness, connectedness and collaboration.

- Young children can learn to take the perspective of another person sooner than previously supposed.

- This stage of development is significant for the beginnings of *social* understanding.

- Allied to this, there is an emergence of a sensitivity to *differences* principally in the areas of *gender*, *race* and *disability*.

- Attribution theory is relevant when considering the cognitive development of the young child, specifically the tendency towards egocentricity. The child's cognitive stage of development, which predisposes him to believe that his own intentions are connected with positive or negative outcomes, places the very young child at risk of developing global negative self-attributions with regard to traumatic events, such as separations.

- The very young child is therefore vulnerable to enhanced feelings of self-blame in the context of experiences of abuse or neglect, or other trauma in the early years.

- Loss in the early years when young children do not have the cognitive abilities to make sense of these experiences has a profound impact.

- Unavoidable separations need to be carefully planned wherever possible for children at this stage and care must be taken to be sensitive to circumstances which may trigger later distress and/or facilitate the ensuing work on the child's 'coherent story'.

- The early identification of developmental delays in young children is vital to trigger careful multi-disciplinary assessment of the possible *causes* of the delays and the early identification of helpful interventions and supports.

- Parents' own difficulties need to be considered carefully when practitioners are formulating relevant interventions, for example presence of domestic violence.

- Services for young children from different ethnic groups, for example nursery and day care provision, need to be sensitive to any additional needs, for example hair and skin care, and should be respectful of the cultural traditions of the families.

- Practitioners need to be aware of the responses of the individual young child to stress. Rather than making assumptions, consideration of temperamental style and personal history in the context of current circumstances will be an important area of assessment.

- Sibling relationships are highly salient and even very young children have the capacity to empathise and seek to support younger siblings, implying an earlier growth of the capacity to take another's perspective than was previously supposed.

- Sibling relationships are often both complex and important and contain the potential for both positive and less positive features. Only careful assessment will illustrate the unique features of the quality of relationship between each sibling pair.

- It is of vital importance for practitioners to listen to parents and to develop supports which are sensitive to their religious, cultural and linguistic traditions.

CHAPTER 7

School Years

Introduction

Early and middle school years are times of tremendous developmental changes. Some of these changes, such as the development of literacy, are a direct result of formal education. Schools also provide the opportunity for significant changes in children's social lives and experiences. At the same time during this period there are surges in physical, cognitive, social and emotional maturation. Children's lives outside the home usually become increasingly important: they have friends, join clubs, are involved in sports and so on. During this period it can become painfully obvious if a child's potential is not being supported. It can also become clear if one child's potential is different from another's. Because of the number of changes to which the child is subject, adversity or abuse can have further dramatic effects on the child's life. At the same time there are aspects of school life in particular that can protect vulnerable children.

This chapter will describe the major developmental changes that usually occur during school-age years. Ages and stages should be taken as a guide only. Each individual child develops at her own pace and trauma and adversity can affect children's development in different ways. Social workers cannot be expected to carry out detailed intellectual assessments alone; these should be done in conjunction with other professionals, especially teachers and educational psychologists.

This chapter draws heavily on psychological literature with the aim of describing individual development; however, when assessing a young person's development it is also important to take account of the wider environmental factors and their impact. The effects of poor housing, poverty and poor community resources can be especially damaging during these years because they restrict opportunities to engage in the activities beyond home and school that are generally open to children as they become more autonomous.

During these years it is also increasingly important to take account of the child's understanding of the situation and to hear her views about events. A school-age child will be making sense of her world and becoming an increasingly active agent. Children are often far more aware of factors affecting domestic circumstances than parents realise. Practitioners should not, therefore, treat children as passive recipients of concern but should include them in decision-making, establish what their understanding of a situation is and ensure that they have accurate information about events that is tailored to their level of understanding.

Attachments

Family remains important throughout the school years. Although school-age children can cope with longer periods of separation from attachment figures, the attachment itself is just as strong as in pre-school children. Experience and increased cognitive powers mean they appreciate that relationships endure over time and distance. However, the family or substitute family's role as the secure base is crucial, especially during the early years of school. Children need to feel that they are exploring the new world of school and friendships from a secure background.

At these ages children can show prolonged grief reactions at the loss of an attachment figure and may find it harder to make new attachments to substitute parents than pre-school children. Separation or loss can create anxiety, and cause children to feel frightened, unwanted and unloved. They may show their upset by impulsive behaviour, or by becoming depressed and withdrawn. They may seek approval from adults, sometimes by making exaggerated claims. Trauma may lead to them regressing somewhat in their behaviour; for example, they may use more 'babyish' language, or ask for help with self-care tasks that they could previously manage. For children who are just adapting to early school years, such regression may be difficult to manage.

In practice, children undergoing loss or separation need to be given as much age-appropriate information as possible that takes account of their level of emotional and cognitive development. Because they are at a stage of considering issues of fairness they may be very concerned with the question of 'Why me?' School-age children should be able to understand that people can have mixed feelings and therefore should be able to explore such feelings with support. In addition they need the comfort and supportive structure of familiar routines (Fahlberg 1994).

School

School is, of course, the crucially important context for many of the key developmental tasks during these years. For those not in formal schooling, education as a process is as important. Schools are very particular social worlds in their own right which therefore have a tremendous impact upon children's social development. In many jurisdictions schools are increasingly expected to take a more active role in the safeguarding and protection of children (see Baginsky 2008 for more information). Meadows (1986) describes the factors that define the school culture:

- Children need very quickly to learn how the social world of school works, which requires understanding the often conflicting demands of peers and teachers. A child can be more or less prepared for the transition to school, depending on the home environment.

- The kind of language between adult and child is different in school from that at home. For example, often the teacher asks questions the teacher already knows the answer to and the child knows that they know the answer. In other words, there is a ritual to checking learning that the child has to learn.

- There are many rules of behaviour that the child has to either learn or infer; for example, to put their hand up before speaking. Children who are not able to or choose not to adapt to school ways are liable to be categorised as 'bad'.

- Children can gain self-esteem and dignity from success at school. These positive self-images can come about from pleasing teachers or through achieving good peer relationships. For certain children these are not compatible goals and a choice has to be made. Some children belong to a group of peers who have a culture of rejecting the teachers' values and choose to mess about instead.

- The children who are most likely to be able to adapt to school culture come from a home background that understands and supports that culture. Good links between home and school are also supportive. Children's school performance is greatly dependent on learning to read. Children also need to have a sense of control over their own learning processes. Anxiety about inability to do the academic work is one of the main reasons behind school refusal.

Rutter (1991) has described the role of school in affecting developmental pathways. The comparison of different schools shows that they have an effect on intellectual performance and on behaviour improvements. The chances of effects lasting into adulthood depend on later circumstances. However, crucially, these later circumstances are themselves partly determined by current circumstances. The lasting effects on children of effective schooling are due to improvements in cognitive performance such as task orientation, persistence, attainment of skills such as literacy and positive effects on self-esteem and self-efficacy which improve competence in school and increase other people's expectations of performance.

Activity 7.1

List ways in which parents or alternative carers could help children to reap the potential benefits of school. How can practitioners encourage parents to hold a positive view of school?

Hints for answers
Many parents whose children have problems at school may themselves have had very negative experiences there. They may avoid going to the school building because of images of school from their childhood. If such parents can be encouraged to visit the school, to see the classroom, meet the head teacher and discuss their child's progress they may feel less intimidated by their child's school problems. Some parents may themselves decide to further their education. Children can be encouraged if someone takes an interest in their school work on a day-to-day basis, asking what they have done at school and helping with homework.

Education can therefore act as a protective factor in the face of adversity. However, it is ironic that those children who could most benefit from this are often those for whom education is most likely to be problematic. A study of the reasons for school exclusion in England, especially with regard to those with special educational needs, looked after children and children from ethnic minority communities, found huge variety in record-keeping about school exclusions (Osler *et al.* 2001). The needs of looked after children and traveller children were overlooked and there was use of unofficial exclusion to mask numbers. Schools with low exclusion rates were found to have an inclusive ethos with a team approach to teaching, to involve children in developing codes of behaviour and in decision-making, to be sensitive to diversity by monitoring attainment and sanctions by gender and ethnicity, and to have strong working relationships with parents and to draw on community resources. Being looked after away from home, and especially the experience of multiple placements, can lead to a downward spiral of educational performance (Jackson and McParlin 2006; Jackson and Sachdev 2001; McClung 2008). The reasons as identified by the Social Exclusion Unit (2003) and cited by Stein (2009) are:

- placement instability

- too much time out of school

- insufficient help with education

- primary carers not being expected or equipped to provide sufficient support and encouragement for learning and development

- many children having unmet emotional, mental and physical health needs. (p.88)

Social workers often have to adopt a role that may be an uneasy blend between being an advocate on behalf of the child, and a partner with the school in planning intervention. It can be helpful if social workers appreciate the reality of the impact that a child's challenging behaviour can have on the rest of the class. Attempts to minimise the problems and explain them away can lead to less effective partnership in tackling the roots of the difficulties some children experience in schooling.

Language and literacy

Language

By the time children start school they can usually understand and use language efficiently and effectively. This includes both the understanding of language and the use of language to express themselves. They already have experience of using language in fun for games and songs. Once in school they start to develop an understanding of ambiguity, verbal jokes and metaphor. By the age of six children can see that language can have multiple meanings and can therefore understand puns, and by eight love riddles and word games. They also understand about narrative and that language can be used to tell stories, not just about events, but also about motives and feelings. However, it is not until about 11 that they can really grasp abstract language (Smith, Cowie and Blades 2003).

During this time children change in the way they think about language. For example, if pre-school children are asked to give the first word they think of when they hear the word 'dog', they will respond with characteristics of a *particular* dog, such as 'black' or 'big'. School-age children tend to respond in terms of categories, for example with 'animal', or another example of the category, such as 'cat'. They also begin to understand common characteristics between words such as 'emerald' and 'diamond' and can distinguish between similar words like 'cousin' and 'nephew'. They develop an understanding of comparatives, such as 'shorter' and 'deeper'. These may seem subtle differences but indicate that children's language moves away from relating simply to their own experiences in the here and now. They also start to have an understanding of the different uses of language (Santrok 2001). Because they are more analytical about language they are also able to benefit from formal teaching and instruction (Berger 2001).

Activity 7.2

Ignoring other cues of communication such as body language, gestures and so forth, listen carefully to the verbal language of children ranging from the ages of five to ten. If possible, get a recording of the language of these children.

1. Listen to the way children use language to express themselves. Note the extent to which the children appear to be aware of their use of language to convey certain messages.
2. Are there obvious differences in the way they use language to themselves, adults and peers?
3. Do the older children demonstrate more sophisticated language forms?

The recent massive growth in global migration has led to an increase in numbers of children whose first language is different from the majority language spoken where they live. It is also common in many countries for children to grow up bilingual. It is a commonly cited statistic that over 300 languages are spoken in London schools (National Literacy Trust 2009). Research with bilingual children has shown that having two languages does not interfere with performance in either language. In fact, it can be associated with a better grasp of some concepts and flexibility of thought (Diaz 1983; Hakuta and Garcia 1989). The optimum stage for learning a second language is between the age of 6 and 11 (Berger 2001). The social and personal development of children moving into a different language environment is supported if they can continue to use their home language. Minority languages may not be accorded respect; for example, in Britain, Asians experience the education system as privileging European languages over Asian languages (Robinson 2007). It can be of benefit to all children, including white monolingual children, to be introduced to the diversity and richness of different languages in school (German 2002).

Most profoundly deaf children have major deficits in spoken and written language and have difficulty speaking and reading at a basic level. However, children who have deaf parents do better on language and literacy skills. The indications are that this is because they have learnt to sign and therefore have a language that parallels spoken language (Schlesinger and Meadow 1972). This early language appears to help with later literacy. These findings are important as about 90 per cent of deaf children are born to hearing parents and therefore grow up in a world dominated by spoken language with which they cannot participate (Bee 1995). Young *et al.* (2008) have reviewed the literature on resilience and deaf children and point to the dangers inherent in conceptualising deafness as an adversity that is 'overcome' by 'resilient' individuals, partly because it reinforces the normal low expectations that society holds such that achievement is seen as exceptional. Rather, they suggest:

> For deaf children and young people, the successful navigation of being deaf in a world which faces them with countless daily hassles and that may commonly deny, disable or exclude them, is a key definition of resilience. For such successful navigation to occur, a range of protective resources and repertoires of skills developed through challenging experiences of risk and responsibility have to be promoted. (p.52)

The importance of language or alternative forms of communication cannot be over-emphasised. It forms the foundation for the continuing development of early attachment and develops into the primary way for children to interact with the human environment. In practice, this means that children may well be able to use language not only to talk about events that have happened to them, but also to relate some of the subtleties of events. Therefore, practitioners must be alert to the level of language use of the children they are working with and take steps to address delays as appropriate. Some children will need specialised speech therapy, while others can benefit from the kind of language stimulation that results from attending a day centre or nursery, for example.

When communicating with children about distressing or abusive events it will be important to assess their level of language comprehension and expression. People who already know the child well should be consulted wherever possible. Children may experience more emotions and recognise more emotions in others than they have the vocabulary to describe. Pictures representing different emotions can, therefore, be used in practice to help communicate about emotions with children.

Thoburn, Chand and Procter (2005) have marshalled considerable evidence to demonstrate that the use of interpreters within child welfare proceedings for children and families where English is not the first language is very patchy and unsatisfactory. Similarly, deaf Asian children have difficulty receiving appropriate support for communication with practitioners (Jones, Atkin and Ahmad 2001, cited in Thoburn *et al.* 2005). No assessment of a school-aged child is complete without effective direct communication with the child concerned that is tailored to his or her communication needs. Practitioners, therefore, have to insist that they are provided with the resources required to facilitate communication.

Literacy

Learning to read and write also affects the way children think about language. Reading systematises language and allows the child access to many new forms of language and variations in its use. Increasing literacy also helps children with logical and scientific reasoning. Figure 7.1 (adapted from Meadows 1986) shows the main stages of reading that can be expected through the school years. Children generally start learning to read and write by six or seven. In order to do this effectively it helps greatly if they come to school with an understanding of the reading conventions. In other words, they need to have some understanding that stories can be written down and that letters make up words that represent sounds. They also need to have the perceptual skills gained from drawing, doing jigsaws, pretend writing and so on (Meadows 1986). A child who has missed out on these experiences for any reason is in danger of falling behind right at the beginning of school; therefore, everything possible should be done to maximise children's chances of gaining these skills before school age.

Stage 0 Up to 6	Prereading, 'pseudo-reading'	Understand thousands of words, but can read few if any. Understand stories read to them.
Stage 1 Ages 6–7	Initial reading and decoding	Level of difficulty of language read by the child is much below that understood when heard. By the end of stage 1 most understand up to 4000 words and can read 600.
Stage 2 Ages 7–8	Confirmation and fluency	Listening is still more effective than reading. At end stage understand 9000, read 3000.
Stage 3 Ages 9–13/14	Reading for learning the new	Reading and listening about equal for comprehension; for some, reading may be more efficient for understanding.
Stage 4 Ages 14/15–17	Multiple viewpoints	Reading comprehension is better than listening comprehension for material of difficult content. For poorer readers, listening and reading comprehension may be equal.
Stage 5 Ages 18+	Construction and reconstruction	Reading is more efficient than listening.

Figure 7.1 The stages of reading at different ages (adapted from Meadows 1986)

Problems with reading are also extremely disabling to a child and can greatly interfere with school adjustment. Language and literacy problems can give rise to considerable adversity in childhood. Conversely, adversity such as abuse may be associated with delays in language development. The evidence is now also very clear about the negative impact of deprivation upon development. For example, a large-scale study of the impact of low birth weight and of the socio-economic environment upon cognitive development showed that both had an effect, but that the effects of deprivation were overwhelming and continued into adulthood (Jefferis, Power and Hertzman 2002). The authors suggest that gains in cognitive development can depend upon attempts to redress disadvantages in the social environment.

A review of research into the features of classrooms and schools associated with effective literacy teaching shows the importance of school climate, including teacher expectations of children and the strategic approach of head teachers (Smith and Ellis

2005). The gap in reading attainment increases with age especially because children with difficulties avoid reading tasks. The review underlines the crucial role of pupil engagement with reading to the extent that it can mitigate socio-economic disadvantage and have a disproportionately positive effect for children from deprived backgrounds. The suggested strategies for teachers to use to improve engagement with reading could easily be adapted to a range of settings:

- reading novels to children
- offering a range of materials, including comics
- giving children freedom to choose books
- discussing books
- not making gender-based assumptions about choice of reading
- promoting interest through reading clubs
- using peer recommendation
- intervening quickly when there are reading problems
- actively building self-esteem and skills
- building on young people's ideas
- using humour and games
- using modelling and scaffolding.

Cognitive development
Piaget

It is now widely accepted, largely because of the work of Piaget (see, for example, Piaget 1952 and 1954), that children's cognitive development is an active and motivated process involving constant learning, unlearning and relearning. Again, it is accepted that children's thought processes are different in some ways from those of adults. Adults, therefore, need to be sensitive to the child's level of understanding in order to relate directly to her. Piaget saw that the main developmental feature was changes in styles of cognitive performance, not levels of achievement. As described in Chapter 6, Piaget's rather rigid stage theory of development has been challenged by experimental findings, but the outline of his theories about this age group will be presented as the concepts are still used widely.

As recounted in Chapter 6, pre-schoolers are described as moving through the *sensory - motor* stage where they have no mental representation of events, and the *pre-operational* stage when internal representations are beginning and can be seen in the use of language and make-believe. So they use some symbolism, but have difficulty with ordering too many objects, ordering by more than one dimension, and with reversibility of operations. Piaget described children at these stages as being essentially *egocentric* and unable to appreciate another person's point of view.

From the ages of about seven up to eleven children move through the *concrete operational* stage. Now children become less egocentric. Their mental functions involve the use of logic and they can think ideas through in order to work out the properties of objects in the world and to make deductive inferences.

Thus, by five or six they are able to understand, for example, that six objects placed in a small heap represent the same number of objects as six spread out in a long row; in other words they develop number *conservation* skills. At around seven or eight they develop mass conservation. This can be tested by rolling a piece of clay into the shape of a ball, then rolling it into a sausage shape. The child is asked whether the sausage contains the same amount of clay as the ball had. Younger children will say that the sausage contains more clay. A similar test can be done for the conservation of volume. A low, wide glass is filled with water which is then poured into a taller, thinner glass. It is usually not until around 11 that children fully grasp that the taller glass contains the *same* amount of liquid and not more.

Using more ecological and naturalistic methods researchers have found that children can, in fact, demonstrate many of these operations earlier than Piaget described (Donaldson 1978). However, the experiments do seem to demonstrate some fascinating shifts in cognitive processes during school-age years. First, the change seems to be a development of the ability to *infer* about underlying reality, rather than simply responding to the surface appearance; in other words, the child can distinguish between what seems to be and what really is. Second, they demonstrate the ability to attend to, and take account of, *all* the features of the situation, not just the obvious change in shape. So, for example, in the liquid test, they observe that the second glass may be taller, but also that it is thinner. Third, the older child is more able to take account of the *transformation*; for example, the act of pouring the liquid from one glass to another. That is, instead of responding to each *state* as a snapshot of the situation as younger children do, school-age children see the dynamics of the *process*. Finally, they grasp that the process can be *reversed*, that the liquid stays the same amount despite the container, and can be poured back into the first glass (Flavell 1985).

As well as being important for academic work in school, all of these developments in cognition will also have an influence on children's social cognitions. So, for example, there will be an improvement in children's ability to look below the surface of another person's action and make inferences about the underlying state of mind and reasons for actions. They should also have a greater understanding of cause and effect and the relationship between their actions and possible outcomes and others' reactions. These skills are now clustered into what is called 'emotional intelligence' (Goleman 1996).

After this stage young people are described as moving into the stage of *formal operations* when abstract thought is possible, hypothetical reasoning becomes possible and logic is more sophisticated.

At all these stages children are described as adapting and organising their thought processes by both assimilation and accommodation. Assimilation requires the taking in of a new idea and fitting it into an existing way of thinking and accommodation requires adjusting the existing thought process to fit the new information.

In practice, therefore, we should expect to see children actively trying to work out how the world they live in works and it is a cause for concern if they are not doing so. Initially in the school years, children's ability to grasp abstract concepts is limited, therefore explanations for what is happening to them need to be couched in concrete terms. If children are not able to assimilate new ideas and concepts their thought processes may be disorganised and unpredictable. Similarly, if they are unable to accommodate their thought patterns to new ideas and concepts, their thinking could be rigid and unchanging.

If children's thought processes seem bizarre or unusual it may be helpful to try and see the world from their own viewpoint and work out what their logic is. For example, some children whose cognitive skills are limited have great difficulty with understanding concepts of family relationships. Many of the young people encountered in practice are part of reconstituted families and may have half and step-siblings. Understanding these relationships may be even harder for children if they are not living at home. To help children understand where they fit in a family network it could be helpful to draw simple family diagrams, or use dolls. They could also be encouraged to play with the concepts by making up other families and working out the relationships. Such practice with logical skills could help a child who is cognitively delayed.

Vygotsky

Piaget underplayed individual differences and the role of the social environment of development. Theories deriving from Vygotsky's work placed much more stress on the social aspects of cognitive development. The use of language is central to Vygotsky's theory, especially the transition from external to internal speech. When children first start using language, Vygotksy argues, it is largely external, and is used to communicate with others. Then between the ages of three and seven years, children develop the ability to talk to themselves, to reflect on their own mental processes and to engage in a form of inner speech. Vygotsky linked the use of inner speech with social competence (Smith and Cowie 1991).

Vygotsky criticised Piaget for concentrating on the *content* of children's thought at the expense of considering the *functional* aspects. He also criticised the fact that Piaget was not interested in the way in which thinking is shaped by education. He claimed that Piaget assumed cognitive development to be a natural process. He considered there to be a complex interaction between the maturation of cognitive processes and teaching so that 'teaching is only effective when it points to the road for development… The school child has to learn to transform an ability "in itself" into an ability "for himself [*sic*]"' (van der Veer and Valsiner 1991, p.331). Teaching can therefore help a child's cognitive development along. Further, learning a specific task will help the child with learning a structural principle that can be applied to other situations. The key is that teaching can precede cognitive development: 'the teacher may faithfully explain a task or concept for six or seven lessons until, suddenly, the child grasps the idea' (van der Veer and Valsiner 1991, p.335). This was an important idea because previously it had been widely considered that teaching should be pitched at the child's *current* level, not beyond it.

The central concept of his theory is the *zone of proximal development* (see Figure 7.2):

The zone of proximal development of the child is the distance between his [*sic*] actual development, determined with the help of independently solved tasks, and the level of the potential development of the child, determined with the help of tasks solved by the child under the guidance of adults and in cooperation with his more intelligent partners. (Vygotsky 1933c/1935, cited by van der Veer and Valsiner 1991, p.337)

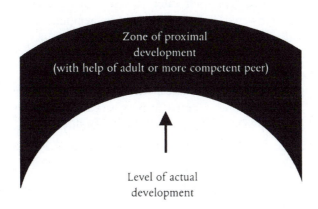

Figure 7.2 Vygotsky's 'zone of proximal development' (Smith and Cowie 1991)

Therefore, according to Vygotsky it is through social interactions that a child gains the tools for thinking and learning. Rather than seeing the child as independently working out how the world works, Vygotsky stressed the importance of the cooperative process of engaging in mutual activities with more expert others. Adults or older children at a more skilful level can help the child's cognitive development with appropriate instruction and demonstration, known as *scaffolding*. It is crucial that the level of help is pitched appropriately: not too close to the child's current ability, but not too far ahead of it. Thus cognitive development is an essentially interpersonal activity occurring within a wider societal context.

As described in Chapter 2, problems with attachment are associated with cognitive delays. This can be understood in the context of Vygotsky's theory that cognitive development is enhanced by a process of sensitive stimulation of thinking by someone who takes an interest in the child and knows her level of functioning. Such are the characteristics of the kind of sensitive parenting that promotes secure attachment. This kind of support need not be confined to parents. Grandparents, teachers, relatives and other interested adults and older siblings could all play a role in providing a child with such support, and this could be especially important for children whose primary attachment is not secure. If a child is looked after away from home the theory should remind practitioners of the importance of involving those who already know the child in sharing information about her. If an alternative carer is to provide appropriate support for cognitive development it is essential that they have an understanding of the child's current level of functioning. There is also a message for intervention with children with disabilities. There may be a temptation to pitch material at the current level of functioning of a child with a disability so that he or she can experience success. However, if it is considered that each child has a *potential* level of achievement, regardless of physical or mental disability, there is a need sensitively to present children with more challenging material.

Social workers often find that their intervention with children is concentrated on socio-emotional issues. However, it is important to remember the complexities of the interaction between the social, emotional and cognitive domains. Children who have undergone trauma or abuse often have difficulty in understanding what has happened to them and in making intellectual sense of the events that may follow, such as moving to foster carers or appearing in court. This can then have an impact on their emotional reaction to events. It is, therefore, essential to be aware of the importance of cognitive factors and that cognitive deficits can act as a real vulnerability factor for children.

Activity 7.3

Using the theory of the zone of proximal development consider ways in which the social worker can either act as the skilled helper or support carers or parents in acting as skilled helpers in 'building the scaffolding' to help the child move to a better level of understanding of events. This would require finding out what the child's level of understanding is and starting from there.

Hints for answers
Any intervention would have to be tailored to the child's level of current functioning. For example, a young child may have difficulty with understanding cause and effect. An adult could spend time with the child playing games such as snooker, while pointing out that hitting one ball into another causes it to move. They could also look for computer games that involve cause and effect and keep pointing out the links. They could also take advantage of real life situations, such as the link between pressing the button on pedestrian crossing lights, the lights changing colour and the cars stopping.

Another example would be a 'looked after' child with a limited understanding of the notion of long-term care. The worker would need to build on the child's current understanding of timescales, for example using the passing of birthdays or Christmas. These measures of time could then be used to mark out a 'long time' in more concrete terms.

Memory

The study of memory is extremely complex because of its many components. Accurate memory depends on first attending to the important features to be remembered, then having the capacity to process and store that information and finally being able to retrieve and reconstruct the information. Memory is used in so many contexts, socially and educationally; there is a great difference between learning information by rote for exams and remembering who your best friend is. There is much research on each of these topics, but for the purposes of practice it is important to know how children's memory can generally be expected to perform. When considering children's memory it is useful to remember that:

- any person's memory will be affected by her thinking and language capacity

- people's memories are better for information that makes sense to them

- people do not store information like computers; memory is an active function that involves processing.

In experiments of *recognition* of previously seen pictures four-year-old children perform as well as adults. However, they are not as good at free *recall* from a list of items. This kind of ability gradually improves in young childhood. By 12 years, short-term memory (that is, quick recall of information) is at about the same level as that of most adults (Flavell 1985). At this age children have more knowledge of memory as a concept and begin to understand that techniques can be used to improve memory; for example, by nine or ten they know that it is easier to tell back a story in their own words rather than word for word as heard. They also become more accurate and realistic in predicting how good their memory will be, while younger children tend to be over-confident about what they will remember (Bee 1995; Meadows 1986).

Long-term memory also improves during middle and late school years. The effectiveness of long-term memory depends, in part, upon the strategies used when processing it in the first place and when retrieving it later on. Children's use of memory strategies increases with age. To some extent strategies can be learnt and formal and informal learning in school will impact upon the development of memory. Flavell (1985) describes four common memory strategies that develop during school-age years:

- *Rehearsal*: Verbal rehearsal of information to be remembered significantly improves recall and its spontaneous use increases between the ages of five and ten. So, for example, school-age children can be seen muttering to themselves in order to remember. Children who do not spontaneously rehearse can be taught the techniques and their recall subsequently improves significantly.

- *Organisation*: When having to remember a number of items it helps to cluster by types; for example, if remembering a shopping list it is easier to cluster the items into categories such as fruit, tins and so on. As children's understanding of categorisation increases so they are able to use this information to improve memory. Again, this is a strategy that can be taught.

- *Elaboration*: Similar to, but developing later than, organisation, elaboration involves more extensive processing of the information to be remembered, maybe by finding a way to associate items, or of linking a word to a personal experience.

- *Retrieval strategies*: As they get older children learn that it may be worth persisting in trying to remember something. They also learn to be more systematic in their memory searches, so for example, if they have to recall three items from each of a number of categories, they will try to get three from one category before turning their attention to the next.

Of course, it is easier to use techniques if one knows in advance that material must be recalled. In everyday life it is rarely important to remember lists of words or to repeat information word for word. However, memory is important within education and if children miss a lot of school because of other problems they may not learn and practise the above techniques. Another important factor in memory is that very young children can exhibit powerful memory for information that they have interest and expertise in. So, for example, young children who develop an interest in dinosaurs can remember a lot of complex names, can incorporate new information quickly and put the information into categories. They are also extremely likely to have a much better memory for information about dinosaurs than many adults. The same is true for children with expertise in particular games or sports, for example chess.

The fact that memory can be improved with help suggests a potential for practitioners, teachers and parents or carers to support a child who is exhibiting difficulties. When helping children who have difficulty with remembering information learnt at school, it may be worth exploring any particular interests and expertise they have, for example knowledge about football or a favourite pop group, both to *reassure* them that their memory can work well and to *encourage* them to consider the strategies they use. The kind of techniques that help memory at any age are the use of imagery, remembering the context of events, thinking about different modalities, such as smells and sounds, changing the order of events in the telling, trying to tell events from another perspective and using mnemonics.

A range of interventions may entail exploring a child's memory of upsetting past events, for example the provision of therapeutic support following trauma or the construction of life-story books. Children who have undergone traumatic experiences may be unlikely to want to recall them, and indeed may well have used techniques to help forget events. However, 5- to 11-year-old children often notice details that adults do not notice and therefore can produce a lot of information under free-recall conditions. Free recall can then be followed up with open-ended specific questions and then increasingly specific questions and finally yes/no questions, if necessary. Saywitz and Goodman (1996) describe two techniques for enhancing children's recall. One is the use of *cognitive* interviewing in which the child is asked to:

- mentally reconstruct the *context* at the time of the crime
- report even *partial* information regardless of its perceived importance
- recount events in a variety of orders, for example describing events in reverse order
- report events from a variety of perspectives, for example by asking what a toy on the shelf would have seen (to be used only from seven years old on, as younger children find it hard to describe from another's perspective).

A second technique is *narrative elaboration* in which children are taught to give a high level of detail about the following, and prompt cards are used to remind them of:

- participants
- settings
- actions
- conversation/affective states.

Forensic interviewing, especially in suspected child sexual abuse cases, is a specialist activity and should only be undertaken following training and following inter-disciplinary consultation. Across many jurisdictions a standard approach to forensic interviewing has now been adopted, based upon research about children's memory development and their potential susceptibility to suggestion. Developed by John Yuille (see, for example, Yuille *et al.* 1993) the *Stepwise* interview technique progresses through stages:

- Rapport building – where neutral topics are discussed; normally also includes:
  - describing two events to explore the child's capacity to talk about neutral past events
  - telling the truth where there is careful introduction of the importance of telling the truth.

- Introducing the topic of concern in a very open way, for example 'Do you know why you have come to talk with me today?'

- Free narrative with use of *open* questions, such as 'Tell me more about that' and 'What happened next?'

- Follow-up questions – where there is some probing and clarification of points that may not have been clear or were inconsistent.

- Closure – concluding the interview with the aim of ending on a positive note with the child thanked for taking part.

Activity 7.4

When children experience family disruption and changes of care-giver they can lose track of events. Consider a child you are familiar with who has undergone such changes. What techniques have you found or would you consider using to help him or her to re-construct a 'coherent story' about his or her life to date? In particular how would you help her to recall good experiences and happier memories that may have become overridden by adverse events?

Hints for answers

For example, you may ask children to recall a particular person with whom they felt safe (who may not have been a member of the family). You could then ask them to remember colours, smells, places, sounds and so on that they associate with that person. The same could be done with places, pets or events such as school trips. Children could also be asked to tell the story of their childhood from the perspective of another person, such as a sibling. Drawings, photos, computer graphics and other games can be used to help prompt memories.

Concept of self

Through social interaction children start to appreciate that others have a view of them, and from this start to build up a view of themselves. The evidence shows that during school years children shift from defining themselves only by external characteristics such as 'tall' or 'fair haired' and start to use internal characteristics such as 'easily upset' or 'having a good sense of humour'. They increasingly use terms of social characteristics and social comparison. By seven they have usually internalised those reactions that depend on the expectations of others, for example shame or pride, and can describe situations that bring these about. By this age they can also describe mixed feelings. From about eight to ten years they become increasingly able to put themselves in another's place and view things from their perspective (Bee 1995; Santrok 2001; Smith, Cowie and Blades 2003).

Gender identity

The most influential model of gender development is Kohlberg's cognitive developmental theory of gender constancy (Kohlberg 1966). The model suggests that by about two years most children have a correct gender *identity*, that is, they can correctly label themselves and others. By four or five they understand gender *stability*, that is, that gender is stable over time, for example that boys grow up to be a man. By the time children start school, gender identity and sex-role behaviour continue to be consolidated. Over the next few years they develop gender *constancy*, in which they understand that gender does not change with change of clothes, hair or activity (Ruble *et al.* 2007). Identity development is also influenced by the extent to which gender is seen to be *central* to who a person is and by the *evaluation* of one's own gender as a group.

The reinforcement of different sex-role behaviour begins very early. By school age most children will have been encouraged to engage in sex-typed activities and to play with sex-typed toys. There will be individual differences between children, but the boys are likely to have played with toys that encourage invention, manipulation and understanding of the *physical* world, while girls' toys encourage initiation, proximity to the caretaker and understanding of the *interpersonal* world. Children will also have engaged in an active process of observing others and working out 'appropriate' sex-role behaviour. The boys are likely to have received the strongest messages about 'appropriate' sex-role behaviour and to have been discouraged from or even punished for engaging in 'girl'-type activity (Golombok and Fivush 1994).

Children will actively avoid playing with opposite sex peers. This pattern can be seen across cultures and in other primates. Boys are particularly rigid in this and control *each other*'s behaviour by using labels such as 'sissy'. Best friends into adolescence are usually of the same gender. Girls' play tends to be in dyads, to be intimate and closer to adults; while boys tend to form larger groups and to play rule-governed games, engage in more rough and tumble and keep further away from adults. In larger groups there tends to be more conflict and competition whereas in dyads interactions are more responsive to each other. During the period up to 12 when children are mixing largely with their own gender the patterns of behaviour diverge to such a great extent that they can be characterised as two different sub-cultures (Maccoby 1998, 2002). Children appear to socialise each other into gender-typed activity and the more time that children spend with their own gender the more the cultures of the two genders diverge.

A study of gender attitudes of children aged from 7 to 19 explored how traditional or flexible they are about others' behaviour and the extent to which it is gender stereotypical. The researchers found that the unfolding of attitudes during these years related to personal and family characteristics. The overall trend was for a decline in traditionality across middle childhood and early adolescence, with an increase in middle to late adolescence (Crouter *et al.* 2007). Boys with parents with traditional views showed little change and held traditional attitudes throughout; boys with less traditional parents showed a decline in traditionality between 7 and 12 but from 15 showed an increase in traditionality. For girls there was a general decline in traditionality throughout middle childhood and adolescence, although those with more traditional parents tended to hold more traditional views overall. Clearly, there are also powerful social and commercial factors at play. Gender-stereotyping in clothes and toys is, if anything, more marked than ever. Popular media, magazines and advertisements are overwhelmingly rigid in their portrayal of sex-role clothes, attitudes and activities across the lifespan.

Girls and boys are both limited by their gender roles (Unger and Crawford 1992). For example, girls are subject to greater adult supervision and are given much less freedom to travel alone outside the home. As they progress through school girls are more likely to opt out of mathematics and science subjects. Those who avoid taking on rigid sex roles fare better, that is, girls who could be described as 'tomboys' are more likely to be popular, creative and to carry on sports into teenage years. Boys may have the advantages of more freedom, more activity-oriented toys and more power. However, the pressure on boys to be 'boys' is very great: it is far more socially unacceptable for a boy to be labelled a 'sissy' than for a girl to be labelled a 'tomboy'. It is often not until adolescence that boys are able to develop close and intimate friendships, and these are usually with girlfriends.

It is difficult to gauge the extent to which gender affects the likelihood of being the victim of different forms of abuse and neglect because official statistics are limited to what comes to the attention of professionals and what is categorised as abusive. In the past, official statistics suggested that more girls than boys are victims of sexual abuse, and more boys victims of physical abuse; however, perhaps because of greater awareness more recent figures are not so starkly different (Department for Children, Schools and Families

2009a). There may be differences in the response to abuse; for example, a study in the US that compared the behaviour at a day camp of 211 maltreated children with 199 non-maltreated children (average age 9.9 years) showed that maltreatment was associated with aggression. However, the aggression was expressed differently by gender with boys showing physical aggression and girls showing relational aggression (Cullerton-Sen *et al.* 2008). Overall, it is important to assess each child as an individual.

The importance of identity tends to be to the fore when working with adolescents but identity is important at all stages and is required to be included in comprehensive assessments of development. Resilience is associated with a lack of rigid gender-stereotyped traits; thus resilience in boys is associated with the ability to express emotions, social perception and nurturance while in girls resilience is associated with autonomy and independence (Werner 1990). The way in which factors are studied in gender research such as that by Ruble *et al.* (2007) and Crouter *et al.* (2007) can be drawn upon in practice for example:

- the *centrality* of gender – which is tested by responses to statements such as 'some girls feel that being a girl is important to them, but other girls do not feel that being a girl is important to them'

- the *evaluation* of the gender as a group, e.g. 'boys are great'

- *rule-based rigidity*, e.g. 'it is *wrong* for girls to play with trucks/boys to wear nail varnish'

- *peer and parental rigidity* – the extent to which children believe that they would be sanctioned for breaking peer-based norms, tested by asking children about the response they would expect if they played with toys that were stereotypically associated with the other gender.

Both male and female social workers can act as role models themselves and they can encourage children to take part in a wide range of activities, including some they may not normally consider to be gender appropriate. Boys can be given the opportunity to care for younger children while girls can be given the opportunity for autonomy and independence. Staff in schools, residential homes, residential schools and foster carers should all be aware of the ease with which gender stereotyping can occur and the power of self-policing by groups of children. For example, any child who demonstrates interest in non-stereotypical activity will need active support.

Ethnic identity

Racial identity was originally linked with biological characteristics but is now seen as more of a social construction and associated with a perceived common heritage (Robinson 2007). Ethnic identity is also viewed as a social construct that relates to a sense of common bond with a group that shares traditions, behaviours, values and beliefs (Dwivedi 2002). The classic model suggests that before adolescence ethnic concepts are not explored in depth, a stage described as '*unexamined* ethnic identity' (Phinney 1993). As described in Chapter 8, it is during adolescence that the implications of race, ethnicity and culture are likely to be explored in depth. None the less ethnic awareness may change and develop during school years. Research on ethnic identity development has been influenced by a series of classic studies by Clark and Clark (1947). In summary studies carried out in white-dominated societies indicate that when four-year-old children are shown pictures of white and black children and asked who they would prefer to play with white children choose white children and black children also mainly choose the picture of the white child. This effect strengthens up to about seven when black children start to choose the picture of the black child and thinking becomes less rigid. Children also tend to segregate by race in their actual play, although the segregation by sex is greater.

By the age of four children can usually recognise their own ethnicity, but on a superficial level. Their understanding of ethnicity as a constant attribute does not fully develop until about eight or nine years (Aboud 1988). As with gender, the sense that is made of ethnic identity depends on a number of factors and the complexities of how children develop both *group* identity and *individual* identity are great. Centrality of ethnicity to the sense of self and evaluation of the ethnic group as a whole will influence development (Robinson 2007). Children may gain strength from being part of an ethnic group, but also experience discriminatory behaviour levelled at individuals and the group as a whole.

The school environment will also be important. In their study of school exclusions Osler *et al.* (2001) found that some teachers and head teachers believed that children from ethnic minority communities could be treated differently in school. They cite Ofsted findings of differences in the characteristics of white and black excluded children. White children were likely to be traumatised, to have lower than average achievement and to be excluded for verbal abuse; whereas black excluded children were more likely to be of above average achievement and to challenge teachers' judgements. The over-representation of black and mixed race children in the care system, and the fact that the care system itself is still predominantly white, may render such children vulnerable to low self-esteem and negative self-images (Robinson 2007).

There is potential for positive work with children on issues of ethnic identity on an individual basis and on tackling racial prejudice at a group level. Maxime (1994) sets out suggestions for supporting children aged 12 and under in the development of positive ethnic identity which include using natural opportunities to discuss race, taking racially motivated incidents seriously and providing children with positive role models. Dwivedi (2002) emphasises the extent to which black children are disempowered by social work services that negate their cultural, racial and linguistic needs. As Robinson (2007) concludes: 'Social workers need to take an active approach in helping black children build positive self-images of themselves' (p.73).

If children have been actively abused then the characteristics of the perpetrator could have an impact on the child's perception of the group. Given that identity is partly influenced by the evaluation of the group it is possible that the gender or ethnicity of a perpetrator of abuse could be attributed to the group as a whole and skew identity development. Part of the assessment of the impact of abuse should therefore include exploration of this issue.

Activity 7.5

Comprehensive assessment of a child entails attention to the child's developing sense of identity. Given that during school years gender and ethnic identity, along with other aspects of self-concept, will be developing in response to individual, family, community and social forces consider ways in which you can explore a child's individual sense of self.

Self and others: self-efficacy, self-esteem and friendships
Self-esteem and self-efficacy

The concepts of self-efficacy and self-esteem are often confused. Self-esteem, in particular, has been defined in many different ways – and the extent to which it is linked to or separated from self-efficacy has been the subject of some debate. For understanding links with resilience, though, an integrated model is more helpful (Miller and Daniel 2007).

Attribution theory helps with understanding self-efficacy – it describes the kind of explanations people give about success or failure on tasks. At any age success on a task can be attributed to one's own efforts or to outside factors such as the intrinsic difficulty of the task or to luck (Heider 1958). Soon after starting school, probably because success or failure is very clear cut in school, children develop an idea of their own relative ability. They become aware of the need for effort and start to distinguish between the relative contributions to success or otherwise of ability, effort and external factors. If they are not accurate in judging these relative contributions then attributions can be confused. Consider, for example, children who always attribute failure to their own inability, even on tasks that no child of their age could be expected to achieve; or children who take personal credit for success on tasks that have been joint endeavours. The way children view the outcome on tasks will then affect their sense of self-efficacy; in other words whether they believe that they have the ability to achieve on future tasks (Bandura 1981).

The main theories about self-esteem can be grouped into two categories – those that focus on self-worth and those that focus on self-competence. Mruk (1999, cited in Miller and Daniel 2007) brought the two together to propose that self-esteem is an integrated sum of self-worth and self-competence such that people need to *both* feel good about themselves *and* feel that they can meet challenges they may face. This model, therefore, allows for close linkage between self-efficacy and self-esteem. Rutter (2000) also emphasises the importance of 'planful competence' which entails a combination of dependability, productivity, self-esteem and ability to interact with others.

Mruk used his two-dimensional model to propose four categories that will resonate with practitioners and which is very helpful when assessing children:

- *Medium* to *high* self-esteem – children with good self-esteem have a positive sense of self-worth and a positive sense of self-competence.

- *Low* self-esteem – those with a low sense of self-worth and low self-competence show classic low self-esteem. These children do not want to take part in activities in the classroom, have a low perception of their own abilities and expect poor outcomes. At its extreme low self-esteem can be manifested as depression.

- *Defensive* self-esteem – where children appear to have good self-esteem but are masking elements of low esteem. It comes in two types:

    ○ Type 1 – children with a high sense of self-worth but low self-competence. These children think highly of themselves, but cannot do age-appropriate tasks, so when asked to do something in class can become defensive. They may brag about small achievements, blame others and use other forms of compensation for lack of skill.

    ○ Type 2 – children with a low sense of self-worth, often associated with traumatic experiences and negative messages from others, coupled with a positive self-competence based upon success on tasks. These children rely on their competence to off-set their low sense of worth. When their ability is threatened they can over-compensate and strive even further to prove their ability, sometimes showing antisocial behaviour in the process. They can be obsessive about demonstrating their competence.

Vulnerable, abused and neglected children will have few opportunities to make choices about their lives or to impact upon the decisions made on their behalf. Neglect, in particular, can render children vulnerable to developing the internal, stable and global pattern of attributions associated with learned helplessness (Seligman and Peterson 1986; Zimmerman 1988). Adult reactions are crucial in the development of self-efficacy. If important adults appear to expect them to fail on a task there is little motivation for them to try. Moreover, the arousal caused from fear of failure can cause failure and further contribute to a lowered sense of self-efficacy. Children who believe that they can have an impact on events, for example that if they study hard for a test they are more likely to do well on it, have greater resilience in the face of adversity. Engaging with children in a way that involves them in assessment and planning, that encourages them to contribute to decisions about their lives and that provides them with positive choices can help to shift such attributions and create the conditions for the development of better self-efficacy (Daniel *et al.* 2008, 2009).

Intervening to enhance self-esteem is not straightforward. There is little evidence that whole school self-esteem programmes are effective and, indeed, there is now concern that crude attempts to raise self-esteem through an over-emphasis on the self and praise are harmful (Newman 2004; Seligman 1995). For individual children there needs to be a nuanced approach to self-esteem that includes development of mastery and achievement through effort, and within schools there needs to be attention to the ethos within the classroom (Miller and Moran 2006; Seligman 1995). Miller and Daniel (2007) suggest a range of strategies to increase self-esteem and resilience. They are aimed at schools where teachers and social workers can develop joint approaches but can also be adapted for a range of settings.

- *Maintain an environment where self-worth is enhanced* – a child's individual sense of self-worth or belief that one is liked and accepted is rooted in early attachment and the experience of caring relationships. Within schools and other settings a focus on creating an inclusive and caring ethos where positive horizontal and vertical relationships are nurtured can enhance a child's sense of self-worth. Practices such as *Circle-Time* can also play a positive role.

- *Focus also on developing self-competence* – fundamental to self-competence is that children achieve their goals. It is essential that children acquire skills and knowledge and recognise their achievements. Practitioners, therefore, need to assist children to learn skills and encourage children to appreciate their attainment. Scaffolding (as described earlier) is crucial here because tasks have to be set at a stage beyond the child's current stage of attainment. There is now an accumulation of evidence to suggest that giving a child tasks that are too easy with the aim of improving self-esteem is, in fact, counter-productive. Brooks' suggestion that one can look for 'islands of competence' for the child can be helpful here (Brooks 1994).

- *Develop activities which develop both aspects of self-esteem* – peer tutoring can enhance both aspects of self-esteem in the peer tutors and tutees. It fosters positive and collaborative relationships and demonstrates to a child that she can offer something to another.

- *Develop and apply a more nuanced understanding of praise* – unsophisticated over-use of praise is not helpful. Different approaches are needed depending upon whether the child needs increased self-worth, increased self-competence or both. To enhance self-worth practitioners should offer affirming messages and show that they are interested in the child as an individual, irrespective of her ability in comparison with her peers. Essentially a child with low self-worth needs to experience warmth and concern. However, praise to increase self-competence has to be honest and contingent. In other words, it has to be linked with improvements on a task, even if very small, and must be proportionate. All of this needs to be within a climate of accepting that mistakes are made – but that they can be learned from.

- *Be aware of defensive self-esteem in the class* – teachers and other practitioners can pool their knowledge about a child to assess the extent to which she may show Type 1 or 2 *defensive* self-esteem and tailor intervention to the child's individual needs.

Peers and friendships

Friendship in childhood has six functions (Gottman and Parker 1987, cited in Santrok 1994):

- companionship
- stimulation
- physical support
- ego support
- social comparison

- intimacy and affection. (p.472)

Just as children change in their descriptions of *themselves* during school years, so children start to describe their *friends* by increasingly referring to internal characteristics. This change parallels the developments in the way friends are chosen. Thus up to about seven or eight years friendships are often based on proximity and common activities and younger children will play rather indiscriminately with other children in the neighbourhood. At about nine or ten children start to see their friends as people with whom they have shared values and interests in common. From 11 to 12 friendships are increasingly based on understanding, self-disclosure and shared interests (Smith and Cowie 1991).

Although good peer relationships can compensate to some extent for poor attachment experiences, there is evidence of an association between the quality of attachments and the quality of friendships. Children with secure attachments tend to relate to peers in a positive, fair and responsive way, whereas children with insecure avoidant attachments either exhibit aggression towards or detachment from peers (Howe 1995).

Most young children show some aggression, although by seven this is mainly expressed verbally. Anger outbursts can be common in infancy, peaking in the second year, accompanied by physical manifestations. This anger can be of two kinds:

- manifestation of *distress*

- to gain something, i.e. *instrumental*.

Instrumental anger, in particular, should decline between the ages of three and seven, while aggressive behaviour normally drops during pre-school years. Before starting school, tantrums, fighting and destructiveness usually decline. By the time children are in school their anger is usually expressed as:

- person-directed *retaliatory* aggression

- *hostile* outbursts.

Persistent aggression is related to irritable and ineffective discipline at home, poor parental monitoring and lack of warmth (Rutter and Rutter 1993).

Dodge (1980) has described a 'hostile' cycle that illustrates how aggressive behaviour can escalate. Pre-school children tend to see all acts as intentional; by school age, children should learn that some outcomes are unintentional. For example, they should be able to differentiate between a child accidentally bumping into them or deliberately pushing them. In other words, their attributions for actions become more accurate. Dodge suggests that some children attribute hostile intent to peers who cause accidental hurt. Because they then retaliate with aggression they are likely to increase their chances of becoming unpopular and therefore of becoming victims of intentional hurt. This cycle can spiral so that the child becomes increasingly rejected.

A classic study exploring children's own ratings of their peers found that children are categorised in one of five ways which can be described as popular, controversial, rejected, neglected or average (Coie and Dodge 1983):

- *Popular* children lead in a cooperative way. In particular, they have better skills at joining in group activity because they participate in a way consistent with the group's activities and do so in a friendly manner that avoids conflict and is open to compromise.

- *Controversial* children may have some leadership skills, but also fight and are disruptive, so although they may be looked up to, they are also feared.

- *Rejected* children are both disruptive and lack cooperative or leadership skills. They tend to join group activities by 'barging in' and may disagree with the group activities and attempt to assert their own ideas and feelings aggressively. Essentially they appear to lack social skills when interacting with peers.

- *Neglected* children are not aggressive, and lack cooperative or leadership skills.

- *Average* children make good friendships and are neither overly aggressive nor shy.

When children were followed over four years 30 per cent of those being originally rated as 'rejected' had shifted to being 'neglected'. Another 30 per cent were still 'rejected'. Ongoing rejection should be a cause for concern for practitioners because of the extent to which lack of friends and a peer group can heighten vulnerability to emotional and behavioural problems.

Aggression can be manifested as bullying of other children, which has, for a number of years, been the biggest reason for calls to ChildLine in the UK. For example, in 2007–2009 32,562 children called about bullying as their main problem and over 5000 other children also mentioned it as one of their problems (NSPCC 2009). Forty per cent of those calling about bullying were aged between 5 and 11. Some children were also dealing with family breakdown and bereavement. Children mainly described physical bullying, name calling and teasing which could occur anywhere where children gather and could involve texting and 'cyber' bullying. Children described a range of effects including 'sadness, loneliness, low self-esteem, fear, anxiety and poor concentration, through to self-harm, depression and suicidal thoughts' (p.7). For some children bullying is identified as the cause of suicide. Only 11 per cent of those who had called about bullying had told a parent and with mixed results. Several said teachers had not helped. Some 406 children called about racist bullying and they did not want to tell parents and thought teachers did not believe them.

Children can be helped to improve their peer skills in a number of ways. These can include social skills and social cognitive training, fostering successful peer relationships and fostering a positive social milieu (Malik and Furman 1993). Children with problems in peer relationships may need a period of more adult supervision than suggested by their chronological age and gradual introduction to structured activities followed by more unstructured activities. In effect, adults can again use scaffolding techniques to help children attain peer skills. Many commercial programmes exist to assist with teaching skills such as listening, handling saying 'no' to stay out of trouble and so on. Each skill is broken down into components which are explained to the child and role play is used to practise skills. Children can also be taught problem-solving styles that encourage them to stop and think before acting impulsively. For example, a study of how practitioners intervene to nurture resilience found that children responded well to techniques including the use of laminated pictures to:

- help children understand about anger blowing up by using the metaphor of a volcano

- teach 'cool-down' techniques using concepts of having a cool drink

- encourage children to count to 10 before responding. (Daniel *et al.* 2008)

As the following quotes suggest, children can understand the point of such techniques:

'We did these cards, like for cool drinks and stuff to calm you down, thinking on a beach – a cold drink.'

'When I was angry and I'd get into fights and get excluded. But [the worker] would say "don't let your anger out, just count to ten and breathe in and out'.

'The cool down techniques have helped me… Yeah, I'm a bit calmer now in lessons and I find the work more easier now.'(Daniel *et al.* 2008, pp.67 and 91)

Activity 7.6

A young boy is referred for additional support because he appears to be socially isolated, to have no friends and to have problems generally in getting on with his peers. He has an older and younger sister who both appear more socially adept, although his parents are somewhat isolated also. Describe a potential package of intervention that includes direct work with the child, support for the parents and work in partnership with other practitioners connected with the child.

Many schools have also now incorporated the use of nurture groups to support the emotional development of children in need of additional support. The children are assessed using the Boxall profile (Bennathan and Boxall 1998). This profile covers the 'developmental strands' of organisation of experience and internalisation of controls and a 'diagnostic profile' that covers:

- self-limiting features
  - disengaged
  - self-negating
- undeveloped behaviour
  - makes undifferentiated attachments
  - shows inconsequential behaviour
  - craves attachment, reassurance

- unsupported development
  - avoids/rejects attachment
  - has undeveloped/insecure sense of self
  - shows negativism towards self
  - shows negativism towards others
  - wants, grabs, disregarding others.

The completed profile for each child identifies areas for further attention which are then the focus of intervention in the nurture group. Social workers and teachers should liaise closely to ensure that parents and carers are aware of the focus of the group so that messages can be reinforced in other settings.

A programme for children with behavioural problems that explicitly involves parents is 'Families and Schools Together', known as FAST (see, for example, McDonald *et al.* 1997). The programme is an interesting blend of techniques from play therapy, family therapy and community development. The programme brings the families of children together in groups that meet regularly for a range of structured activities with the aim of assisting with parenting, but also building networks of mutual support and strengthening community ties. Evaluations of the programme are positive and it is being rolled out in a number of countries.

The NSPCC (2008) suggest a number of strategies to tackle the specific problem of bullying:

- incorporate the UN Convention on the Rights of the Child throughout national curricula
- include tackling bullying in initial teacher training courses
- implement and enforce school-wide anti-bullying policies and create a safe environment
- undertake regular anonymous questionnaires in schools
- check the 'hidden spaces' in schools where bullying occurs unobserved
- provide information about ChildLine and ensure that independent counselling services are available to all children
- implement local authority supported community mediation services using restorative justice concepts to tackle bullying in the community
- use awareness-raising campaigns and safety software to tackle cyber-bullying.

Development of morality

Lying, stealing, cheating, disobedience and cruelty to younger siblings or peers are the kinds of behaviour that social workers are frequently presented with in children both living at home or in alternative care. They all represent difficulties with some aspect of moral development. 'Some aspect' is the key expression here as morality encompasses a complex interaction of a number of different factors. It begins at a very young age, continues throughout school age and adolescence and depends on cognitive, emotional and behavioural maturation.

Cognitive

Moral development depends in part upon children's increasing *understanding* of the difference between right and wrong within the context of societal conventions. They need to appreciate that there are rules for governing behaviour and that there are reasons for such rules. They also need an appreciation of the fact that other people have thoughts and feelings and that their own actions may have consequences for others.

As described in Chapter 6, by the time children reach school years they should have developed a 'theory of mind', that is, they should know that others have independent inner worlds and are thinking and feeling beings. This is one vital part of the social knowledge required for moral development. However, considerable empirical work has also been carried out to explore the development of children's moral *reasoning*. It was again Piaget who first systematised the study of this aspect of cognitive development (Piaget 1932). He used a combination of methods, including observing children at play, asking them to explain the rules of their games and setting them moral problems in the form of stories. He concluded that children move through three stages of moral reasoning, as outlined below.

PRE-MORAL JUDGEMENT

Up until about four years of age children have no systematic understanding of rules or the reasons for rules.

MORAL REALISM

Between the ages of four and nine or ten, rules are seen as absolute and unchangeable and laid down by a higher authority such as God or parents. The seriousness of an action is judged by the amount of damage, rather than the intent behind the action. Punishment, similarly, is seen as related to the amount of damage and is inevitable. So, by this reasoning, a child will consider that it is worse to accidentally break three cups than to deliberately break one.

MORAL SUBJECTIVISM

From about nine or ten, children begin to realise that rules are made by people and, in certain circumstances, can be changed. Thus, a group of this age may decide to change the rules of a game, for example by agreeing to go down the ladders and up the snakes! They also exhibit a clearer understanding of the importance of intent rather than outcome for judging the seriousness of an action and realise that certain moral principles underlie rules.

As with other aspects of Piaget's work, some of the elements of the more advanced moral reasoning has been demonstrated at younger ages. Using similar methods, Kohlberg refined the stages of moral reasoning (Kohlberg 1969). He paid more attention to the reasoning people gave for their answers than the answers themselves and discerned six stages of moral reasoning which he placed into three levels.

LEVEL ONE: PRE-CONVENTIONAL MORALITY

This level represents the thinking of most children up to the age of nine, and of some adults. Stage one (obedience and punishment orientation) is similar to Piaget's moral realism in that morality is based on obedience to those in authority. In stage two (individualism, instrumental purpose and exchange) children judge morality as that behaviour which meets one's own needs, but begin to recognise intention as important.

LEVEL TWO: CONVENTIONAL MORALITY

Stage three (mutual interpersonal expectations, relationships and interpersonal conformity) represents obedience in order to please and help others. Judgement by intention is further developed. Stage four (social system and conscience), similar to Piaget's moral subjectivism, represents the recognition of law and the need for maintaining social order. Most adolescents and adults respond at this level.

LEVEL THREE: POST-CONVENTIONAL MORALITY

Stages five and especially six represent levels of moral reasoning that few attain. Stage five (social contract or utility and individual rights) allows for laws to be broken in order to preserve such basic values as life and liberty, although there is an acceptance that rules are needed to preserve order. By stage six (universal ethical principles) laws are seen as relative and as such can be broken if they conflict with basic ethical principles according to individual conscience.

Both Piaget and Kohlberg have been criticised for an apparent over-emphasis upon *justice* in what could be described as a male orientation to morality based on rights and rules (Gilligan 1993). As a result of the detailed study of women's approaches to various moral dilemmas, Gilligan suggested another important component of morality whereby decisions are based on principles of *responsibility* to others, taking account of feelings and interpersonal issues:

> In this conception, the moral problem arises from conflicting responsibilities rather than from competing rights and requires for its resolution a mode of thinking that is contextual and narrative rather than formal and abstract. This conception of morality as concerned with the activity of care centres moral development around the understanding of responsibility and relationships, just as the conception of morality as fairness ties moral development to the understanding of rights and rules. (p.19)

Affective

In addition to the intellectual understanding of the need for moral behaviour, children also need to develop the facilitative *feelings* of empathy and concern for others and feelings of well-being and positive self-esteem for doing the right thing, as well as the inhibiting feelings of guilt and remorse after doing the wrong thing.

EMPATHY

In order to behave in a way that is 'pro-social', that is in a caring and helpful manner towards others, children need to feel empathy. Most important, children need to realise that, like themselves, others can feel pain, distress, happiness and so on. Empathy depends on developing a sense of self in relation to others and the ability to see things from another's perspective. Although much younger children demonstrate empathic feelings and behaviour, during school years empathic behaviour becomes increasingly based upon an understanding of other people's perspectives. In the early school years, up to about eight, children realise that other people have a social perspective and that it may not necessarily be the same as their own, but they find it difficult to coordinate different viewpoints and therefore tend to focus on one.

From eight to ten, children not only know that each individual is aware of another's perspective, but also know that this awareness affects people's views. They, therefore, know that it is possible to judge another's intentions, purposes and actions by putting oneself in their place. Because they know that someone's reaction may be different from their own they are able to respond more appropriately to another's distress. For example, although they may like physical comfort when in distress, they can realise that another child in the same position may prefer to be left alone. They can use objective ideas about fairness, using more universal principles. During later school years they develop a greater appreciation of the effect of life circumstance and feel empathy for people in less fortunate circumstances than their own (Santrok 2001).

Schaffer (1996) summarises the main findings about the kind of parental factors that are associated with pro-social behaviour in children (citing Zahn-Waxler, Radke-Yarrow and King 1979; Robinson, Zahn-Waxler and Emde 1994). Like morality itself, these factors include cognitive, affective and behavioural components, suggesting that children need support with their development in each of these domains.

- Pro-social behaviour in children is associated with the provision of clear rules and principles for *behaviour*, with an explanation of consequences.

- The manner in which such messages are given also seems to have an impact; thus, contrary to what some might suppose, pro-social behaviour is associated with parental messages given not in a calm, cool way but with a strong *emotional* component.

- Children who are attributed with good intentions, for example described as 'helpful', are more likely to incorporate such *attributions* into their self-definition and live up to them.

- Caretakers who behave in a moral way towards others provide positive models for children.

- Finally, what Schaffer describes as 'the most essential attribute, i.e. the existence of a warm and responsive relationship between parent and child. Those parents who behave in a loving, accepting manner towards their children are most likely to have children with high rates of pro-social behaviour' (p.276).

CONSCIENCE

As well as the positive feelings of empathy that encourage moral behaviour, children also need to experience feelings that will *inhibit* immoral actions. In other words, they need to develop a conscience. Fahlberg (1994) firmly locates the development of conscience in early attachment. Children, in trying to please attachment figures, gradually internalise their values, standards and constraints. By the age of five children have an internal critical voice, but, because of their lack of self-control, they still require adult supervision which prevents misbehaving. At this stage it is crucial that children receive consistent and appropriate messages of approval and disapproval, otherwise they have nothing on which to base their own conscience development. By nine or ten they have the cognitive ability to consider alternative possibilities and to imagine possible outcomes. By this age their sense of right or wrong is normally strong enough to prevent them from misbehaving without adult supervision. From then on conscience continues to be refined and modified as values develop.

Fahlberg also describes three main types of problems of conscience, all of which may be seen in children within the care system:

- Some do not feel guilt because they do not believe they could survive the experience of guilt.

- There are those, described as psychopathic, who appear to feel no guilt and show no restraint or remorse.

- Most commonly seen is the problem of those who feel guilt after the act, but whose conscience does not warn and/or restrain them in advance.

Behavioural

Knowing and feeling also need to be put into *action*. Some children may feel remorse after an action, but not be inhibited from doing wrong again. Others may know that their actions are wrong, but do them anyway. In younger children action is mainly monitored by adults; increasingly, children need to learn to exert control over their own actions.

It is therefore evident that the underlying reasons for immoral behaviour can be very complex and require detailed assessment. Ryan (1979) provides a specific discussion of lying and stealing in children being looked after by foster carers. She points out that very few people are totally honest all of the time. She explores some of the reasons as to why children may lie and steal. For example, children may lie about their family to present a different picture than the unbearable reality, some children will have witnessed their parents lying, and others may have been lied to themselves. Children may steal because they have not had their needs fulfilled or because of a lack of appropriate experiences at home.

In practice, we should expect school-age children to be developing more sophisticated thinking about moral issues. They may believe that it is important to be good in order to live up to the expectation of family and important others and appreciate that morality is socially defined. They should also start beginning to appreciate that intention is a factor in making decisions about action.

As with other cognitive skills, one could expect there to be a zone of proximal development for moral reasoning. This would mean that there is scope for children's moral reasoning to be encouraged by appropriate scaffolding. So, for example, as described in the section on peer relationships, some children may get into fights because they do not appreciate the difference between deliberate and accidental actions. It is unlikely that simple statements such as 'Don't hit John, he only accidentally bumped into you!' will change such cognitive processes. Instead, it would be necessary to explore their understanding of terms such as 'accident' and 'deliberate' and 'intent'. Support would then need to start from their point of understanding, perhaps by using simple scenarios in the form of cartoons or stories to help them disentangle issues of intention.

Children who have difficulty in understanding their own feelings and emotions (as is the case with many children who have suffered abuse or neglect) are also likely to have difficulty in understanding other people's feelings and emotions. Experiences of abuse and neglect may therefore impede the development of empathy. If such children have to be looked after away from home, carers need to provide an environment as described above that will foster the development of empathy. For children living at home, practitioners need to consider all attachment figures as possible sources of support for the development of empathy. Other adults such as social workers themselves, teachers, home visitors and volunteer befrienders could also provide such input.

Fahlberg (1994) suggests that school-age children with conscience problems may need to be supported as a younger child would be. They can be helped by providing sufficient supervision to monitor behaviour and giving them the consistent messages of approval and disapproval they have missed. These messages are more effective if constructed in the 'I' form, for example saying 'I don't like it when you do...' rather than 'you are naughty to do...'.

Key messages

- During school years a secure *attachment* base remains important. Because of the burgeoning of cognitive processes young people experiencing loss or separation are likely to try to make sense of events. They need information, and crucially, care has to be taken to make sure that they do not blame themselves for loss. They need a coherent story that explains life events, and social workers can play a part in checking that children can account for changes in their lives.

- During any disruption practitioners need to ensure that as much continuity can be maintained as possible, for example children should have the opportunity to keep contact with their family, even if they move away from home.

- School features strongly during these years; for some it may act as a source of support. For others, school problems may be the reason for referral for social work intervention. The fact that school experiences have such long-term implications means that prompt intervention is essential when school has become a source of difficulty for a child. The intellectual, emotional and social aspects of school should all be taken into account when assessing a child's overall school experience.

- Exclusion from school has a devastating effect on a child's education. The key aim has to be to prevent exclusion wherever possible, which entails good inter-disciplinary relationships and purposeful work to reduce the behaviour triggering exclusion.

- During school years *language* use should become increasingly sophisticated, and children increasingly incorporate abstract concepts. Language delay has to be appreciated as a factor that will render a child vulnerable to problems in school and in communication with friends and adults.

- Practitioners must recognise the importance of language, and find help for the child who has problems in communication. Similarly, they need to be alert to the potential impact of adversity upon the development of language.

- When working with a child it is absolutely essential to find a way to communicate. Rather than seeing a child as having communication 'problems' we must consider what additional supports the practitioner requires in order to be able to communicate with the child in a form that suits him or her.

- Reading provides the fundamental underpinning for nearly all school subjects, and, as such, is crucial. However, it also allows children to take part in other aspects of peer culture, for example reading books, comics and magazines. Many computer games and activities also require some literacy skills. Problems with reading must therefore be tackled as soon as possible. Joint planning with educational staff is essential.

- The development of reading skills can be greatly promoted by interest from home and parents or carers may need encouragement to be involved in the process of improving reading ability. If they are not, then it is important to find someone who will take that role.

- Cognitive development not only underpins engagement with learning, but also engagement in the social world. Attention to cognitive development must be progressed in parallel with other priorities such as ensuring security of attachment.

- During school years children's ability to use *memory*-enhancing techniques improves. As children move into adolescence their memory performance may approach adult level. No assumptions should be made about a child's level of recall, because of the diversity of factors that can impact on memory. It is important to ensure that a child has emotional support if she is in a process of recalling disturbing events.

- Children develop their *gender* and *racial* identity within the context of family, peers, school and society. These layers of influence all exert powerful forces, which if restrictive, negative or undermining are significant adversities that may increase vulnerability. Assessment at any age and stage must explicitly explore these vital aspects of self-concept.

- Along with secure attachment experiences, *self-esteem* and *self-efficacy* form the foundations for resilience. During these years problems with self-esteem can become entrenched, especially if school experiences are difficult. At the same time there is scope for positive intervention.

- Imagination is needed to help find 'islands of competence' for a young person. Clubs, hobbies, sport, arts and drama all provide fruitful avenues to explore.

- Friendships should play a large part of the school-age child's life. The implications for practice depend on whether children have friends or not. If children have friendships they must be taken seriously. The obvious first step is to ask children who their friends are and start from this point. Friends can be an important source of resilience during adverse life events and every effort should be made to support and nurture children's friendships.

- If children do not have friends then there must be careful assessment as to why. It may be due to different factors including lack of confidence, lack of self-esteem, overt aggression, an insecure inner working model of relationships and so on.

- Moral development depends on cognitive, emotional and behavioural maturation. It parallels development in these domains, so for example, as a child's cognitive skills evolve, they are able to engage in more sophisticated moral reasoning. Moral development can be supported by the social environment, particularly through encouragement to feel empathy and to act pro-socially. Children's moral development is also influenced by observation. Adults' and other children's behaviour will be copied. Residential staff and other carers need to work towards creating an atmosphere of mutual respect and responsibility.

CHAPTER 8

Adolescence

Introduction

With increasing affluence and longer periods of education in the Western world the gap between childhood and independence has been prolonged and has been called adolescence. Some consider adolescence to be a political and social construction (Steinberg 1993). Nevertheless, there are important biological, cognitive and social changes to which all young people are subject. Although individual responses to these changes may differ, an awareness of how development can usually be expected to progress along the path from childhood into early adulthood will be helpful for practitioners.

Adolescence is subject to stereotypical phrases such as 'identity crisis', 'generation gap', 'acting out', 'typical adolescent' and 'raging hormones'. Though they may contain a grain of truth most of these stereotypes are misleading or wrong. Usually they act as a shorthand way of 'explaining' a difficulty that a young person may have. To attribute behaviour solely to the fact of being adolescent is not particularly helpful when trying to help young people and parents in distress.

Activity 8.1

Think about the young people you have worked with.

1. Recall ways in which their behaviour was described and explained by family, other professionals, the young people themselves and you.
2. List the range of stereotypical views that may underlie these accounts.

Understandings about adolescence are characterised by dichotomies largely because of ambiguities about this transitional phase and whether the young people are viewed as 'children in need of support' or 'threats to others' or 'adults who should take responsibility for themselves'. This chapter will explore the key developmental tasks of adolescence within the context of three common dichotomies and associated practice issues.

Attachment, identity and well-being: smooth transitions or time of crisis?

Maturing relationships

The central dichotomy in adolescence lies in the potential tension associated with negotiating changes in overt dependence on primary attachment figures. In popular discourse this tension underlies the concept of a generation gap. While adolescence is certainly a time of transition, the evidence suggests that the concept of a generation gap is much exaggerated. In reality young people often hold similar values and aspirations to their parents and normally conflict is generated in relation to differences about day-to-day issues of clothing, tidiness and so on. Conflicts usually arise when parents define an issue as a matter of custom, for example in relation to suitable clothes for school, whereas the young person sees it as a matter of personal choice (Berger 2001; Smetana 1989). The concept of 'independence' is unhelpful at any developmental stage – is it a rare person who survives totally independently; healthy adult functioning normally depends on having a network of support, including partners, friends, peers and colleagues. Instead it is preferable to see adolescence as a time of moving towards more mature inter-dependence (Holmes 1993).

Parents continue to be important three-quarters of young people interviewed in one study said they felt they could count on their parents and that if they had children in the future would hope their own families would be similar to the one they grew up in (Steinberg 1993). Indeed, Schaffer (1996) stresses that during adolescence parents are often the main source of support and that a good relationship with one or both parents can help ameliorate the effects of adverse life events. Parents can buffer young people against some of the stresses of the teenage years, especially if they are able to maintain a close relationship despite the inevitable changes. In other words, a good parental relationship can be a *protective* factor in the face of adversity. If parents assume that there will be a generation gap they may miss the opportunity to use the positive aspects of their relationship with their children in dealing with difficulties. Parents may need to hear that adolescents can still value their views and opinions.

None the less, all involved have to adjust to changes in family and wider relationships. The tantrums associated with striving for more autonomy in adolescence have been likened to the tantrums exhibited by toddlers as they simultaneously explore the world while trying to maintain a link with the secure base (Fahlberg 1988). Transitions are supported by good communication and support from parents. Connectedness or the sense of closeness is also important. Young people are likely to strive for more autonomy and freedom, but parental monitoring is essential for the prevention of serious problems (Berger 2001). Monitoring is not the same as curtailing activity, so it can be difficult for parents to attain the appropriate balance between *knowing* what their young people are doing, where and with whom; and *forbidding* certain activities. The wider context is also important because parents living in disadvantaged areas where there may be more community-based risks often have to set greater limits than parents in more affluent areas. A study of parenting in disadvantaged areas in Scotland, for example, showed that parents and young people were all able to articulate the levels of risk posed in the community and, although young people resisted their parents' attempts to keep them in, they understood the motivation (Seaman *et al.* 2005). The importance of balance is highlighted by Berger (2001):

> adolescents have *never* been found to benefit from families that are permissive to the point of laxness *or* strict to the point of abuse... Families that are high in conflict, or parent–child relationships that are low in support, are almost always hard on the adolescent. (p.442)

When presented with difficulties in family communication that have emerged during adolescence, it will be helpful to look for the continuities with earlier behaviour. Attachment theory suggests that the quality of family relationships develops from very early interactions between the child and his caretakers. Therefore, a problem in adolescence can be viewed as the expression of a well-established pattern of family communication rather than a symptom of adolescence itself. When there are communication problems, other significant adults can play a role, perhaps by acting as a mediator to help each person put over his point of view.

Attachment relationships with the family form the foundation for other social contacts; young people explore their peer attachments from the secure base of attachment to parents (Feeney and Noller 1996). Adolescents who currently have or have experienced secure attachments are likely to be better adjusted and more socially competent (Rice 1990). The *quality* of relationship a young person has with his parents may also affect the quality of relationship he has with his peers. The importance of peers increases during adolescence, but they do not usually become more important to the young people than parents.

Activity 8.2

Consider a young person with whom you work whose relationships with his peers seem to be affected by the type of relationships he or she has at home.

1. Examine the quality of the different relationships the young person has and list which aspects are similar and which are different.
2. Consider what opportunities there are to assist the young person to develop good peer relationships despite poorer familial relationships.

A popular view not fully supported by research is that adolescents are somehow uniquely susceptible to 'peer pressure'. The pressure to conform with a peer group rises in early adolescence but only until 14 (Coleman and Hendry 1990). In fact peer relationships often help young people negotiate adolescence and can ease the transition away from childish behaviour. Sometimes young people do lead each other into trouble, but this can often relate to peer solidarity rather than pressure (Berger 2001). For example, Seaman *et al.* (2005) found that gatherings of young people in the streets were described by members of the community as gangs whereas for the young people they were seen as protective groups of friends.

If a young person's family and peer relationships are both stressful practitioners will need to assess what is going wrong. Even if it seems too late to mend the family relationships, there may be scope for young people to learn skills in making friends. They may benefit from the chance to reflect upon their habitual responses to others and change them. For example, if young people find that they often feel criticised by others, they can practise monitoring whether they are over-sensitive. Role play and group work can be useful methods of helping young people to experiment with different ways of responding to others.

Social workers dealing with young people also need to avoid falling into the trap of attributing lack of communication purely to adolescence. It is not uncommon to encounter a young person in difficult circumstances who presents as surly and uncommunicative. Describing this as typical teenage behaviour may mean that not enough time and care is taken to establish sufficient trust to enable more meaningful communication.

Attachment and looked after adolescents

Messages from Research, based on a series of studies of children's services in England, is highly recommended for further information and suggestions for practice in relation to looked after children (Stein 2009). Many young people received into care in adolescence have troubled relationships with their parents. Indeed it can often be during adolescence that attachment problems become most pronounced. One of the important aspects of the attachment relationship is that it provides a secure base from which the child can explore the world. The lack of a secure base, or an insecure base, will make the natural urge for the teenager to explore the outside world more complex and often frightening for the young person. If an adolescent is looked after away from home, he or she not only has to deal with the loss of what may be complicated and unsatisfactory attachment relationships, but he or she also has to negotiate new relationships. Attachment theory suggests that an internal working model of relationships develops from early relationships, which, in turn, influences later relationships.

Having a secure attachment with at least one adult, not necessarily the parent, can improve outcomes for children leaving foster care and different attachments can help with different domains, such as education (Stein 2009). However, despite decades of recognition of the negative effects of instability upon attachments, the evidence suggests that young people are still experiencing too many changes of placement. A large-scale study (of 7399 looked after children) in 13 English councils found that 13 per cent have three or more placements in a year, and of those looked after for over two and a half years only two-thirds stay in the same placement for two years or more (Sinclair *et al.* 2007).

Downes (1992) has written extensively about the ways in which foster carers can help adolescents with attachment disorders (see also the work of Howe *et al.* 1999). She describes particular patterns of attachment behaviour which are stimulated by the threat of separation. Facing even brief separations across the family boundary, young people often demonstrate a particular pattern of attachment behaviour which illustrates the nature of their internal working model of relationships with the important people in their lives. Downes postulates that particular types of considered responses on the part of parents or carers can build and develop a young person's ability to use support effectively.

SECURE ATTACHMENT

This type of attachment relationship is characterised by the ability of the adolescent to use adult support appropriately at times of stress or challenge and in particular prior to or following brief separations, for example visits to birth family, and crossing the family boundary, for example at school or college.

INSECURE/AVOIDANT ATTACHMENT

Typically the young person exhibiting this pattern of attachment seeks to avoid intimate contact with parents or carers and support needs to be offered in a very sensitive manner in order to allow the young person to make use of any benefits of nurturing. Often the young person will maintain emotional and physical distance from carers. They may be isolated with few friends. They may be either low in self-reliance, or fiercely self-reliant with problems with intimacy.

Carers need to help the young person experiment with being close by offering responses at times of crisis which allow for more intimacy, without scaring the young person away. For some carers, though, it can be more demanding to offer such unrewarded help than to deal with actual delinquency. They need to be able to cope with receiving little feedback from the young people.

INSECURE/AMBIVALENT ATTACHMENT

The adolescent who has ambivalent feelings towards his attachment figure simultaneously both wants and fears closeness and support from adults. Typically, he will vacillate in his capacity to use the secure base and will appear to want nurturing but not to be able to use this in preparation for his or her explorations at school, college or in the community. This young person may attempt to sever the connection with carers prematurely in an attempt to establish his independence while often demonstrating clearly his inability to deal with the stresses he faces.

The aim of the carer's work is to try to reduce the oscillating pattern and to enable the young person to pause between the feeling of the need to go and the going. Carers need to maintain a consistent stance without recrimination. They need to be able to welcome the young person back after an absence. However, the adolescent's behaviour can be very effective in achieving the aim of destroying those good relationships he may be establishing with carers. Carers therefore require considerable patience and understanding to cope with the undermining of their offers of support. It is most important that they are able to resist falling into hostile patterns with the young people.

INSECURE/ANXIOUS ATTACHMENT

The behaviour which characterises this pattern of attachment is indicative of the adolescent's preoccupation with the presence or availability of adults or carers. The young person typically exhibits significant problems in separating with any feeling of security from his secure base and venturing into the adult world without displaying a high level of anxiety and distress.

If the carers are seen as the attachment figure then they need to be able to tolerate this kind of dependency upon them as a secure base and be available and reliable. The evidence suggests that this will not make the young person over-dependent; rather, the reassurance of the carer's availability will allow him to become more self-reliant.

If the parent or other family member is seen by the young person as the attachment figure then the carers will need to understand the ways this may affect his behaviour. For example, in times of stress he may go to great lengths to seek that person out. Carers need to resist entering into loyalty conflicts, and if possible maintain good communication with the young person's attachment figure.

Activity 8.3

Foster carers may need support and training to help with recognition of different attachment patterns. List the opportunities there may be for carers and practitioners to observe behaviour in a range of everyday circumstances that would help with identification of attachment style.

Hints for answers
Natural times of separation and reunion may be illuminating, for example when leaving for or returning from school. Another example would be to compare a young person's interaction with a stranger as opposed to with a known adult. The extent to which a child is able to spend time away from the carer, for example on a school trip or with friends overnight, will give some indications about capacity to tolerate short separations. Patterns of either clinginess or apparent remoteness will help with distinguishing different types of insecure attachment.

Moving back and moving on

In most cases the aim is for young people to return home, but again the evidence suggests that preparation for reunification is poor. A two-year follow-up of 180 looked after children in England showed that the return home was planned for only 40 per cent of children; for many there was no assessment (Farmer, Sturgess and O'Neill 2008). Crucially, 90 per cent had experienced abuse or neglect at home, but in many cases there had been no effective ongoing work with the family of origin in order to tackle the problems that led to the young person having to be looked after in the first place. Parents wanted help with drug or alcohol problems, help with behaviour management, respite care and direct support for the child. The factors found to be associated with stability on return included:

- multi-agency assessment before return
- conditions being set for return
- ongoing multi-agency supervision
- frequent visits by the social worker
- problems that led to being looked after being addressed
- good parenting on return

- close bond with at least one parent

- family not socially isolated. (Stein 2009)

Another important developmental issue is that of moving to more mature dependence and an adult lifestyle. For most young people this is a gradual and unproblematic process that builds from earlier experience. However, for young people who have experienced disruption, and particularly those who have been looked after by the local authority, this process may not be straightforward. Many of these young people experience considerable difficulties with the transition to independence, one of their main problems being social isolation (Biehal *et al.* 1995; Stone 1989; Triseliotis *et al.* 1995). Attention to supporting the development of inter-dependency skills is therefore essential.

In relation to adolescents specifically, three distinct 'looked after' groups have been identified, each with different needs (Sinclair *et al.* 2007). The first group are young people who have a secure base in care, are happy there, have the contact they need and plan to move to independent living from care. The next group comprises asylum seekers and older young people who have fallen out with their parents. They need practical support and an enduring base. They also benefit when there are good inter-agency links. The final group have no reliable base and have experienced a high level of disruption and moves and are desperately in need of more intensive support and assistance to obtain some sense of security.

The difficulties for young people in establishing supportive networks when their attachments have been disrupted during childhood are well known. There is a need for more consideration of the friendship networks of vulnerable young people and, in particular, *how* they can actually be fostered. Social workers are often not well informed about teenagers' social networks, and policies for young people should take account of their need for a permanent social base and their need to develop a support network in order to cope with adulthood (Biehal *et al.* 1995). Those helping vulnerable young people need to help them to develop positive networks of support *despite* having experienced disruption in family relationships and should try to maximise their skills and opportunities for ameliorating adverse earlier experiences.

Activity 8.4

Looked after young people with no sense of a secure base or permanence are likely to experience the greatest problems of transition to an adult lifestyle and mature dependence. They require a considerable amount of support, and at the same time may find it difficult to establish trusting relationships.

Note ways in which intervention could address the complex array of needs including the establishment of a trusting relationship with someone in a position to offer helpful support; access to practical advice and guidance on finance, employment, leisure and housing; a chance to gain some experience of stability; development of peer relationships; enhancement of cognitive skills such as problem-solving and information-processing; and development of social competence.

Hints for answers
Your description is likely to be fairly long and beyond the capacity of one practitioner. Consider ways in which practitioners from statutory and voluntary organisations can be linked with informal supports and family members to build a network of support around the young person to help him or her through transition to an adult lifestyle.

Identity and well-being

A popular idea is that an 'identity crisis' occurs during adolescence. This was formalised by Erikson in his theory of human development that sets out a series of psycho-social crises to be resolved at each stage of development (Erikson 1959). In adolescence this involves the crisis of identity versus identity confusion. That is, in adolescence a process of reflection occurs and choices are made about the different aspects that contribute to a sense of self.

Marcia (1966, 1980) developed two dimensions – the degree to which young people have made commitments to some specific role or ideology and the degree to which they are engaged in a 'crisis' in the sense of a re-examination of values – to produce four categories or 'identity statuses':

- *Identity achievement*: achievement of a coherent sense of identity following questioning and commitment.

- *Moratorium*: being in a state of questioning or 'crisis' without commitment.

- *Foreclosure*: being in a state of having made commitments without a period of crisis or experimentation.

- *Identity diffusion*: being in a state of having made no commitments and experiencing no active experimentation or crisis.

Herbert (2005) discusses the development of a 'subjective public identity' and suggests that it is underpinned by three components: how a young person views his abilities, status and roles; whether he has an acceptable body image; and whether he sees himself fulfilling aspirations and becoming what he would like to become. Young people gain information about themselves through interaction with others. For example, if they find that others tend to confide in them, they may incorporate the notion of themselves as 'sympathetic' into their self-image. By the same token, young people whose interactions with others are characterised by abuse or neglect could well incorporate notions of themselves as unlovable and unworthy.

It is clear that during adolescence there is a preoccupation with self in relation to others. As cognitive development matures towards formal operational thinking young people have a greater capacity to reflect on their own thoughts and also to think about the thoughts of others. However, this process can lead to 'adolescent egocentrism' in which the young person may believe that other people are thinking about, and preoccupied with, the same things as he is (Elkind 1967, cited by Berger 2001). So, for example, if the young person is thinking about his appearance, he may assume that other people are also thinking about his appearance. This means that young people can be preoccupied with anticipating the reactions of others who become, in a way, an 'imaginary audience'. Further, a preoccupation with the imaginary audience can be associated with an adolescent believing his own thoughts to be very special and unique. Thus a 'personal fable' is constructed:

> In essence this is the individual's story about himself [sic], the story he tells to himself, and it may well include fantasies of omnipotence, and immortality. It is not a true story, but it serves a valuable purpose, and is exemplified in some of the most famous adolescent diaries. (Coleman 1980, p.32)

Of more concern is the 'invincibility fable' which can entail a 'foolish sense of security' (Berger 2001). This can be manifested in risky behaviour and the belief that 'nothing bad will happen to me'.

It is not so clear that adolescents necessarily experience a crisis of identity, nor that identity issues are always addressed in adolescence rather than in early adulthood (Bee 1995). Coleman (1980) argues that the majority of teenagers appear to move to adulthood without necessarily suffering identity problems and crises. Although the majority of young people do not have an identity crisis as such, it is likely that young people whose family relationships have been troubled, particularly if they have not been living at home, will need support in exploring their identity as a family member.

The young people known to practitioners typically may have fewer opportunities for building a positive self-image than their peers. Many have difficult relationships with peers and family and their experience of interactions with others may frequently be negative, making it more difficult to develop a positive identity. This provides a role for the practitioner in maximising opportunities for young people to experience positive feedback from those around them.

Bearing in mind Marcia's four categories may help when assessing a young person's current identity. For example, a young person who is desperate to be accepted by an important family member may choose early on to identify with them, without any questioning, that is, he may be in identity *foreclosure*. Another young person who is exposed to conflicting opinions of himself, for example a positive view from school teachers and a negative view from a parent, may be in a state of questioning without commitment or identity *moratorium*. It is also worth noting the potential for young people to revise their self-identity after adolescence. This potential could be maximised if the young person moves to a situation where he receives positive experiences, perhaps in further education or in a successful relationship, or as a parent.

An exploration of a young person's personal fable and the kind of thoughts he may attribute to an imaginary audience could be helpful in understanding some behaviour. For example, a young person who has been sexually abused in childhood and who is acting in a sexually inappropriate way towards others may have many thoughts about sex. He may then believe the 'imaginary audience' also to be obsessed with sex and attribute sexual connotations to interactions. This could be coupled with a personal fable of unique badness.

Coleman has proposed a 'focal' rather than 'crisis' theory of development which suggests that adolescents cope best by tackling different issues at different times, rather than trying to change everything at once. Therefore, they may focus first on exams, and then on negotiating to stay out later. The focal model could also be helpful when considering troubled adolescents. For example, far from being able to tackle issues one at a time, young people who are looked after may often have to deal with many issues all at once. Indeed, many young people feel the need to leave accommodation and move to independence at a time when their counterparts are using their secure home base to explore issues of identity and sexuality. Also, some adolescents living at home in difficult circumstances are required to leave by one or both parents at a young age. Facing the overriding issue of finding somewhere to live and coping with bills and so on is likely to force a young person to cope with too many issues all at once. The distress he feels can be expressed in ways that could be described as 'typical teenage moods'. If young people are exhibiting strong mood swings it could well be attributable to the stress they feel at being required to mature too quickly. There is a role here for practitioners in planning transitions so that changes are paced and ensuring that issues can be tackled one at a time.

Racial and ethnic identity

In countries where the population is predominantly white the development of a white ethnic identity is a relatively smooth and unconscious process. However, for young people who are part of a minority ethnic group, the development of ethnic identity is, perforce, more of a conscious process, especially during and beyond adolescence.

Phinney (1993) describes three stages in the development of ethnicity. As described in Chapter 7, before adolescence there is a lack of exploration of ethnic concepts, described as '*unexamined* ethnic identity'. During early adolescence there may be a period of 'ethnic identity *search*' in which previous attitudes are questioned and political consciousness is heightened. This period has been elaborated by Rodriguez, Cauce and Wilson (2002) to encompass first 'emerging awareness' due to 'a sober realisation that in society people of colour are treated differently' (p.306) and then 'exploration' of cultural heritage. Young people may need to resolve stereotyping and prejudice and negotiate potential clashes of culture while carrying a bi-cultural value system (Chávez and Guido-DiBrito 1999). By late adolescence young people may have a clear and confident sense of their own ethnicity, reflecting 'ethnic identity *achievement*'. There may be commitment to an ethnic identity, although the process of exploration may be re-visited during adulthood (Rodriguez *et al.* 2002).

The development of ethnic identity is affected by the normally positive immersion in cultural traditions through family and local community; and the more negative media and wider social messages about difference (Chávez and Guido-DiBrito 1999). The development of this identity is not necessarily problematic, but it does require the young person to make decisions about how to operate within a culture of racism and how to deal with encounters with racism. It also requires the capacity to de-personalise racism (Banks 2002). The capacity to understand the context of racism will also be affected by the development of cognitive skills.

Some young people may need support to counter the negative messages that may have impacted upon identity development. Dwivedi's edited book (2002) includes many useful pointers for practitioners and is recommended for further reading, as is Robinson's book on cross-cultural child development (Robinson 2007). In England (as in many jurisdictions) practitioners are legislatively required to consider aspects of race and ethnicity, but Dwivedi (2002) argues that practice is still largely filtered through white, Eurocentric perceptions. Child protection statistics in England 'suggest an over-representation of African/Caribbean and mixed-parentage children and an under-representation of Asians' (Barns 2007, p.1428). However, based upon a detailed review of the research literature about child protection referrals, Chand and Thoburn (2006) conclude that the evidence is contradictory and insufficient to indicate whether a particular ethnic group is more or less likely to be referred under a specific category in England. Practitioners have, therefore, to be aware of the dual dangers of either over-intrusive action based on perceptions of dysfunction or non-intervention based on false interpretation of cultural norms.

Banks (2002) suggests that practice should be underpinned by a number of principles:

- intervention should be based upon knowledge of the developmental stage of the young person and pitched at the right level

- the aim must be to meet the needs of the child rather than a personal 'politicised' agenda

- work must be based upon assessment of individual needs rather than a 'cookbook' approach

- at the outset a good working relationship should be established

- the parents and carers should be involved wherever possible, and preferably work should focus on supporting them to support the young person.

Katz (1996) advocates the use of a biographical or life history approach which aims to obtain a narrative or life story from someone and help him make sense of the way in which he views himself in relation to culture and society. The resulting narrative is seen as an account, not of the objective truth, but of a subjective understanding of life events. This approach could be very fruitful in work with adolescents experiencing difficulties with forming a 'coherent story' of their lives. Using non-directive, open-ended interviewing the young person could be asked to tell his own story. This story could then serve as a jumping-off point for joint work on a number of issues, including identity.

There have long been concerns about the over-representation of children from a minority ethnic background who are looked after and accommodated. The question of race 'matching' in placement raises many issues. In relation to the placement of children with carers Barns (2007) cautions that 'crude matching based on essentialist notion of race must give way to a more nuanced approach which takes into consideration the short and long-term needs of children' (p.1428).

Young people, carers and practitioners interviewed by Rodriguez *et al.* in the US suggested that contact with the birth family can provide powerful opportunities for ethnic identity affirmation. Drawing on a range of outcome studies Zeitlin (2002) also questions the benefits of crude matching by race and ethnicity and summarises the factors linked to good adjustment within transracial placements:

Good communication with mother

Early ego-enhancing treatment

Assistance in verbalising racial material

Supportive interest in expression of racial ambivalence

Multiracial associations

Interracial label for child

Early age of adoption. (p.245)

Body image

The dramatic and speedy changes in body shape and size during adolescence force young people to be keenly aware of their body and issues of body image may affect the development of identity. Although perhaps more overt in young women, preoccupation with body image affects both genders and there is a recurrent theme in the research of distorted and negative perceptions of the body in adolescence.

Weight gain is a necessary part of maturation for girls, but perversely Western society places high value on youthful and slim bodies. Popular debates about the influence of 'size zero' models reflect the mixed messages young women can receive. Body dissatisfaction is so widespread among young women that it has been called 'normative discontent' (Levine and Smolak 2002, cited in Mooney, Farley and Strugnell 2009). A focus group study with 124 young women aged 15–16 in the Republic of Ireland revealed high levels of body dissatisfaction and dieting (Mooney *et al.* 2009). The media appears to have a significant influence, with young women aspiring to be like celebrities and following their reported dieting regimes including skipping meals, snacking and crash dieting (whether they need to lose weight or not). There was evidence of heavy peer influence, with girls reporting girls being very hard on each other. The young women were convinced that boys preferred thin girls and that it was more important than personality – part of dieting was to attract boys.

Based on a study of 359 young men and women in their first year at a US college (around 18 years of age) Grossbard *et al.* (2009) found body dissatisfaction in both genders. They explain that individuals differ in the extent to which their self-esteem is 'contingent' – that is, based upon living up to external expectations and standards of physical appearance, performance and gaining others' approval. They found that the more self-esteem is contingent upon factors such as perceived ideal weight and perceived social values about appearance, the more likely the young person was to indulge in unhealthy eating patterns and dieting. For young men the patterns may be less obvious because some want to lose weight, whereas others want to gain the kind of weight associated with muscularity – some used steroids, diet supplements and high-protein foods. They suggest that some of the anxiety and depression associated with body image could be countered by intervention aimed at encouraging greater self-determination and enhancing 'true' self-esteem that is less based upon external standards and expectations. Given the pervasive nature of body image concerns in the general population, it is highly likely that problems could be magnified for young people with troubled backgrounds when adolescence will be a time when difficulties can become more pronounced and intense.

In summary, rather than characterising adolescence as problem-laden, it is more useful to ask why concerns are raised once young people reach adolescence. Problems that may already have been present can become much more obvious and disturbing in teenagers. They may be manifested because of the growth in the ability of the young person to challenge his parents, to make comparisons, and to articulate his thoughts better. Situations may be more frightening simply because adolescents are big and physical containment can no longer be a last resort (or first resort) solution for parents. Finally, it is precisely because adolescents are so close to being adult that parents become so concerned and frightened about how they will cope when they are more independent.

Activity 8.5

The establishment of an identity with which one is content is not confined to the period of adolescence. However, it is during these years that there may be an emerging awareness of self in relation to others and an exploration of concepts of identity and body image. Taking into account the experiences of adolescents in the general population, list the factors that may particularly influence the identity development of young people encountered within practice.

Sexuality: healthy development or risky behaviour and exploitation?

The recognition of oneself as a sexual being, and the development of intimate relationships, is an important part of the development of personal identity and of identity in relation to others. As children reach adolescence they become subject to physical changes that can force them to become aware of their sexuality. These developments are overlaid by a range of social forces – many highly gendered – that are also powerful influences upon sexuality.

Moore and Rosenthal (2006) provide a comprehensive and accessible overview of the development of adolescent sexuality which is recommended for further reading. They highlight the gap that results from much earlier maturation coupled with much later adoption of adult roles in contemporary Western society, suggesting that 'sexuality is a normative event in adolescent development with the potential for both positive and negative consequences' (p.2). It is this potential for both positive and negative consequences – sometimes co-occurring – that underpins this particular dichotomy in adolescent development.

It is very difficult to make statements about what constitutes normal sexual development since it is so open to societal pressure and shaping by experience. Aspects of sexual expression start well before adolescence and depend on personal, familial and cultural ethos, values and beliefs. Cavanagh Johnson (2001a, 2001b) has developed a typology of childhood sexual behaviour before puberty (which on average begins between 10 and 12) ranging from healthy to less healthy expressions of sexuality. This allows for *early* identification of a problematic sexual developmental trajectory and for provision of therapeutic intervention before behaviours become entrenched into adolescence and beyond:

a) *Group I* includes children engaged in natural and healthy childhood sexual exploration;

b) *Group II* is comprised of sexually-reactive children

c) *Group III* includes children who mutually engage in a full range of adult sexual behaviours

d) *Group IV* includes children who molest other children. (Cavanagh Johnson 2001a, p.2)

Natural and healthy exploration (I) is characterised by light-hearted and 'giggly' mutual exploration of bodies and differences and is part of a spectrum of curiosity about the world. Children who have been overly exposed to sexually explicit material or behaviour, though, may show more anxiety and guilt about sexuality and engage in more overt and explicitly sexual behaviour such as public masturbation and overt sexual behaviour towards adults (II). Some children who have been sexually abused and live in sexually charged settings engage in more pervasive and entrenched sexual activity including a full range of adult sexual behaviour. They tend to show a rather blasé attitude to sex and have little trust in adults (III). Finally, some children, even those under 12, engage in coercive sexual abuse of younger children and require specialist therapeutic treatment (IV).

The onset of puberty is triggered by increases in sex-related hormones and changes in the balance of hormones. These changes are accompanied by a dramatic growth spurt and the development of the primary sex characteristics – in boys, growth of the testes and penis; in girls, breast budding and growth in the ovaries. Secondary sex characteristics for boys include growth of pubic hair, underarm and facial hair, coarsening of the skin, activation of sebaceous glands and changes in voice pitch. In girls they include changes in the shape and size of the hips, breast development and growth of pubic hair (Slee 2002). Girls experience onset of menstruation and boys the production of live sperm. Immediately preceding puberty there is also a further significant spurt in brain growth followed by 'pruning back' during the next few years (Giedd *et al.* 1999). It is suggested that these brain changes may be associated with temporary problems in impulse control and decision-making, increased sensitivity to some recreational drugs but also increases in capacity for reasoning, planning and rationality (Moore and Rosenthal 2006).

Little is known about the extent of masturbation but self-report studies suggest that for over half of children it represents their first explicitly sexual experience, that erotic fantasies are an important element in adolescent sexuality and that for two-thirds of boys masturbation will lead to their first experience of ejaculation (Katchadourian 1990). While masturbation in private is normal, compulsive masturbatory activity or sustained public masturbation can be a sign of some form of emotional disturbance. It may not necessarily be indicative of sexual abuse, and therefore the reasons should be carefully assessed.

The trends over the last few decades have been towards an increase in reported teenage sexual activity and an average drop in the age of engagement in sexual intercourse. The lead time from 'petting' to full intercourse is also shorter. Such trends mean that the experience of the parental generation in each era is different from that of their offspring's generation. An 'average' age of first experiences of sexual intercourse may be rather unhelpful given the extent to which it varies across cultures; however, the studies cited by Moore and Rosenthal suggest an average of around 15 to 16 and a study in Britain found 55 per cent of 16- to 17-year-olds had had at least one experience of sexual intercourse (Breakwell, Fife-Schaw and Clayden 1991).

There appears to be a relatively standard sequence of increasing intimacy leading to intercourse with the desire for increased intimacy growing from the first date to 'going steady' (McCabe and Collins 1990). The age of commencing this sequence is less standard; thus, if a person starts going out with someone in early adolescence, they are more likely to start having sexual intercourse earlier than those who start dating at a later age. Young people will also report engaging in a wider range of sexual activities and with more partners than in previous generations. One significant development is in attitudes to, and practice of, oral sex. Many young people engage in oral sex earlier than sexual intercourse; in a study of young people in high school in Australia 50 per cent reported giving or receiving oral sex in the previous year with one partner, and 38 per cent with two or more (Smith, Agius, Dyson, Mitchell and Pitts 2003). As Moore and Rosenthal point out, it is important to know this because young people may not describe oral sex as 'sex' which means that they may not register that messages about 'safe sex' also include oral sex.

There is more likely to be sexual activity in a relationship that is seen as committed, especially for girls. Both girls and boys will cite loving, caring and affection as being important in relationships, although girls are more likely to define love as being the reason for having sex. Boys are more likely to cite the satisfaction of sexual urges as the reason for sex. Most adolescents tend to engage in serial monogamy. So for most adolescents sexuality is expressed in the context of a relationship. Interestingly the same opposite-sex relationship can be described by the girl as committed and by the boy as casual.

Despite the number of messages about safe and protected sex, and increased knowledge about condoms, many young people still do not use condoms, especially in early or 'casual' sexual encounters. Young people may have a reasonable understanding about, for example, HIV/AIDS, but not apply the messages to themselves. The reasons for non-use often relate to the 'invincibility fable' described above. In more committed relationships the concept of protection is largely viewed as prevention of pregnancy rather than of disease and the expectation is upon the girl to use the contraceptive pill. Choosing to use contraception requires recognition of the risks, a sense of control and the choice and implementation of a particular contraceptive method. As summed up by Moore and Rosenthal: 'Everything we know tells us that much of teenage sex is unplanned and that explanations of teenage sexual behaviour do not fit easily into rational decision-making or problem-solving models' (p.34).

While development of sexuality is a normal part of adolescent development the trajectory of that development as positive or negative can be affected by family, peer and social factors. Undoubtedly there are significant biological changes resulting from puberty but, contrary to popular belief, biological changes do not necessarily have a direct effect on behaviour or the expression of sexuality. There are complex interactions between biological and social forces – and those forces have a different impact upon the genders. For example, whether an increase in sex drive related to hormonal changes is acted upon may be influenced by the actions of the peer group and other social factors, especially for girls. Frequently young people's difficult behaviour is attributed to uncontrollable urges and biological changes. This explanation could well mask the fact that a young person is suffering mood swings because of emotional distress. It is likely that such biological changes will be harder for a young person to manage if their self-esteem is already low and they lack secure attachments. For example, a girl reaching puberty at a younger age than her peers may be vulnerable to feelings of embarrassment and confusion. These feelings can be exacerbated if she is in transition between placements and has no trusted female adult to turn to. In such circumstances it can sometimes be a professional such as a school nurse who can provide support and advice.

Parents may believe that they can educate their children about sex and influence their behaviour, but the efficacy of their messages against the wider backdrop can depend very much upon the quality of existing communication within the family. Parents consistently underestimate the level of their own child's sexual behaviour and overestimate use of condoms and levels of parental communication and influence (Rosenthal and Collis 1997). They may feel they have provided helpful information whereas, in fact, they may not have. The issue can be fraught with embarrassment even where family relationships are close and supportive, but when family relationships are strained and confrontational this is even more likely to be the case. One study showed that 69 per cent of 17- to 20-year-olds discussed sexual issues with their friends and that 61 per cent got their sex education from peers in comparison with 33 per cent who turned to their mothers and 15 per cent who turned to fathers (Moore and Rosenthal 2006). This is important because frequently the information gained from peers about sex is inaccurate.

The prevailing family context appears to have a greater influence than parents 'telling' young people what to do. Sexual activity can be associated with the overall level of warmth and an authoritative parenting style, the amount of joint activities, the availability of parents, levels of supervision and monitoring, parents' own attitudes to sex and their own behaviour. Later dating is related to relative affluence and higher engagement with education. The quality of romantic relationships and resilience in the face of a break up are associated with secure attachment experiences. On the other hand, early sexual encounters seem to be associated with behaviours such as drinking, smoking and truancy and delinquency. They are also associated with risk-taking in general and risky sexual behaviour in particular. It appears that young people engaging in such activities tend to show impulsive and sensation-seeking characteristics. Young people engage in more sexual activity where they lack familial closeness and support – so sex perhaps becomes part of asserting independence (Moore and Rosenthal 2006).

During adolescence young people may engage in same-sex encounters. Sexual *activity* need not necessarily be directly related to sexual *identity* or to sexual orientation – young people who consider themselves to be homosexual may not engage in homosexual relationships for a number of reasons, and others may define themselves as heterosexual despite having homosexual experiences. However, a proportion of young people will experience primarily homosexual orientation and begin to adopt this as their sexual identity. Studies in Australia and the USA suggest that between 8 and 11 per cent of young people report same-sex attraction (Hillier, Warr and Haste 1996; Lindsay, Smith and Rosenthal 1997). Those who define themselves as homosexual are not usually confused about their gender identity and show the same range of feminine and masculine characteristics as those who define themselves as exclusively heterosexual. The expressed desire for long-term romantic relationships is no different.

Over the last decade in many Western countries there have been dramatic shifts in attitudes, policies and legislation with regard to homosexuality. In some countries, including the UK, this shift has been marked by the introduction of civil partnerships that enable same-sex partners to be accorded legal recognition, rights and responsibilities. This backdrop should provide a more liberal context for today's adolescents; however, there are still prevailing prejudices against homosexuality. Homophobic language is prevalent in society and popular media, and within school is common as a form of verbal bullying.

Practitioners need to recognise that adolescents may question their sexual orientation and may need support in resolving this process. Young men who have been sexually abused by men may also question their sexuality and will need support with their sexual identity development.

If young people define themselves as homosexual then they may well need support in coping with family disapproval and possibly rejection. They may also need help in developing a supportive social network. Support organisations for young people who are gay and lesbian can offer social, emotional and practical help.

Supporting healthy sexual development

Developing a sexual identity is a normal part of adolescence. Being involved in sexual activity is not normally associated with psychological disturbance, unless it begins unusually early or is in the context of an exploitative or abusive situation. Parents frequently cite concerns over sexual activity as sources of extreme conflict with their children and they can be given as a reason for parents to eject children from the home or to request alternative care. Social workers, therefore, can help parents and alternative carers to consider the realities of adolescent sexual exploration and to set an individual's behaviour into context. It is helpful to assess the whole family's attitude towards, and early experiences of, sexual relationships. At the same time, practitioners need to be aware of the factors that can be associated with early-onset sexual activity and provide young people and families with information and support to help prevent risky behaviour and ameliorate the dangers associated with very early sexual activity.

With regard to sex education, peer-based programmes may be more effective than relying on parent-based education. Social workers, teachers, foster carers and key workers in residential units can play a vital role in counteracting some of the distorted sexual information gained from friends. The starting point has to be establishing the current level of information. It is easy to make assumptions about young people's knowledge about sex, especially in a group context where there may be reluctance to show ignorance or fear of being laughed at. Young people need accurate, straightforward information, which can be given by verbally and backed up with leaflets and so forth. It is not possible to 'do sex education' on a one-off basis – it has to be part of an ongoing process of social and emotional education and support. Although adolescents are more usually able to cope with abstract concepts than younger children, it is often not until an issue touches them personally that it will be seen to have real relevance. Therefore, they need plenty of opportunities to come back and ask questions at another time.

Sex, gender and violence

Representations of sex surround us. Sex is used in advertising, films and television. Childhood sexuality, particularly that of girls, is used in advertising and film and television. Widespread use of the internet has led to an explosion of access to sexual material from around the world. In a survey of 16- to 17-year-olds in Australia 73 per cent of boys claimed they watched X-rated films; 2 in 5 boys had searched for sex sites; and 84 per cent of boys and 60 per cent of girls said they had been accidentally exposed to internet sex sites (Flood and Hamilton 2003). Such material invariably portrays gender-stereotyped images of sexual activity, often de-coupled from relationships or intimacy and frequently coupled with violence.

There is considerable evidence to suggest that gender-based double standards are still in force in young people's relationships. Boys' sexual urges are still regarded to be more natural and uncontrollable than those of girls. The concept of 'sexual scripts' first described by Gagnon and Simon (1973) is still relevant. Young women are likely to have internalised a 'female' sexual script that associates sex with love, whereas young men gain a 'male' script that condones a right to be sexually aggressive. Lees (1993) describes gender power differences as a 'force field' that traps both boys and girls. In her interview study with girls the importance of reputation was summed up by one young woman: 'It's a vicious circle. If you don't like them, then they'll call you a tight bitch. If you go with them they'll call you a slag afterwards' (p.27). Young women who are confused about intimacy as a result of insecure attachments may seek sexual relationships in the hope of finding intimacy. However, because of their difficulties with attachment, they may find it hard to sustain relationships. If they then find themselves to be the victims of hostile social judgement, their self-esteem can be further undermined. Young men with low self-esteem may not have the self-confidence to feel secure in challenging a male peer group's negative attitudes towards women.

Even more worrying is the extent to which sexual scripts and double standards are played out in the relationships of young people today. Barter et al. (2009) surveyed 1353 13–17-year-olds and interviewed 62 girls and 29 boys across England, Scotland and Wales about their experiences of partner violence. In the survey 88 per cent reported some form of intimate partner violence, especially girls. A quarter of the girls and 18 per cent of boys reported some form of physical violence; three-quarters of the girls and half of the boys reported some emotional violence; and a third of the girls and 16 per cent of boys reported some sexual violence. Four per cent had a same-sex partner and this was associated with an increased risk of reported violence. In the interviews the girls described greater levels of all forms of violence and were more likely to report that it affected their well-being. They experienced high levels of coercive and controlling behaviour, including by mobile phone and text messaging. Girls tended to blame themselves and reported that ending a relationship could lead to escalation of violence. Highly significant for practitioners is the finding that factors associated with either instigating or receiving violence were experiences of child maltreatment, domestic abuse and aggressive peer networks. Those who had experienced family violence were also more likely to have experienced a relationship at an earlier age, and for girls this was more likely to be with an older partner, defined as at least two years older. Young people tended to tell friends about their experiences and not adults – although some had told learning mentors in school. All of the girls in a relationship with a boy or man at least two years older than them experienced violence, prompting the authors to suggest that a girl in such a relationship should be considered to be a 'child in need'.

Practitioners, therefore, need to consider ways in which they can challenge the prevailing gender stereotyping that can contribute to the acceptance of violence within young people's relationships. When working with more troubled young people there are also a number of implications for practice. Some young people will have grown up in households where the adult male was physically and sexually aggressive towards the female adult and possibly towards them also. The exploration of their own sex-role identities is likely to be influenced by such experience and this should be explored with them. The impact of their own gender and the particular social pressure upon them should also be considered.

Within schools and mixed residential settings staff may find that young men and women adopt traditional sex-role stereotypes. There is potential for positive work with groups of young people during the time when they are exploring their own sexual identities to help both genders with the development of mutual and satisfying sexual relationships. Some young women who become the subjects of social work intervention do not follow the traditional 'female script' and may act in a sexually assertive or aggressive manner. Practitioners need to be alert to the possibility of such young women being subject to greater moral disapproval than young men engaging in similar behaviour.

Activity 8.6

The evidence suggests that unhealthy patterns of gender relationships are far from uncommon in the teenage population, with young women in particular reporting concerning levels of intimate partner violence. Describe ways in which practitioners can help support both young women and men to establish healthy and respectful relationships.

Hints for answers

Young people with different characteristics and with different life experiences are likely to require different blends of information, relationship skills, values and knowledge. Be specific about the different ways you may be able to support, for example, a young woman or young man who has grown up in a household characterised by domestic abuse; a young man who has been physically abused by his father; a young man who has been sexually abused by a woman; a young woman whose first relationship is with a man much older than her, and so on.

Teenage parenthood

It is difficult to present a clear picture about teenage conception and parenthood because of statistical, cultural, socio-economic, international and national variations. It is important to distinguish between pregnancy rates and birth rates. When looking at birth rates it seems that, contrary to popular belief, the proportion of births to teenagers as opposed to older women has *not* been rising over recent years. Most studies indicate a rise in the 1970s with a subsequent decline (Moore and Rosenthal 2006). The UK tends to have higher rates than other parts of northern Europe, but the figures for England suggest that the problem may be over-represented in the popular media. In England conception rates in 2007 for 15–17-year-olds were 41.7 per thousand (i.e. around 4%) representing a 10.7 per cent *drop* since 1998 (Office for National Statistics 2009). For 13–15-year-olds the conception rate in 2007 was 8.3 per thousand (around 0.8%) representing a 6.4 per cent *drop* since 1998. During the same period the rate of abortions of these conceptions has risen in both age groups to 50.6 per cent for 15–17-year-olds and 61.9 per cent for 13–15-year-olds. Therefore, the overall birth rate to young women has fallen. Information about the fathers is harder to collate but they tend to be older than the mothers.

Berrington *et al.* (2007) undertook secondary analysis of two large cohort studies to examine the effects of teenage parenthood on the mothers, fathers and children. In their analysis they defined teenage mothers as 19 years or younger and fathers as 22 or younger. The findings were congruent with those in relation to early sexual activity – the likelihood of becoming a young mother (and father to an extent) was associated with factors measured at age 10, including having a conduct disorder, having poor reading ability, and having a mother with low educational aspirations for her children. Half of the births to teenagers in the 1990s were to lone mothers. By age 30 women who had been teenage mothers were more likely to suffer from physical and mental ill health associated with partnership breakdown and living in households with no-one in paid employment. They were also more likely to be living in social housing, to be dissatisfied with their neighbourhood and to lack emotional support. The fathers were more likely to be unemployed and not to be living with their children, although many had contact and paid some form of maintenance. The children were doing as well as other children in language development at 38 months and in social development, gross motor or fine motor skills and pro-social development at 42 months. They had experienced more accidents and exhibited more behavioural problems – but these were shown to be associated with higher levels of maternal anxiety and depression rather than youth as such. Berthoud *et al.* (2004) also found that children of teenage mothers when young adults exhibit lower educational attainment, a higher risk of economic inactivity and higher likelihood of becoming a teenage mother themselves. They attribute this to the experience of a lower standard of living (see also Phoenix 1991). The key implications here are the need for attention to the mental health of young mothers, to provide support for the maintenance of the parental relationships and for support with factors such as housing and employment. Resilience of children is enhanced if there is wider spacing between children which suggests, also, the need for ongoing contraceptive advice for young mothers (Werner and Smith 1992).

The implications for practice are many. Social workers and health practitioners are likely to be involved in supporting the teenage mother (and possibly the father) as well as assessing the probable impact upon the child if born. In addition, the concerns of many other people will need to be considered, for example the young woman's parents, siblings, extended family, carers and residential staff.

- In the first instance the young woman will need access to specialised advice about her alternatives as *early* in the pregnancy as possible. Practitioners will need to help the young person obtain all the information she requires and encourage her to think through the consequences of all possible choices. She may then need help with presenting her choice to her family.

- Teenage mothers and their child have an elevated risk of complications during pregnancy and birth, probably attributable to poor antenatal care (Moore and Rosenthal 1991). Therefore, it is essential to ensure that the pregnant teenager receives good and prompt antenatal care. She is likely to need considerable support with the actual practical and emotional factors involved in attending clinics.

- The long-term consequences for teenage mothers can be to lose out on schooling, to have lower occupational achievement and to be economically disadvantaged. For some, school problems will have already been a feature before pregnancy. However, long-term negative effects can be ameliorated if the young woman can remain in education and establish a stable relationship. The potential positive effects of school are clear and here the message is reinforced: that resilience can be fostered by good educational experiences. Clearly there is a responsibility for all professions involved to make a concerted effort to provide good educational opportunities for pregnant teenagers and young mothers.

- The material circumstances of the young woman must be seen as a priority, and not just over the short term. This will include maximising income, advocating with housing agencies and supporting maintenance arrangements.

- For some young women who perceive themselves to have few career options, motherhood may be a positive choice. For some young women who have limited contact with their families because of being looked after away from home, a baby may serve as a bridge to increased contact (Biehal *et al.* 1995). There will be opportunities for practitioners to build on the optimism and plans for the future that the birth of a baby can spark.

- Even though the parental relationship may break up, practitioners can play an important role in supporting a young father and/or his family in maintaining a relationship with the child.

- A protective network should be assembled around the child according to their needs. Often extended family members who have a difficult relationship with the mother can, none the less, be a resource for the child.

Sexual abuse

What the figures on normative development fail to capture is the fact that for some young people their first experiences of intercourse will be in the context of child sexual abuse (see also Chapter 5). A comprehensive review of research suggests that in developed countries the cumulative prevalence of any sexual abuse (including non-contact and contact) is 15–30 per cent for girls and 5–15 per cent for boys; and of penetrative sexual abuse: 5–10 per cent for girls and 1–5 per cent for boys (Gilbert *et al.* 2009).

Young people who have been abused may exhibit problems in expressing adolescent sexuality and engaging in healthy experimentation. Some may avoid sexual exploration, while others may enter into a number of unsatisfying sexual encounters. Some of the problems exhibited by young people that are attributed to adolescence may in fact be the expression of the effects of childhood sexual abuse. These may include persistent running away, extreme hostility, family discord, low self-esteem, difficult peer relationships, involvement in prostitution and so on.

Summit's *accommodation syndrome* is a five-stage model that describes why young people often do not tell anyone about sexual abuse and accounts for some of the behaviour that they may exhibit (Summit 1983). Much of this behaviour may become particularly evident during adolescence when young people are forcibly aware of issues of sexuality and may be exploring sexual relationships with their peers for the first time. The five stages and their implication for practice are:

- *Secrecy*: The secrecy surrounding abuse means that the child is dependent upon the abuser for explanations of what is happening. Considerable force or threat of force is frequently used to ensure secrecy, and the longer children keep the secret, the harder it is for them to speak out. Enforced secrecy, often involving threats, is likely to distort the development of trust in attachment relationships, especially if the abuser is a family member. Also, during adolescence, young people can develop close and intense friendships. Having to keep such a secret about their lives is likely to interfere with the process of shared confidences that forms a part of such friendships as they move through adolescence.

- *Helplessness*: Abusers make full use of adult power to reinforce the child's helplessness. Other adults may not pick up on messages that a child is trying to give. Or, worse, they may underestimate the power imbalance and blame the child for the abuse, or for not speaking out sooner. It is not hard to imagine how damaging it would be for a young person's self-concept as he reaches adolescence to feel such powerlessness. It is ironic that it is possible that increased awareness in recent times of child sexual abuse may make it more distressing for young people as they enter teenage years and understand the inappropriateness of their experience.

- *Entrapment and accommodation*: If sexual abuse is an ongoing experience and if it is kept secret, then the child learns to accommodate it by adapting and surviving. They may 'structure' reality to protect an abusing parent, often by defining the parent as 'good' and themselves as 'bad'. The process of systematic entrapment and the child's attempt to cope by accommodating to and incorporating the experiences into his life could affect several developmental tasks. For example, the child's cognitive processes must be distorted by the attempt to view such distressing experiences as normal. Many young people (especially young women) develop self-harming behaviours, while others (especially young men) behave in an aggressive and antisocial fashion. As Summit points out, 'much of what is eventually labelled as adolescent or adult psychopathology can be traced to the natural reactions of a healthy child to a profoundly unnatural and unhealthy parental environment' (p.184). It would also be difficult for a child to develop a coherent system of moral understanding under such circumstances. Finally, if the child is being abused at home, the home cannot then act as a secure base from which to explore the world of school and beyond.

- *Delayed, conflicting and unconvincing disclosure*: It is difficult for adults to believe that a young person would tolerate sexual abuse and it is also difficult for non-abusing parents to accept the enormity of a disclosure. If a young person is already behaving in a way that is causing difficulties, then there is more reason for adults to disbelieve him. If a young person is not believed by those he is close to then this could compound the process of distortion of cognitive, moral and emotional development.

- *Retraction*: It is frequently the case that young people retract allegations of sexual abuse, especially if the reactions of those around them confirm what they have been told by the abuser, for example that they and possibly siblings will be taken into care, that their mothers will be deeply hurt, that they will be blamed and so on. It is therefore not surprising that retraction so often occurs. The trauma of being involved in a sexual abuse investigation can in itself cause great distress. In addition, children, and especially adolescents, have a tremendous fear that their peers will find out and that they will be stigmatised.

MacMillan *et al.* (2009) reviewed intervention studies for different types of maltreatment, including sexual abuse. It has to be first noted that there is a lack of systematic research into the outcomes of different types of post-abuse support and many studies do not use robust methodology. With that backdrop the evidence tends to come mainly from studies of psychological approaches aimed at treating internalising, externalising and sexualised behaviours, especially the cognitive-behavioural model. This model draws on the link between thoughts, feelings and behaviour; for example, a young woman who *thinks* that she was to blame for being sexually abused may *feel* as if she is a bad person and then may *act* aggressively. Treatment involves uncovering thoughts and related feelings and replacing the thoughts with more appropriate ones. The aim is for the young person to be able to account for the events and to recall the events without undue distress. In other words, the aim is for the young person to have a 'coherent story' for the trauma he suffered. The review summarises the characteristics of the most promising treatment programmes as being trauma-focused, delivered by trained professionals and focusing on 'skills in expressing feelings, coping, recognising links between feelings and behaviours; gradual exposure through developing a child's narrative; reprocessing the abuse' (p.9).

Sexual Exploitation

Often associated with childhood sexual abuse, sexual exploitation can range from young people being given small rewards in exchange for sex through to much more structured prostitution (Barnardo's 2008). The paths to prostitution vary, but a common characteristic is that the young person (girl or boy) has unhappy, unrewarding, hostile and sexually abusive experiences. The young people may have to cope with problems of family stress, poverty, crime, substance abuse, lack of education and/or unemployment – any or all of these are likely to lead to prostitution as a means of survival. Young women, especially those being looked after away from home, are vulnerable to exploitation by older men who initially form a 'boyfriend' relationship with them that then shifts to that of pimp as they encourage them to engage in sex with others for some form of reward.

In a study of teen prostitution in the USA, 61 14–19-year-old young men and women were interviewed. They described violence, abandonment and sexual abuse in the family of origin and then ongoing physical violence and continuous sexual victimisation from clients and from pimps (Williams 2010). The young people developed a range of survival skills, including characteristics that could be unlawful or unappealing, and were resistant to being labelled 'victims'. They could come to the attention of services as 'victims', 'survivors' or 'offenders' and therefore evoke ambivalent responses from a range of services: 'Instead of a sad-eyed crying victim they confront a strong, willful, survivor who looks and acts quite differently from the victims portrayed in the media.' (p.251) These young people often see the streets as preferable to the kind of services that may be on offer, and have very good reason not to trust adults.

Clearly the ideal would be for practitioners to spot the signs of exploitation early and help the young people onto a different trajectory, but those who have become heavily involved in prostitution need highly flexible and creative services that respect the extent to which they have already survived life-threatening circumstances. The briefing by Barnardo's (2008) sets out useful information for practice and asserts that services need to provide:

- good access
- consistent and persistent attention to the needs and priorities of the young people
- assertive outreach
- advocacy with other services.

Activity 8.7

Staff at a local care home for young people have expressed concerns about an older man who has befriended a series of young women accommodated in the home who have gone on to become involved in prostitution for money. The latest young woman, aged 15, is adamant that the man in question is kind and is the only person who really understands what she has been through. She also says that she has really good fun with him, they go to lots of parties in nice houses and he is going to help her find work. Consider an intervention for the young woman, but also what can be done at a more systemic and strategic level with other professionals and community groups to address the wider issue of sexual exploitation in the area.

Young people who abuse

Finally, young people's early sexual experiences may be as perpetrators or victims of peer abuse. Gil and Cavanagh Johnson (1993) suggest five criteria that should be used to help differentiate between age-appropriate sex exploration between children and an abusive situation:

- *Age difference* – An age difference of greater than three years can be an indication of an abusive relationship, particularly if an adolescent initiates sexual activity with a child who is not yet an adolescent.

- *Size difference* – If one child is much bigger and stronger than the other, then there is the possibility that undue force is involved in sexual encounters.

- *Difference in status* – Status differences could include one young person being the babysitter for the other or holding a role with status in school.

- *Type of sexual activity* – Although there is a huge variety in the type of sexual play and exploration, sexual behaviour that does not follow the pattern described above may be an indication of problems.

- *Dynamics* – Rather than the spontaneity and laughter associated with experimentation, problematic sexual behaviour may be characterised by more anxious and intense dynamics.

Practitioners, therefore, need to be alert to signs that young people are either abusing others or are the victims of abuse from peers or siblings. Prompt access to specialist therapeutic help is vital for young people who demonstrate such behaviour.

In summary, the development of *sexuality* is a process and is affected by biological and social forces. It does seem that teenagers are engaging in sexual activity at a younger age than did their parents' generation, but their values about the importance of the context of a committed relationship are not markedly different. Therefore, it is important to assess the behaviour of an individual adolescent within the context of that of his peers. This means not assuming that if a young person has sex at a young age he is unusually precocious. On the other hand, just because 'everyone else is doing it' does not mean that the individual young person has the maturity to cope with a sexual relationship. Practitioners have a key role to play in supporting young people to develop healthy and respectful intimate relationships.

Social competence: prosocial and antisocial behaviour

During the 1990s and early 2000s the predominant public image of young people has been that they are out of control, show no respect, are antisocial and commit crime. The prevailing discourse about young people as a group is one of fear, especially in relation to the use of public spaces. In particular the concept of young people 'hanging around' appears to incite disapproval and anxiety in adults (Hayden 2007). Derogatory terms such as 'hoodies' and 'feral kids' abound in the media. Hayden discusses the ambiguities and paradoxes evident in social attitudes towards young people. As she says, 'for most children and young people, getting into trouble is part of the normal business of growing up, testing the boundaries and finding one's place in the world' (p.2).

In reality, the proportion of young people whose behaviour is sufficiently challenging to warrant professional intervention is small; rather, for the majority, it is a period of burgeoning cognitive skills, social competence, self-control and autonomy.

The cognitive capacity to move beyond the concrete into more abstract concepts assists with both formal learning and understanding of social situations. Adolescents are able to think about possibilities, not just realities, so that they can analyse situations and consider different possibilities and solutions. Young people move to what Piaget called the *formal operational* stage, in which logical thinking is more sophisticated. Formal operational thinking involves the consideration of a number of possible solutions to a problem. When they have reached this stage, young people can construct hypotheses and check them out with reality before coming to a conclusion. They can also think in purely abstract terms (Flavell 1985). They develop deductive abilities which means that they can start from general principles and apply them to specific problems. Overall, this allows for intellectual advancement, but also allows young people to consider a range of possible options for their own futures. As Berger (2001) puts it: 'Adolescents can, and do, break free from the earthbound, traditional reasoning of the schoolchild, soaring into contradictory notions and ethereal dreams quite apart from conventional wisdom' (p.408). This means, of course, that they are less likely to accept adult assertions and will want to challenge, question and assess them for themselves.

Although this may be tiresome in some situations for parents, teachers and carers, the absence of such enquiry should be a cause for concern. The attainment of such thinking is not necessarily automatic and not all adults use formal operational thought. Many of the young people encountered in practice have problems with logical thought. Cognitive development, like other domains of development, needs to be nurtured, encouraged and supported by interested adults. Children who have been neglected or abused may enter adolescence without having moved through the cognitive maturation described in the previous chapter. However, the development of formal operational thinking can be supported by education and other opportunities to practise logical and abstract thought

(Smith, Cowie and Blades 2003). Therefore practitioners need to ensure that there is a careful assessment of cognitive skills during adolescence.

Conduct disorders, antisocial behaviour and delinquency

The terms 'conduct disorders' and 'antisocial behaviour' are psychiatric diagnostic categories that are also used more widely and loosely in the media and policy documents and within the professional network. The diagnosis of conduct disorders (CDs) is based upon the presence of at least 3 of 15 behaviours in the previous six months under broad categories of:

- aggressiveness to people and animals

- property destruction

- deception or theft

- serious rule violations. (DSM IV, American Psychiatric Association 1994, cited in Herbert 2005)

It overlaps with diagnosis of oppositional defiant disorders (ODDs) in which the level of defiance of authority is a key feature. Between 6 and 15 per cent of children may demonstrate conduct disorders (Hayden 2007). The existence of a conduct disorder is a prerequisite for later diagnosis of 'antisocial personality disorder' in adults (Utting, Monteiro and Ghate 2007). As a diagnostic category in DSM IV 'antisocial personality disorder' requires indications of a 'pervasive pattern of disregard for and violation of rights of others from 15 years'. The individual needs to be at least 18 and to have a past history of conduct disorder before 15.

Hayden reflects on the extent to which the 1990s in the UK were characterised by a sharp focus on disruptive youth. The introduction in England of *Acceptable Behaviour Contracts* (ABCs) and *Anti-Social Behaviour Orders* (ASBOs) in the Crime and Disorder Act (1998) allowed for a very broad definition of antisocial acts that spills beyond traditional diagnostic categories. Rutter, Giller and Hagel (1998) reserve the term 'antisocial' for behaviour that is a criminal offence (whether detected or not), but ASBOs can be served on children committing 'nuisance' acts from as young as ten and 'general loutish and unruly conduct such as verbal abuse, harassment, assault, graffiti and excessive noise' (Home Office 2003, p.11, cited in Hayden 2007). The *breach* of an ASBO does constitute a criminal offence, even if the precipitating behaviour for the order did not, which increases the risk of criminalising young children.

One of the challenges in practice, therefore, is to avoid contributing to the labelling of young people when their behaviour is on a normal spectrum. Adolescence, for the majority of young people, represents a time of increasing social competence, autonomy and self-control. Although many may engage in some 'troublesome' activities, they tend not to persist. A number of young people, however, exhibit behaviour that causes concern to those around them, and often to themselves. Practitioners need to be able to identify whether the behaviour is beyond the bounds of normal adolescent testing and also whether it is likely to persist. Hayden (2007) has developed a very useful typology that helps set behaviour into the context of expected developmental pathways (see Figure 8.1).

The majority – testing the boundaries/experimentation and growing up
Nearly all will be in trouble with their parents or carers at some point
Many will have been involved in one or two minor offences – stealing from a shop, fare-dodging, and so on (e.g. 26% of 11–16-year-olds in school commit some offence in a year)
Many will experience occasional instances of being formally 'told off' in school, the odd detention, sometimes being late for school, truanting once or twice
Two-thirds (67%) will have drunk alcohol by the age of 16.

Temporarily lost the way
A fixed-period of exclusion at secondary-school level
More frequent truanting at secondary-school level
Likely to be underachieving at school
Some conflict at home and/or at school
Experimentation with drugs such as cannabis (15% of 11–16-year-olds in school)
Minor criminal acts which may include vandalism as well as stealing and fare-dodging; behaviour that is often seen as 'anti-social'

In trouble (up to 10%)
Multiple fixed-period exclusions and regular truanting, starting at primary-school level (2.6% of all school pupils had a record of one or more fixed periods of exclusion in 2003–04)
Underachievment at school very apparent, academic qualifications highly unlikely
More likely to associate with delinquent peers and have involvement in criminal activity; serious offences likely (assault leading to injury, theft, burglary, robbery, TWOC)
More regular use of drugs and/or alcohol, use likely to be more problematic
Warnings and reprimands, community-based punishments
Runaways (around 100,000 yps a year)
Mental health problems likely

In serious trouble (up to 3%)
Not attending school/dropped out or 'disappeared' (e.g. around 10,000 between 15 and 16 years old)
Some will attend a pupil referral unit (around 12,000 yps at a time)
Very likely to have been permanently excluded from school (around 9,500 yps a year)
Likely to have a long history of problematic behaviour, fixed-period exclusions and severe underachievement at school, likely to have no useful record of achievement
Time spent in secure estate (around 6,000 ypd a year)
Frequent serious offending (assault leading to injury, theft, burglary, robbery, TWOC)
Alcohol or drug use problematic; drug use more likely to include class A drugs
Mental health problems very likely

Figure 8.1 Typologies of children and 'trouble' (reproduced from Hayden 2007)

Note: yps = young people, derived from an interpretation of statistics by Hayden.

A consistent finding is that early-onset problems are more likely to persist than later-onset problems. Figure 8.2 shows the pattern of 'escape' and inflow starting from the 15 per cent of five-year-olds who show symptoms of ODD and ending with a much smaller group of 17-year-olds with conduct disorders.

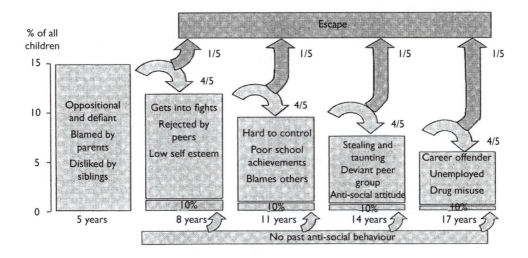

Figure 8.2 Continuity of antisocial behaviour from age 5 to 17

Source: Research conducted by Stephen Scott (2002) for the Home Office (unpublished), cited and reproduced in Every Child Matters (Department for Education and Schools 2003, p.19).

Not all the challenging behaviour of young people is criminal, but young people do commit a disproportionate amount of crime – around 25 per cent of known offenders are under 18 (Hayden 2007). But there is a distinction between 'adolescent-limited offenders' whose criminal activity commences in adolescence but stops by 21 and persistent offenders whose criminal behaviour starts early and continues into adulthood (Moffit 1997, cited in Berger 2001).

Utting *et al.* (2007) set out the risk factors associated with children 'whose conduct disorders place them at risk of developing persistent and intractable patterns of problem behaviour later in life, including poor physical and mental health and criminal behaviour, alongside economic poverty' (p.9). They also set out the protective factors that are not just the opposite of risks, but rather moderate the impact of risks.

The *individual risk* factors include:

- hyperactivity and impulsivity
- low intelligence
- cognitive impairment
- chronic ill health
- attitudes condoning offending and drug misuse
- antisocial friends and peers.

Family risk factors include:

- low birth weight
- poor parental supervision and discipline
- family conflict
- family history of antisocial behaviour
- parental attitudes condoning antisocial behaviour
- low income, poor housing and large family size.

School risk factors include:

- low achievement beginning in primary school
- aggressive behaviour, including bullying
- lack of commitment to school, including truancy
- school disorganisation.

Community risk factors include:

- disadvantaged neighbourhood
- availability of drugs.

Protective factors include:

- being female
- resilience, self-efficacy and an outgoing temperament
- social bonding
- adults setting healthy standards of behaviour
- opportunities for involvement, social and reasoning skills and recognition and due praise.

Such problems therefore need detailed and prompt intervention. Intervention also requires effective inter-disciplinary agreement. Any intervention needs to be consistent across all settings in which the child or young person operates. Intervention also requires good communication and partnership with the family, who need to accept and understand the rationale for that intervention.

Activity 8.8

There is often a difficult balance to strike between providing prompt intervention as a result of behaviour that might be considered antisocial and over-reacting or contributing to unhelpful and premature labelling of a young person as 'delinquent'. List the factors you need to take into account when planning your response to a referral of a 15-year-old young man who has come to the attention of the police as part of a group of young people who were alleged to have damaged a number of cars in a neighbouring district.

Cigno (1995) argues persuasively for intervention based on behaviourist techniques, seeing it as consistent with partnership with, and empowerment of, parents, because behavioural intervention in the home requires:

- parents to be informed and involved

- parents to be partners in therapy

- specific, agreed goals

- a lack of mystique

- intervention that is task-centred

- close attention to the detail of what parents are telling the young person

- a focus on the 'here and now' of problems.

Put simply the social learning approach suggests an ABC model of the reinforcement of problem behaviour. First, there is an *antecedent*: for example, a parent might ask a young person to help with the washing up. This is followed by the *behaviour*: for example, the young person flies into a tantrum, says he is expected to do everything and refuses. Finally there are the *consequences*: in this case the parent may feel too exhausted for a fight and to avoid the escalation will do the washing up him- or herself. The aim of intervention is to help parents or carers create an environment that both discourages the problem behaviour and encourages positive behaviours. Herbert (1987) provides a 12-step guide to the process of which the two main components are:

- *Assessment*: A detailed, longitudinal and functional assessment of the child and his behaviour in the context of the environment is fundamental. For behavioural treatment to work the initial assessment must be precise in identifying behaviour and its antecedents and consequences. The situation in which behavioural problems occur also needs to be specified. The assessment asks 'what' the child is doing, not 'why'. Aggression, non-compliance and hyperactivity are pinpointed as commonly presented problems.

- *Behaviour modification:* If it is decided that the behaviour problems require treatment they are ranked in order of priority and the initial focus is on the one that most concerns the parent. A programme of treatment is negotiated with the parents and young person. Techniques will vary according to the individual situation, and include the use of rewards, punishment, modelling, skill training, cognitive approaches, group work and so on.

Much of the approach can seem like common sense. But there are factors that often undermine the common sense approach; for example:

- The *assessment* process is crucial. Intervention will not work unless considerable time has been spent on assessing the problems *in detail* and planning the programme *in detail*.

- People often underestimate the extent to which the target behaviour can *increase* before it decreases as the child escalates his attempt to get the desired response. The temptation may be to switch to another method, or give up, both of which *reinforce* the behaviour that was supposed to be reduced.

- Parents/carers, despite their best intentions, may be *inconsistent* in their application of rewards and sanctions.

- There can be problems when people are required to reward a child for what may seem very small improvements.

- There can be difficulties if the parents/carers are not committed to the process, do not understand the rationale, or have doubts that it will be effective.

In summary this theory suggests that behaviour problems are a clear message that the young person is struggling to cope with his environment. However, the ways he has used to cope are antisocial and cause him more problems because they are not adaptive. A review of the impact of neglect during adolescence has highlighted the extent to which it can be associated with challenging behaviour (Stein *et al.* 2009). Young people who exhibit conduct disorders often have difficulty in manipulating abstract concepts. They may also find it difficult to learn from experience and therefore engage in self-defeating behaviours. This suggests that practitioners need to pay attention to supporting the cognitive skills that should be maturing in adolescence that underpin information processing and forward planning. Helping young people to re-connect to school or education of another form is also highly protective as there is a positive association between the young people's assessment of the quality of care, their satisfaction with school and their general happiness (Berridge *et al.* 2008).

If the young people are accommodated away from home, alternative carers can instigate clear behavioural frameworks to change maladaptive behaviours. However, Fahlberg (1994) urges caution when planning rewards and sanctions for young people being looked after away from home. Young people who have already been separated from those to whom they are attached may not respond well to sanctions involving further separation, for example time out in a bedroom; instead time out could be carried out in the same room as the adult. They also may not change their behaviour in order to gain a reward because they do not believe they deserve good things and because they do not have an attachment to the carer and therefore lack the urge to please them. Fahlberg recommends that assessment is needed to understand the reasons for difficult behaviour; the focus should then be on meeting the child's emotional needs and encouraging positive behaviours.

Delinquency is, therefore, not a necessary part of adolescence. The majority of adolescents do not become involved in delinquent behaviour, or else do so only on a small scale and do not continue to offend as adults. The small minority who show serious and persistent behaviour problems in adolescence are very likely to have already had problems. Therefore a detailed assessment of preceding childhood experiences is essential. What is clear is that early intervention is crucial before adolescence with young people whose conduct raises concern.

Activity 8.9

Read the case study and using the information you have been given in this and the previous chapters consider the questions that follow.

Case study
Paul is 14 years old and has been in residential accommodation for two years. His parents are both heavy drinkers and have had a violent relationship since Paul's early childhood. His reception into local authority accommodation was precipitated by a battle with his father during a marital row: Paul was hit by his father and ejected from the house. He is a tall, well-developed boy for his age, one of the earliest maturers in his school year. He is very conscious of his size and also of the fact that he closely resembles his father in appearance.

He has chosen to have no contact with his father but does see his mother regularly. These are very sad meetings when Paul takes on his mother's worries; he comes back to the residential unit burdened by anxiety about her. He has recently confided to a trusted staff member that he was sexually abused in an atmosphere of physical threat by a paternal uncle when he was at the pre-pubescent stage. This abuse began with threats and favours but later shifted to a relationship of intimidation.

This would fit with confusing accounts in the case notes of a worrying and sudden deterioration in Paul's school work in his late primary school stage. Paul thought he had tried to tell a member of primary school staff, but his communication skills are fairly poor and it is quite possible the disclosure was unclear. Paul is now extremely anxious about possible police action in relation to his disclosures and when anxious he can become very touchy and aggressive. He does have a guidance teacher in whom he is beginning to confide. Paul also has friends who have moved through primary into secondary school with him. They are now puzzled by his aggressive behaviour and are beginning to withdraw from him at school break times. He is dependent on them for his social life as a number of the other residents in the unit are older than Paul or involved in trouble with the police in the local community.

Paul's father is outraged at the disclosures, but his mother has managed to convey her belief in him.

1.   In what respect may Paul have experienced emotional abuse and neglect alongside the physical and sexual abuse?

2.   How might maturational tasks he now faces be further complicated by his previous history and current circumstances?

3.   What does he need to support him in the current crisis and who might offer this?

Hints for answers

For example, you should consider the effects of growing up in an atmosphere of family discord. The fact that Paul left the house rather than his father after being hit could lead him to feeling guilty for what happened and to his self-esteem being low. The fact that his attempt at disclosure was unsuccessful could further undermine his self-esteem and efficacy. At this age Paul could be expected to be exploring the outside world from the security of a home base. However, he may feel a lack of security from his home and from the alternative care. He may need help in exploring issues of sexuality. Finally, in considering positive aspects for intervention, it would be important to build on his relationships with his mother, his friends and guidance teacher.

Young people arrive at adolescence already some way along a developmental pathway. This pathway will have been influenced in different ways by many people. Some young people will have encountered continuous setbacks which have impacted upon their ability to respond to opportunities in adolescence. However, the direction of future pathways can be hugely influenced by constructive intervention by adults who rise to the challenge of seeking out and enhancing any areas of potential resilience both within and around the young people they care about.

Key messages

- The developmental tasks of adolescence are often likened to those during toddler years. From the perspective of attachment theory the main interest lies in the process of *transition* from childhood to adulthood and how well this process is supported by earlier experiences.

- During adolescence attachment networks are usually becoming wider, building on a base of family relationships and friendships. Family relationships remain essential to most young people. Even if they are not able to live at home, many young people retain strong ties to family members, including extended family. Careful assessment of the importance of family relationships is necessary without making assumptions about who is of importance.

- All young people need a supportive network, which, if the family cannot provide it, should be provided by others. The finding that social workers often lack knowledge about young people's friendships acts as a reminder to pay attention to this area. The aim should be to help them to attain mature dependence on friends and family, especially if they are looked after away from home.

- Those faced with the challenge of caring for adolescents who cannot be looked after by their family know the extent to which inner working models developed in early childhood can impact upon current relationships. Planning for the care of young people must be based on a bedrock of as much information as possible about their past. This does not mean just a list of family facts and of placements (although these are important), but detailed assessment of attachment experiences with all significant people in their life history.

- Adolescence can be a time for exploration of *identity*. This need not lead to a crisis of identity for young people who have security and positive self-esteem (which are closely associated). Young people with a low sense of self-efficacy and poor self-esteem will be predisposed to experiencing identity problems. It could be helpful to explore the personal fables of young people with efficacy and self-esteem problems using self-narrative techniques described.

- If the family has been a site of conflict and distress the young person may feel a lack of family identity, and may actively reject values espoused by his family. In this situation other adults may be identified with, for example, social workers, residential staff, parents of friends and teachers.

- All young people, regardless of gender, race or sexual orientation, have a right to a positive identity which is supported and reinforced by adults around them. Care must be taken to be sensitive to this; for example, criticisms of family of origin may be perceived as criticisms of self; derogatory comments about the part of town young people come from may also be damaging. The expression of sexist, racist or homophobic opinions by people in positions of trust can be similarly undermining.

- The prevalence of body-image problems suggests that it is highly likely to be a factor in young people encountered in practice. As with younger children, all potential 'islands of competence' should be explored as avenues for boosting self-esteem and identity. Any interests, hobbies and skills should be encouraged and supported.

- There is a complex interaction between *hormonal* and environmental influences on mood during adolescence. The *biological* changes of teenage years are overlaid with *social* meanings. 'Adolescence' is essentially a *social* construction and, as such, has different meanings in different countries and cultures.

- Young people require support with the physiological changes experienced during puberty. Young people who have experienced neglect or abuse may have difficulty with interpreting their own physiological indicators. For example, they may not accurately interpret feelings of hunger or tiredness. During puberty they may require extra support in attuning to their own internal states. Some may need accurate, clear information about puberty.

- All young people, whether they are involved in sexual relationships or not, should have access to clear, age-appropriate information about sex, relationships and contraception. Practitioners should ensure that each young person can identify one trusted adult that he would feel able to discuss sexual matters with. Carers may themselves need access to information and support if they are to adequately support and educate the young people in their care.

- Young people's relationships may be characterised by violence and lack of respect. In particular, there is clear evidence of double standards for young women and young men. Violence in teenage relationships must be taken as seriously as domestic violence in adult relationships.

- Young people who have already been abused or neglected and who lack a secure attachment base are highly vulnerable to sexual exploitation, both within the context of relationships and commercially. Boosting resilience in these young people so that they have the confidence to withstand such exploitation is a challenge to practitioners. Examples of ways to intervene include role play to practise interpersonal skills, assertiveness training, same-sex groups which explore gender issues, couple counselling and support with informing the police about attempts at recruitment into prostitution.

- Delinquent behaviour that springs out of nowhere during teenage years is unusual. As with other areas of adolescent development it is the *continuity* with earlier experiences that is most informative. Although some young people become involved in delinquent activities for the first time in teenage years, this usually wanes as they mature. When the roots of delinquency can be traced back to earlier conduct problems the need for intervention is strongly indicated. A combination of material, familial and peer group factors are associated with such problems, as is boredom, non-attendance at school and lack of opportunities for constructive activity.

- It can be easy for parents and professionals alike to feel despair in the face of persistent delinquent behaviour by a young person. It is highly likely that the young person is also distressed by the behaviour. This can be a good starting point in intervention and will involve including the young person in planning.

- If used thoughtfully and in conjunction with attention to the young person's emotional needs, behavioural approaches can be very effective. They are most effective if based on reward for positive change rather than punishment for failure.

- Helping the young person to find constructive ways to occupy his time has to be the main approach. Educational provision should be the first priority, both because it provides current occupation, and also because it can interrupt the trajectory towards more criminal activity in adult life. Other activities should probably, at least initially, be structured and supervised by adults, for example schemes for young 'joyriders', outdoor activity schemes and sports clubs.

- Overall, it may be necessary to set very small goals for improvement. Often young people are expected to make too many changes too quickly and with insufficient intensive support from adults. Failure on these goals simply serves to reinforce their own belief that delinquency is the best choice.

CHAPTER 9

Conclusions: Stress and Support in the Lives of Children Facing Adversity

Introduction

In this concluding chapter, some of the key themes of the earlier text are revisited. Of all the stressors that children may face, perhaps the one most easily under-estimated is that of loss. Yet loss experiences may have enormous significance in the lives of vulnerable children. The chapter emphasises the resources and supports that children can call on in responding to the impact of loss and other challenges in their lives. It highlights the importance of social support for vulnerable children and young people, and especially social support from informal sources outside formal service systems. It flags the relevance of children's own agency in how children access such support. It also considers the relevance of attachment and our conceptions of who constitutes attachment figures, the importance of holistic assessments, the value of a strengths focus in assessment, and the relevance of developmental pathways and developmental outcomes in planning, and assessing the value of, interventions. The reader is reminded of the significance of these themes and is given some practice guidance tips.

Dealing with loss

Social workers should assume, until proven otherwise, that any child client has been affected by significant and enduring loss in some way: loss by bereavement, loss by separation, loss by rejection, loss by betrayal of innocence, loss by failed expectations or dashed hopes. Loss may arise from misfortune or specific social stressors; or it may arise from displacement through, for example, forced migration, or placement in care. It can violate a child's trust in attachment figures and her belief in the very trustworthiness of the people and the world around her, profoundly troubling territory for children who are often already rendered fragile by life's circumstances. Serious loss of this kind can undermine a child's sense of belonging to people who care about her and thus her sense of value and lovability; it can also undermine a child's sense of connection to place, and thus her sense of order and predictability in everyday life. Serious unresolved loss may also be at the root of violent or very troubled behaviour. For many such young people their 'deep reservoir of unrequited sorrow is the smouldering emotional underbelly to their violence' (Crenshaw and Garbarino 2007, p.247). Much of the challenging behaviour of children, about which carers may complain to social workers, can be traced to unresolved losses in the child's life, and the knock-on effects of such losses. This framework of understanding related to the themes of loss and grief can be a most valuable frame of reference for the harassed social worker.

Working in a manner sensitive to this issue of loss requires knowledge of the significance of attachment and loss in children's development; of likely reactions to severe and unresolved loss; and of likely influences on such reactions that may aid or impede ultimate recovery. In particular, professionals must never lose sight of the shattering impact of parental rejection for a child's sense of self-worth. Trying to empathise with a child's sense of loss, whatever its source, will also require workers to draw honestly on their own personal experiences of loss in order to try to sensitise themselves to some degree to the child's plight. In acknowledging the power of loss in children's lives, we must also recognise the healing energy that lies within the child and ordinary everyday experience. Adaptation to, or recovery from, loss relies more on support than 'therapy' of a highly specialised or clinical type. While sometimes necessary, too ready recourse to such therapy may exert a very high price in stigma or undermining of natural coping skills and resources.

Activity 9.1

1. How can a worker begin to prepare him- or herself to tap in to the depth of a child's sense of loss?

2. Reflect on the impact of separations in the worker's own childhood (due to hospitalisations, illness, death of loved ones, summer holidays, summer camps, boarding school, parents' divorce, etc.).

3. Reflect on appropriate sources in literature, film, songs or poetry which address themes of loss.

Working effectively and sensitively with the child's issues of loss will also require a comprehensive understanding of the child. This will be built up through a thorough gathering of information about the child and her social context, and a careful sifting/ assessment of the significance of that information. The work will also require a capacity to identify and negotiate with those adults in the child's life who are well placed to assist the child to begin to process unfinished business about past loss. This may involve helping a child to prepare for and carry out a visit to the grave of a departed relative. It may involve a carefully orchestrated setpiece meeting with a parent where the child hears an honest and fundamental explanation as to why the parent had been unable to care for the child and how this had led to the child entering the care system. Even more painfully, it may require the child being faced honestly and sensitively with the news that her future does not involve the realisation of any treasured fantasy about returning home, but in fact entails remaining in care, or placement for adoption. It may also be the case that the process of transmitting such sensitive information needs more than one setpiece meeting. It may take a longer process over time for both parties to formulate and absorb what has to be said and heard.

The importance of this focus on loss has implications not only for the priorities of social workers' own professional practice. It also raises issues for the quality of professional supervision available to them and for the quality of commitment which agencies have to the importance of these issues in the lives of their child clients.

Key questions for practice

- What major losses has this child suffered?

- How can information about these be gathered (information from parents, key care-givers, agency records, hospital records, etc.)?

- At what developmental stage did these losses occur?

- What opportunities has this child had to process her reaction to these different losses?

- What are important sources of continuity in the child's life despite the losses?

- Are there ways in which the social worker can strengthen the connection to such threads of continuity?

- Does the child need to do any active work on grieving for losses at this point?

- And on a related point, does the child have a need for fuller or more accurate information concerning the circumstances surrounding any key past losses?

- If so, are there people of significance to the child who the child trusts and who may be able to help in the process of working through the loss?

- Can these people be helped to ready themselves to support the child in this process?

- Are current care-givers properly briefed on the child's history of loss and the likely psychological reactions to such patterns of loss?

- Have the care-givers or other adults playing a significant role in the child's life (e.g. a key teacher) had a chance to have training and discussion about the precise nature of loss and its likely impact in the child's life?

The importance of social support in children's lives

Social support may take different forms, alone or in combination: practical material help, advice, emotional support in hard times. Knowing that support is there to be called on may be as important as actually receiving it. A crucial issue may be an openness to receiving help, a stance which may be challenging for young people whose experience has made them sensitive about appearing to need or ask for help. For children and parents, support flows through *relationships*. These relationships may be enduring or tentative, but always they are built on some degree of connection, commitment and trust. The relationships can unleash great positive energy and capacity in the development of the child as the National Scientific Council on the Developing Child in the US has noted:

> Stated simply, *relationships* [emphasis added] are the 'active ingredients' of the environment's influence on healthy human development. They incorporate the qualities that best promote competence and well-being – individualized responsiveness, mutual action-and-interaction, and an emotional connection to another human being, be it a parent, peer, grandparent, aunt, uncle, neighbor, teacher, coach, or any other person who has an important impact on the child's early development. (2004, pp. 1–2)

These valuable relationships may sometimes be with supportive peers but a 'strong relationship with an adult' is especially significant for vulnerable young people generally (Luthar, Sawyer and Brown 2006). The critical point for professionals to realise is that most help flows through naturally occurring networks and relationships. The message for professionals is to recognise and strengthen such 'natural' sources of helping.

The importance of attachments and a child's sense of having a secure base from which to explore the world

While most relationships can have some positive potential for a child, attachment relationships have particular meaning. A child's experience of attachment-type relationships may have implications for many aspects of her functioning including her capacity to trust, learn, concentrate, play and socialise. Positive attachment relationships are important because they give children access to responsive adult care. That responsive care, in turn, helps children to form an internal working model of relationships as being potentially supportive and positive. In other words, through good experiences of attachment relationships, children can learn that it is positive and safe to trust and be close. Through good (or bad) attachment experiences, children learn how to be comfortable (or not) with closeness, intimacy and distance in relationships more generally. As we mention below, however, it cannot be assumed that all attachment relationships yield safe, protective and supportive caring all of the time.

Social workers should always remember that *attachment relationships are important*. A successful primary attachment may be especially important and ideally it should occur in the first year. A primary attachment figure is a familiar person whom the child seeks out, and whose proximity and comfort can console the child in moments of extreme distress. However, it is not necessarily an all or nothing scenario. If the child does not form a primary attachment to an adult in the first year, it may still be possible, although more difficult, for the child to experience a primary attachment experience through a later relationship. It is important to bear in mind that attachments are not dependent on the gender of the carer, the quality of care, or the frequency of contact. Primary attachments may form with more than one adult. They may form despite abusive behaviour on the part of the adult. The context of the attachment relationship and the responsiveness of the attachment figure are two key factors in the nurturing of an attachment relationship. A child may thus form an attachment to an adult who abuses her in the absence of alternative attachment figures and because the abusive relationship also contains elements of warmth, responsiveness and support which the child desperately craves.

It is vital for social workers to realise that children are likely to have a hierarchy of attachment relationships to other important figures in their lives (Trinke and Bartholomew 1997). It is profoundly unhelpful, in our view, to conceive of a child's attachment needs solely in terms of one or two precious relationships. The frequent fragility of primary relationships in the lives of children enduring serious adversity such as life in care should surely highlight for us the importance of developing a cast of adults who may play different and important parts in the drama which is the child's life (Scales and Gibbons 1996). Children in care themselves seem to want such a range of adults with whom to relate (Sinclair and Gibbs 1996). Professionals should recognise children need people to whom they are special: carers, family members, teachers, social workers, sports coaches and so on. It is best not to put all the eggs into one basket in terms of such special relationships since we cannot guarantee individual people or relationships are forever.

Children may form a range of meaningful attachments with different people, and the degree of such attachments may vary. It may be helpful to think of secondary attachments as serving an important safety net function should any primary attachment(s) fail to materialise or should it collapse for some reason. A key professional task for social workers in work with children at risk is to ascertain which people make up their attachment network. This attachment network in a sense serves the child as a secure base from which to explore the world and to which to return in moments of crisis. This attachment can also usefully be considered as a potential safety net which prevents the child falling deeper into difficulty in times of crisis.

Siblings are likely to be significant members of a child's attachment network especially in conditions of family stress (Gass, Jenkins and Dunn 2007). Siblings may be drawn together in their common struggle to cope with parental frailty and familial distress. The intensity of some sibling relationships in such circumstances may be double edged. Some sibling relationships may be unhelpful to both parties where negative family dynamics intrude and corrode the more positive tendencies often present in sibling relationships. Social workers may sometimes have to assess – and somehow regulate – the nature of sibling relationships where elements of emotional or other abuse have crept in. This question may be posed most sharply in whether to place certain siblings together, or in determining the extent of contact between siblings placed apart. While there may be good reasons sometimes to keep siblings apart for a period, the guiding principle should be to keep siblings placed in care together or at the very least in very active contact. Connections between siblings may be a very precious resource for the young adult after leaving care or later in mid-life. That longer-term perspective should inform these critical decisions about the nature and extent of sibling contact for youngsters in care. Another area that may sometimes be contentious is a child's contact with a father who has somehow not lived up to expectations or has harmed the child in some way. It is important to bear in mind that decisions geared to tackling immediate issues should also be assessed for their long-term implications. Will cutting links with a father now deprive both parties of meaningful connections when the young person is an older teen or a young adult and better able to cope with the father's frailties? Will cutting off the father now also risk cutting off half of the child's extended family (on the father's side) – an often unintended side effect of such decisions about fathers?

Activity 9.2

Consider a child or young person you are concerned about.

1. Who is important to the child or young person:

    •   at home

    •   in the extended family (grandparents, aunts, uncles, cousins)

    •   in school (teachers, ancillary staff, friends)

    •   in the neighbourhood (adult neighbours, friends, church members, shopkeepers, etc.)

    •   in clubs (sports, cultural, musical)

    •   elsewhere (workplace or training centre)?

2. What kind of relationship does the child have with his or her sibling(s)?

3. What can be done now to help strengthen that relationship for the long term?

4. What might be the longer-term legacy of a decision taken today to limit or block contact with a certain family member?

5. Will this decision serve to enhance or diminish the level of support the young person can call on in later life?

In working with children in distress it may be helpful to remember that the greater the distress and disruption, the greater the need for a sense of having a secure base. In decision-making about where children are to live professionals should strive to preserve threads and relationships in children's lives – the price of help should not be the severing or demeaning of past ties. Even where past ties contain negative elements, the professional challenge is to help the child to tap safely into the positive elements of such ties.

It is important in planning for children to establish which relationships are meaningful in secure base terms by getting to know the child – children will tell you, if you can listen to and hear all their messages. This will help the worker to identify and support those members of a social network whose relationships with the vulnerable person may provide a sense of secure base. While attachments occur predominantly through relationships with other human beings it is also important to recognise how, in addition to relationships with people, memories, symbols, animals, stories, images, places, language and events can all contribute to a child's sense of having a secure base. For some children, the impact of adversity may mean that ties to attachment figures or their sense of secure base may be very tenuous. In such instances, symbols or objects which evoke positive connections to the past may assume special importance. Social workers and others need to be especially sensitive to this point in their practice with children in crisis or transition. It is also important to acknowledge that children may be deeply attached to people who have harmed them, wittingly or unwittingly. Attachment does not depend on the quality of care. The protection of the child must be secured in a way which remains sensitive to the meaning of that attachment relationship for the child.

Ways to enhance a sense of secure base for a child in crisis

The secure base can be supported by:

- bringing a familiar object from one placement or care-giver to another (a toy, photograph, etc.)

- having the endorsement of a valued attachment network member for a move

- having sight of comforting religious or ethnic symbols (where relevant and meaningful)

- having adults involved in the transition honour scrupulously promises and commitments made to the child.

However tempting it might be in the face of a child's pain and emotional void, it is inappropriate for a professional to serve as anything more than a *transitional* secure base offering a relationship which in some instances may appropriately help a child 'cross the bridge' from one permanent carer to another. It is not feasible or appropriate for a professional to pose as a longer-term secure base, thus possibly obstructing or supplanting naturally occurring potential secure base relationships in the child's social ecology. One of the most sensitive tasks in social work with children is the management of transitions from one care-giver to another, from one living arrangement to another. If one thinks of how much care is required to transplant a human organ or a young tree or plant, then one has a sense of the vulnerability of the child in transition and the care and attention to detail which should attend the move.

Important issues to bear in mind

A move is not just a logistical challenge – finding a placement, booking it and managing transport. It involves for the child loss of the familiar, and fear of the unknown. It may reawaken buried memories, fears and anxieties; it may tap into barely hidden emotional fault lines in the child's make up. Many questions will arise for the child, such as: Will I see loved ones again? Will I ever get out of the new setting? How will I be treated? What will happen to me? What are the rules in the new setting? Who will protect me if I get a hard time from other children or adults? What about contact with siblings? What about school? Children will need the opportunity to process over time the emotional and the practical effects of a move. It will be easier for the child to cope, the less that is unknown, the more she feels some influence or control, and the more that is familiar. Certain things may help the child to come to terms with what is happening: discussion and consultation about the new setting and practical arrangements; visits beforehand; handover by familiar adults; scrupulous adherence to arrangements (this symbolises certainty, order); bringing favourite toys, photographs, clothing (these symbolise continuity); visits back to previous setting; and visits to/from familiar people. It helps for everyone to 'sing from the same hymn sheet', that is, for the adults – social worker, carers and family of origin – and the child to have a clear and common understanding of the *plan*.

Activity 9.3

Considering the child or young person you have reflected upon answer the following questions.

1. Who are the people who serve as attachment figures in this child's life?

2. Who does the child seek out for consolation in distress?

3. Who has a partisan commitment to the child?

4. Who might be said to be the people who make up the child's attachment network?

Holistic assessment

Each child is an individual and each child's story is unique. Children each experience the world differently. They react to and act on it in their own way. Each child plays some part in shaping her own destiny. Each child is an agent in her own development and exercises that agency in her own particular way. Assessment must strive to help us know this child – and particularly her strengths, capacities and preoccupations. Assessment must seek to know and represent the whole child. Assessment of children and their needs must not be preoccupied only with deficits, problems or pathology. Too often, we would suggest, assessment is absorbed with the negative. It must instead adopt a rounded approach looking at both positives and negatives, strengths and weaknesses, resources and deficits, and protective and risk factors. As two key American researchers in the field of resilience research put it, assessment must

> focus not only on the risk factors in the lives of these [vulnerable] children but also on the protective factors. These include competencies and sources of informal support that already exist in the extended family, the neighbourhood, and the community at large and that can be utilised to enlarge a child's repertoire of problem solving skills and self esteem and self efficacy. (Werner and Smith 1992, p.208)

A satisfactory assessment must not only focus on problems as defined by somebody else or even by the child. It must not focus only on difficult behaviour or past failings. It must seek out qualities, interests and talents which the child has, and about which the child and other people feel good. A comprehensive assessment which attends to strengths as well as deficits will highlight resources not only in the child's own personal profile but also in her social ecology: people who care about her, take an interest, help her. An assessment must focus not only on the trigger for referral; it must also focus on the child. It must also address the ecology or social context within which the child has developed and within which problems have emerged or been defined.

Activity 9.4

Seeking out strengths in assessment, consider the following:
1. What talents does this young person have?
2. What qualities does this young person have which other people find attractive?
3. Which of the young person's qualities are helpful in dealing with adversity?
4. Who are the people to whom this young person matters?
5. What should be included in a list of this young person's social skills and accomplishments?
6. Who or what constitute resources in assisting this young person to negotiate adversities and to make her way in the world?
7. What cultural assets and supports can the young person tap into?

Developmental pathways

A very hopeful message from developmental research is that children's fate or destiny is not cast in stone at conception, birth or some other critical deadline in their development. What happens next is certainly influenced by what has happened earlier, but positive factors may emerge, sometimes unexpectedly, to counteract previously negative trends. Even in unpromising circumstances, there may be unexpected turning points that shift development in a positive direction. The turning point may arise from a combination of opportunity and response (Gilligan 2009b).

It may be useful to think of a child's developmental pathway as being rather like that of the intended course of a sailing yacht (see Figures 9.1 and 9.2). If conditions remain as predicted then the course will be close to that expected at the outset. The yacht's course will follow that plotted on the maps before the journey begins. Similarly the child's progress will follow the path predicted by the 'deal of the cards' at birth in terms of height, weight and temperament. What makes the pathway interesting of course for sailors or people concerned with child development is that life is rarely that simple. Severe weather may occur, winds may blow the boat off course, the boat may suffer damage, a key crew member may be injured. On the other hand, adverse developments may be counterbalanced by favourable shifts in weather or winds which cancel out and outweigh earlier problems. Similarly, illness in the child or care-giver, stress in the home environment and unplanned separations may all adversely affect the child's progress. This may lead to the child 'underachieving' in terms of the expected path of progress. Children whose projected developmental trajectory is veering off course because of a surfeit of stress may be drawn back onto, or closer to, course by a critical moment or experience. A move to a supportive school, a relationship with an aunt who takes a new and deep interest, success at sport and the care of a foster carer may all be examples of how a child's progress may be turned around.

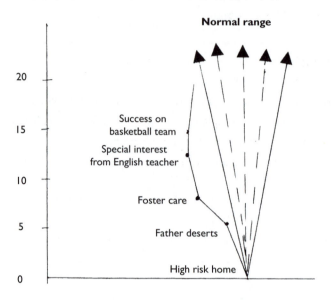

Figure 9.1 Key turning points in developmental pathways (1) (Gilligan, after Bowlby 1988)

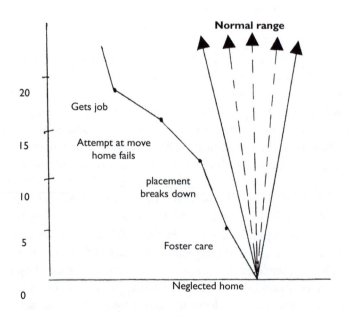

Figure 9.2 Key turning points in developmental pathways (2) (Gilligan, after Bowlby 1988)

It may often seem puzzling that some children apparently exposed to the same adversity react differently, as we discuss earlier in the volume. One child may seem permanently scarred in terms of loss of confidence and self-esteem. Another – even in the same family – seems to bounce back. There may be two sets of related reasons for the difference between the two children. First, the cumulative number of adversities experienced by the two children may be different despite their sharing at least one in common. There is various evidence to suggest that children may escape one or two adversities in their lives relatively unscathed, but that after the third, fourth or further adversities, the child begins to buckle under the pressure and her developmental progress and functioning become severely compromised. Children may also differ in their reaction to stressors because of their innate quality of resilience. Resilience – this vital capacity to bounce back in the face of stress – is both constitutional and social in origin.

These two points about the weight of adversity and the importance of resilience are not merely abstract insights remote from the concerns of everyday practice. One may think of a set of scales where there is on one side an accumulation of negative weights representing stressors or adversities in the child's life and a series of positive weights on the other side representing assets and protective factors in the child's life. Bearing in mind the importance of avoiding adversities creeping above two in number, it may be important for the social worker or other professional to be able to target one adversity which can be more easily removed from the negative side of the scales, or possibly indeed to add a new positive weight to the other side in order to cancel out the effect of the negative weight. While the constitutional element of resilience is beyond the reach of the social worker, it is possible that the social worker can influence the level of social resilience displayed by the child. Social resilience can be enhanced by secure attachments, self-esteem and a sense of self-efficacy. All of these may be amenable to influence by actions by the social worker or by other significant adults in the child's caring network who may be encouraged in this task by the social worker.

Developmental outcomes

Practitioners need to remember what we are here for – improving the lot of the child. It is a modest aspiration – but let us at least try to ensure that the young person leaves our agency's supervision or care with somewhat fewer problems than when she entered. In our view a key message of the resilience paradigm for work with children in care is dealing with the small elements as well as the big elements. One of us has written elsewhere about the limitations of relying excessively on permanence as a guiding principle in this work (Gilligan 1997). Permanence is a big idea, with many merits, but in the real world professionals cannot guarantee permanent outcomes for placements for children. Therefore, planning for placements needs to proceed with a wise balance of humility and realism. Developmental outcomes depend on a perspective that bears developmental pathways and influences in mind, that emphasises care planning and that attends to both the small details and the big picture. The following pointers are worth considering.

Attend to the value of education and school experiences

Success at school academically is invaluable for cognitive development, self-esteem, general social competence, social status and job prospects. But school is also an important source of opportunities to acquire friends, hobbies, sporting and cultural interests and general social skills and confidence. Thus the social worker should be alert to how the child is enjoying school overall as well as to the importance of matters such as homework, reasons for school difficulties (possibly due to unidentified problems such as dyslexia and learning difficulties) and levels of literacy, numeracy and school attendance in children for whom they are responsible. Personal contact with teachers and close attention to school reports will help brief the social worker on the child's motivation, attainments and possible special tuition requirements relative to other children in the school. The value of fresh direct evidence from the school underlines the importance of school representation at setpiece meetings such as case conferences and reviews. For children in care, it is important that there is clear communication and an agreed division of labour between social workers and carers about school issues and contact with the school.

Remember the therapeutic power of the everyday, the ordinary, the routine

We are too easily preoccupied with the 'problem' and too readily seduced by the idea that referral to some specialist service, some expert, some exclusive therapy will unlock the problem. Meanwhile we blissfully ignore questions such as: Does the treatment or placement or therapy, or whatever, work? Does the child want it? Does the young person understand its purpose? Does the specialist really understand the child's lived reality? Does referral generate stigma, and stigma, resistance?

It is almost inevitable that a child labelled special in some way will feel different and be seen as different. The sense of stigma resulting from this feeling of negative difference is very corrosive of self-esteem and social confidence. Referring on to specialist provision also risks ignoring the potential of naturally occurring resources within the child's ecology. Moreover, it does not face up to the problems of successful reintegration into the natural environment especially where intervention has meant full- or part-time withdrawal from the same. We would suggest that social workers and other professionals should be much more ready to search out naturally occurring supports in a child's wider social habitat. For example, the reassuring and familiar structure of a sensitively laid out and consistently managed primary school classroom and a warm relationship with a responsive teacher may do more for a child's craving for a secure base than elaborate efforts around weekly one-hour sessions of therapy. We must learn to recognise and value the therapeutic power that is all around us. A child who has a talent for swimming recognised and encouraged may thrive in the structure and attention which regular daily or twice weekly coaching or training sessions offer. A child who loves horses may blossom through encounters with the thrill – and fear – of horse-riding. The concentration, responsibility, courage and discipline required will earn precious affirmation for the child and from people other than those who are professionally obliged to support the child.

Remember that problems usually have complex causes, and are therefore likely to require complex or multi-faceted solutions

Beware simple answers to complex questions. The serious problems which prove most challenging usually have multiple sources and causes. Few are amenable to single responses. An effective intervention will require a sufficiently comprehensive plan which embraces a number of approaches and which also attends to a lot of the little details. A plan will be all the stronger for carefully drawing on the capacities that child brings to the situation and on the energy and commitment of supportive adults and peers in the child's network.

Remember that behaviour is often a coded language about the child's inner world and the (mis)fit between his or her needs and the responses the adult world has managed to produce

As has been discussed earlier, when children behave in ways which numbers of adults find difficult, it is most likely that the child is communicating distress. It is important for practitioners to view behaviour as a form of communication which often contains many layers of significance and meaning. The challenge for professionals is not just to react to the surface behaviour but to discern the underlying meaning and pain behind the behaviour. Experience has taught this child certain messages about her own worth or the reliability of caring adults. A child's behaviour invites us to search out the messages which experience has taught a given child. Behaviour which is difficult is often a device for seeking attention, and for communicating emotional pain and distress. Heeding the underlying significance of difficult behaviour is vital. Appropriate attention to the child's unmet needs rather than to the challenging or provocative behaviour may be the most constructive strategy to adopt.

Remember that social experience and development are important but so also is cognitive development

Children's behaviour may reflect conclusions they have drawn about what has happened to them or who has done what to them. Or more accurately, behaviour may reflect the child's inner story or explanations of what she thinks has happened. It is important that children are helped to have a 'coherent story' (Dowling 1993) about the progress of their lives and the incidents and events which have shaped their destiny. It is important that children have a story which helps them know where they stand, where they have come from, and where they are going. It is important that they do not shoulder blame for the actions of others, or that they do not attribute wilful malice where in fact a problem such as alcoholism explains a parent's errant behaviour. A coherent account and understanding of what has happened will help the child more effectively to have a command of the experience. A firm grasp of a coherent story pulls disjointed fragments of experience into a more integrated whole and helps a child to make more sense of what has happened and what is happening. A child is lucky if her level of intelligence helps her to interpret accurately what has happened more easily, and to attribute causes and influences to their proper sources. But all children in such circumstances will need to have their own efforts supplemented with the assistance of sensitive adults attuned to their needs. Social workers should always be alert to the educational and therapeutic opportunities which enhance children's cognitive skills and which minimise barriers to their proper understanding and processing of emotional experiences.

Enhance the young person's coping and self-efficacy by helping the child to rehearse, observe and discuss problem-solving skills and strategies

Some of this strengthening of the young person's coping and self-efficacy can be done in an explicit and direct way. For instance, it might involve taking young people through a customised course on coping with life in care, or a course on dealing with being bullied. Other parts of it might be done through activities which indirectly achieve the desired effect. For instance, joining a project to develop a course about life in care or afterwards for other young people may help the course designers with an actual background of life in care to grapple with and perhaps resolve more subtly issues which a full-frontal course for them might not achieve. Carers can play an important part in this regard, by sensitising them to the young person's needs. They can be helped to encourage the young person to take advantage of everyday opportunities that may present themselves.

Devices which allow young people in care simultaneously to meet other people's needs as well as their own seem likely to be very helpful. Examples of these might involve matching the needs of the young people and students where they both have complementary needs, for instance through journalism students working with young people in care to produce a newspaper or radio programme about life in care, or drama students doing similar in relation to a play about adolescence, or photography students working on a photo essay about young people's needs, and so forth. In a different context, health promotion workers might cooperate with young people in care in the production of health promotion materials, a process which might produce a valuable end product as well as much useful learning for the young participants.

It is clearly important to involve children in discussions about their needs and about their future. In one sense this is not something necessary to say to readers of a book such as this but it is still important to stress it. We must constantly work to find ever more effective ways of helping young people contribute to care plans and reviews. This entails giving clear information to the young person. It requires ensuring that the young person knows about:

- the reasons for the young person entering and remaining in care

- the young person's rights while in care

- future plans for the young person and how the young person can influence these.

We need to regard young people as resources in the process of seeking solutions in their lives or milieux. We must encourage them to make choices and declare preferences in everyday living. We must coach young people in how to resolve conflict with peers without recourse to bullying or violence. These various opportunities and experiences can teach them that their opinions are of value and help them learn some of the skills of influence, negotiation and problem-solving. Perhaps we have much to learn from the fields of negotiation and mediation. Skills from those areas could be very useful to care-givers in everyday living and could also be very valuable to consciously pass on to young people in their care.

Final practical tips for intervention

While it may be very difficult to alter the whole picture, it may still be possible to make a difference. Reducing by one the number of weights on the risk side of the scales and adding one or more weights to the protective side may have quite a dramatic effect on the functioning of a young person. Even more importantly it may alter the perception which the young person and those around her have of the potential for positive change and development. Some key changes prompted by skilful and targeted intervention may switch a vicious circle of gloom and despair into a virtuous cycle of growth and hope. These are as follows:

- identify who is important to the child

- try to help build and sustain those relationships

- find who the child knew in the past who may still be willing to keep contact with the child

- try to find out what interests and talents the child has

- try to encourage these

- find adults in the natural networks of the child who may be willing to play a mentoring role for the child in terms of talents or interests

- help the young person to acquire valued social roles (e.g. as part-time worker, volunteer, sports committee member, choir member). (Gilligan 2008)

Accomplishment in some hobby, sport or cultural pursuit enhances the child's self-esteem, offers a constructive use of time and perhaps most important is likely to link a vulnerable child into networks of social relationships which may eventually endure and develop. Attend also to how important school is not only for academic learning but also as a site where vulnerable children may receive precious adult interest and support, where they may learn esteem-enhancing knowledge or skills and acquire friendships or the social skills and opportunities which promote them.

The final message of the book must be to underline yet again the child's social context as a source of decisive experiences and influences, and of resources to assist the child, and the practitioner seeking to help the child. Even in the most barren social landscape there are likely to be at least some resources and supports which can be tapped into. To the discerning and optimistic eye, the child's natural social context is a reservoir of informal supports and resources often lying ready to be tapped and mobilised (Gilligan 1999). To understand the children and their needs and history, and certainly to intervene effectively in their lives, it is vital that social workers – and child welfare professionals more generally – attend to the significance of children's social ecology in the origin and resolution of needs and problems. Problems will make more sense when seen against the background of children's social context. Solutions will seem more possible when seen in the light of the naturally occurring resources waiting in the same social context.

References

Aboud, F. (1988) *Children and Prejudice.* Oxford: Blackwell.

Ahmed, B. (1991) 'Setting the Context: Race and the Children's Act 1989.' In S. MacDonald (ed.) *All Equal under the Act?* London: Race Equality Unit.

Ainsworth, M.D.S. and Bowlby, J. (1991) 'Attachments and Other Affectional Bonds across the Life Cycle.' In C.M. Parkes, J. Stevenson-Hinde and P. Marris (eds) *Attachment Across the Life Cycle.* London: Tavistock/Routledge.

Ainsworth, M.D.S., Bell, S. and Stayton, D. (1971) 'Individual Differences in Strange-Situation Behaviour of One Year Olds' In H. Schaffer (ed.) *The Origins of Human Social Relations.* New York: Academic Press.

Ainsworth, M.D.S., Blehar, M., Walters, E. and Walls, S. (1978) *Patterns of Attachment.* Hillsdale, NJ: Erlbaum.

Aldgate, J. and Rose, W. (2008) 'Assessing and Managing Risk.' In *Getting it Right for Every Child.* Edinburgh: Scottish Government.

Alejandro-Wright, M.N. (1985) 'The Child's Conception of Racial Classification.' In M.B. Spencer, G.K. Brookins and W.R. Allen (eds.) *Beginnings: The Social and Affective Development of Black Children.* Hillsdale, NJ: Erlbaum.

American Psychiatric Association (1994) *Diagnostic and Statistical Manual of Mental Disorders* (4th edition). Washington, DC: American Psychiatric Association.

Argent, H. (2008) *Placing Siblings: Ten Top Tips.* London: BAAF.

Azar, S.T. (1997) 'A Cognitive-behavioural Approach to Understanding and Treating Parents who Physically Abuse their Children.' In D.A. Wolfe, R.J. McMahon and R.D. Peters (eds.) *Child Abuse: New Directions in Prevention and Treatment Across the Lifespan.* Thousand Oaks, CA: Sage.

Baginsky, M. (ed.) (2008) *Safeguarding Children and Schools.* London: Jessica Kingsley Publishers.

Balbernie, R. (2007) 'Circuits and circumstances: The neurobiological consequences of early relationships.' Presentation to the Presidents' Conference, Judicial Studies Board.

Baldwin, N. and Spencer, N. (1993) 'Deprivation and child abuse: Implications for strategic planning in children's services.' *Children and Society 7,* 4, 357–375.

Baldwin, N., Johansen, P. and Seale, A. (1989/90) *Race in Child Protection: A Code of Practice.* Kirklees Social Services Department, UK: Race Equality Unit, Black and White Alliance.

Bandura, A. (1981) 'Self-referent Thought: A Developmental Analysis of Self-efficacy.' In J.H. Flavell and L. Ross (eds.) *Social Cognitive Development.* Cambridge: Cambridge University Press.

Banks, N. (2001) 'Assessing Children and Families who Belong to Minority Ethnic Groups.' In J. Horwath (ed.) *The Child's World: Assessing Children in Need.* London: Jessica Kingsley Publishers.

Banks, N. (2002) 'What is a Positive Black Identity?' In K.N. Dwivedi (ed.) *Meeting the Needs of Ethnic Minority Children.* London: Jessica Kingsley Publishers.

Barlow, J. (1999) 'What Works in Parent Education Programmes?' In E. Lloyd (ed.) *Parenting Matters: What Works in Parenting Education?* Barkingside: Barnardo's.

Barnardo's (2008) *Effective Work with Sexually Exploited Children and Young People.* Barkingside: Barnardo's. Available at www.barnardos.org.uk/effective_work_with_sexually_exploited_children_young_people_2008-2.pdf (accessed on 16 July 2010)

Barns, R. (2007) '"Race", ethnicity and child welfare: A fine balancing act.' *British Journal of Social Work 37,* 1425–1434.

Barter, C., McCarry, M., Berridge, D. and Evans, K. (2009) 'Partner exploitation and violence in teenage intimate relationships.' Available at www.nspcc.org.uk/Inform/research/Findings/partner_exploitation_and_violence_summary_wdf68093.pdf, (accessed on September 2009).

Baumrind, D. (1972) 'Socialization and Instrumental Competence in Young Children.' In W.W. Hartup (ed.) *The Young Child: Reviews of Research, Vol. 2.* Washington, DC: National Association for the Education of Young Children.

Bee, H. (1995) *The Developing Child.* New York: HarperCollins College Publishers.

Benard, B. (2004) *Resiliency: What Have We Learned?* San Francisco, CA: WestEd.

Bennathan, M. and Boxall, M. (1998) *The Boxall Profile: A Guide to Effective Intervention in the Education of Pupils with Emotional and Behavioural Difficulties.* Manchester: AWCEBD on behalf of Nurture Group Consortium.

Bentovim, A., Cox, A., Bingley Miller, L. and Pizzey, S. (2009) *Safeguarding Children Living with Trauma and Family Violence.* London: Jessica Kingsley Publishers.

Berger, K.S. (2001) *The Developing Person Through the Lifespan.* New York: Worth Publishers.

Berliner, L. (1990) 'Clinical Work with Sexually Abused Children.' In C. Howells and C. Hollins (eds.) *Clinical Approaches to Sex Offenders and Their Victims.* London: Wiley.

Berliner, L. (1997) 'Intervention with Children who Experience Trauma.' In D. Cicchetti and S. Toth (eds.) *Developmental Perspectives on Trauma: Theory, Research and Intervention.* Rochester, NY: University of Rochester Press.

Berridge, D., Dance, C., Beecham, J. and Field, S. (2008) *Educating Difficult Adolescents: Effective Education for Children in Public Care with Emotional and Behavioural Difficulties.* London: Jessica Kingsley Publishers.

Berrington, A., Stevenson, J., Ingham, R. with Borgoni, R., Cobos, Hernandez, M.I.C. and Smith, P.W.F. (2007) *Consequences of Teenage Parenthood: Pathways which Minimise the Long Term Negative Impacts of Teenage Childbearing.* Teenage Pregnancy Research Programme Research Briefing No. 8. London: DfES/DH.

Berthoud, R., Ermisch, J., Fransesconi, M., Liao, T., Pevalin, D. and Robson, K. (2004) *Long-term Consequences of Teenage Births for Parents and their Children.* Teenage Pregnancy Research Programme Research Briefing No. 1. London: DCSF/DH.

Biehal, N., Clayden, J., Stein, M. and Wade, J. (1995) *Moving On: Young People and Leaving Care Schemes.* London: HMSO.

Bolger, K.E., and Patterson, C.J. (2003) 'Sequelae of Child Maltreatment: Vulnerability and Resilience.' In S. Luthar (ed.) *Resilience and Vulnerability: Adaptation in the Context of Childhood Adversities.* Cambridge: Cambridge University Press.

Boushel, M. (1994) 'The protective environment of children: Towards a framework for anti-oppressive, cross-cultural and cross-national understanding.' *British Journal of Social Work 24*, 173–190.

Bower, T.G.R. (1977) *A Primer of Infant Development.* San Francisco: W.H. Freeman and Company.

Bowlby, J. (1969) *Attachment and Loss, Vols. 1 and 2.* New York: Basic Books.

Bowlby, J. (1988) 'Developmental psychiatry comes of age'. American Journal of Psychiatry 145, 1–10.

Brandon, M., Belderson, P., Warren, C., Howe, D., Gardner, R. and Dodsworth, J. (2008) *Analysing Child Deaths and Serious Injury Through Abuse and Neglect: What Can We Learn? A Biennial Analysis of Serious Case Reviews 2003–2005.* London: DCSF.

Brandon, M., Howe, A., Dagley, V., Salter, C., Warren, C. and Black, J. (2006) *Evaluating the Common Assessment Framework and Lead Professional Guidance and Implementation in 2005–6 Research Report.* London: Department for Education and Skills. Available at www.dcsf.gov.uk/research/data/uploadfiles/RR740.pdf (accessed on 21 July 2010).

Breakwell, G.M., Fife-Schaw, C. and Clayden, K. (1991) 'Risk taking, control over partner choice and intended use of condoms by virgins.' *Journal of Community and Applied Social Psychology. Special Social Dimensions of AIDS 1*, 2, 173–187.

Bronfenbrenner, U. (1989) 'Ecological systems theory.' *Annals of Child Development 6*, 187–249.

Brooks, R.B. (1994) 'Children at risk: Fostering resilience and hope.' *American Journal of Orthopsychiatry 64*, 4, 545–553.

Calder M.C., Goulding S., Hanks H., Regan L. and Rose K. (2000) *The Complete Guide to Sexual Abuse Assessments.* Lyme Regis: Russell House Publishing.

Cavanagh Johnson, T. (2001a) 'Understanding the sexual behaviour of children: Part I.' *Cyc-Online Reading for Child and Youth Care Workers 30.* Available at www.cyc-net.org/cyc-online/cycol-0701-toni1.html, accessed on 24 September 2009.

Cavanagh Johnson, T. (2001b) 'Understanding the sexual behaviour of children: Part II.' *Cyc-Online Reading for Child and Youth Care Workers 31.* Available at www.cyc-net.org/cyc-online/cycol-0801-toni2.html, accessed 24 September 2009.

Chand, A. and Thoburn, J. (2006) 'Research review: Child protection referrals and minority ethnic children and families.' *Child and Family Social Work 11,* 368–377.

Chávez, A.F. and Guido-DiBrito, F. (1999) 'Racial and ethnic identity and development.' *New Directions for Adult and Continuing Education 84,* 39–47.

Chess, S. and Thomas, A. (1977) 'Temperamental individuality from childhood to adolescence.' *Journal of Child Psychiatry 16,* 218–226.

Cigno, K. (1995) 'Helping to Prevent Abuse: A Behavioural Approach with Families.' In K. Wilson and A. James (eds.) *The Child Protection Handbook.* London, Philadelphia, Toronto, Sydney and Tokyo: Baillière Tindall.

Clark, K. and Clark, M. (1947) 'Racial Identification and Preference in Negro Children.' In T.M. Newcomb and E.L. Hartley (eds.) *Readings in Social Psychology.* New York: Holt.

Cleaver, H., Nicholson, D., Tarr, S. and Cleaver, D. (2006) *The Response of Child Protection Practices and Procedures to Children Exposed to Domestic Violence or Parental Substance Misuse.* Summary Report. London: DfES.

Cleaver, H., Unell, I. and Aldgate, J. (1999) *Children's Needs – Parenting Capacity: The Impact of Parental Mental Illness, Problem Alcohol and Drugs Use, and Domestic Violence on the Development of Children.* London: The Stationery Office.

Cohn Donnelly, A. (1997) 'Early intervention efforts to prevent physical abuse and neglect.' Paper delivered at the Sixth European Congress on Child Abuse and Neglect, ISPCAN, Barcelona.

Coie, J.D. and Dodge, K.A. (1983) 'Continuities and changes in children's social status: A five year longitudinal study.' *Merrill-Palmer Quarterly 29,* 261–282.

Coleman, J.C. (1980) *The Nature of Adolescence.* London and New York: Methuen.

Coleman, J.C. and Hendry, L. (1990) *The Nature of Adolescence* (2nd edition). London: Routledge.

Conte, J. and Berliner, L. (1988) 'The Impact of Sexual Abuse on Children: The Empirical Findings.' In L. Walker (ed.) *Handbook on Sexual Abuse of Children: Assessment and Issues.* New York: Springer Publishing.

Cooper, A., Hetherington, R. and Katz, I. (2003) *The Risk Factor: Making the Child Protection System Work for Children.* London: DEMOS.

Cooper, C. (1985) *Good Enough Parenting.* London: BAAF.

Cox, A.D., Puckering, C., Pound, A. and Mills, M. (1987) 'The impact of maternal depression in young children.' *Journal of Child Psychology and Psychiatry 28,* 917–928.

Crenshaw, D.A. and Garbarino, J. (2007) 'The hidden dimensions: Profound sorrow and buried potential in violent youth.' *Journal of Humanistic Psychology 47,* 160–174.

Crittenden, P.M. (1995) 'Attachment and Psychopathology' In S. Goldberg, R. Muir and J. Kerr (eds.) *Attachment Theory: Social, Developmental and Clinical Perspectives.* Hillsdale, NJ: Analytical Press.

Crittenden, P.M. (1996) 'Research on Maltreating Families: Implications for Intervention.' In J. Briere, L. Berliner, J.A. Bulkley, C. Jenny and T. Reid (eds.) *The APSAC Handbook on Child Maltreatment.* Thousand Oaks, CA, London and New Delhi: Sage Publications.

Crittenden, P.M. and Ainsworth, M.D.S. (1989) 'Child Maltreatment and Attachment Theory.' In D. Cicchetti and V. Carlson (eds.) *Child Maltreatment: Theory and Research on the Causes and Consequences of Child Abuse and Neglect.* Cambridge and New York: Cambridge University Press.

Cross, M., Gordon, R., Kennedy, M. and Marchant, R. (1993) *The ABCD Pack: Abuse and Children who are Disabled.* Leicester: ABCD Consortium.

Crouter, A.C., Whiteman, S.D., McHale, S.M. and Osgood, D.W. (2007) 'Development of gender attitude traditionality across middle childhood and adolescence.' *Child Development 78*, 3, 911–926.

Cullerton-Sen, C., Cassidy, A.R., Murray-Close, D., Cicchetti, D., Crick, N.R. and Rogosch, F.A. (2008) 'Childhood maltreatment and the development of relational and physical aggression: The importance of a gender-informed approach.' *Child Development 79*, 6, 1736–1751.

Cummings, E.M. (1987) 'Coping with background anger in early childhood.' *Child Development 58*, 976–984.

Cummings, E.M. and Davies, P.T. (1994) 'Maternal depression and child development.' *Child Psychology and Psychiatry 35*, 73–112.

Daniel, B. and Rioch, C. (2007) 'Parenting Issues and Practice in Child Protection.' In K. Wilson and A. James (eds.) *The Child Protection Handbook*. London: Baillière Tindall.

Daniel, B. and Taylor, J. (2001) *Engaging with Fathers: Practice Issues for Health and Social Care*. London: Jessica Kingsley Publishers.

Daniel, B. and Wassell, S. (2002a) *Adolescence: Assessing and Promoting Resilience in Vulnerable Children 1*. London: Jessica Kingsley Publishers.

Daniel, B. and Wassell, S. (2002b) *The School Years: Assessing and Promoting Resilience in Vulnerable Children 2*. London: Jessica Kingsley Publishers.

Daniel, B. and Wassell, S. (2002c) *The Early Years: Assessing and Promoting Resilience in Vulnerable Children 3*. London: Jessica Kingsley Publishers.

Daniel, B., Vincent, S., Farrall, E. and Arney, F. (2008) *How is the Concept of Resilience Operationalised in Practice with Vulnerable Children?* Final Report to the British Academy. Stirling: Stirling University.

Daniel, B., Vincent, S., Farrall, E. and Arney, F. (2009) 'How is the Concept of Resilience Operationalised in Practice with Vulnerable Children?' *International Journal of Child and Family Welfare 12*, 1, 2–21.

Darlington, Y., Feeney, J. and Rixon, A. (2005) 'Practice challenges at the intersection of child protection and mental health.' *Child and Family Social Work 10*, 239–247.

Dent, H. and Stephenson, G. (1979) 'An experimental study of the effectiveness of different techniques of questioning child witnesses.' *British Journal of Social and Clinical Psychology 18*, 41–51.

Department for Children, Schools and Families (2007) *Aiming High for Disabled Children: Transforming Services for Disabled Children and their Families*. London: DCSF.

Department for Children, Schools and Families (2009a) *Referrals, Assessment and Children and Young People who are the Subject of a Child Protection Plan, England – Year Ending 31 March 2009*. London: DCSF. Available at www.dcsf.gov.uk/rsgateway/DB/SFR/s000873/index.shtml, accessed on 21 July 2010.

Department for Children, Schools and Families (2009b) *Safeguarding Disabled Children*. Nottingham: DCSF.

Department for Education and Schools (2003) *Every Child Matters*. Cm 5860. London: The Stationery Office.

Department of Health (1991) *Patterns and Outcomes in Child Placement: Messages from Current Research and their Implications*. London: HMSO.

Department of Health (2000) *Framework for the Assessment of Children in Need and their Families*. London: The Stationery Office.

Derman-Sparks, L. (1991) *Anti-bias Curriculum: Tools for Empowering Young Children*. Washington, DC: National Association for the Education of Young Children.

Devore, W. and Schlessinger, E.G. (1987) *Ethnic-sensitive Social Work Practice*. Ohio: Merrill Publishing Company.

DHSS (1995) *Child Protection: Messages from Research*. London: HMSO.

Diaz, R.M. (1983) 'Thought and two languages: The impact of bilingualism on cognitive development.' *Review of Research in Education 10*, 23–54.

DiClemente, C. (1991) 'Motivational Interviewing and the Stages of Change.' In W. Miller and S. Rollnick (eds.) *Motivational Interviewing*. London: Guilford Press.

Dodge, K.A. (1980) 'Social cognition and children's aggressive behaviour.' *Child Development 51*, 162–170.

Donaldson, M. (1978) *Children's Minds*. London: Fontana.

Douglas, J. (1989) *Behaviour Problems in Young Children*. London: Tavistock/Routledge.

Dowling, E. (1993) 'Are family therapists listening to the young? A psychological perspective.' *Journal of Family Therapy 15*, 403–411.

Downes, C. (1992) *Separation Revisited: Adolescents in Foster Family Care*. Aldershot: Ashgate.

Dubowitz, H., Black, M.M., Starr, R.H. and Zuravin, S. (1993) 'A conceptual definition of child neglect.' *Criminal Justice and Behavior 20*, 1, 8–26.

Dunn, J. (1993) *Young Children's Close Relationships: Beyond Attachment*. Thousand Oaks, CA, London and New Delhi: Sage Publications.

Dunn, J. and Kendrick, C. (1982) *Siblings: Love, Envy and Understanding*. Cambridge, MA, and London: Harvard University Press.

Dunn, J. and Plomin, R. (1990) *Separate Lives: Why Siblings are so Different*. New York: Basic Books.

Dunn, J., Brown, J., Stankowski, C., Teska, C. and Youngblake, L. (1991) 'Young children's understanding of other people's feelings and beliefs: Differences in their antecedents.' *Child Development 62*, 1352–1366.

Dwivedi, K.N. (2002) 'Introduction'. In K.N. Dwivedi (ed.) *Meeting the Needs of Ethnic Minority Children*. London: Jessica Kingsley Publishers.

Edwards, J. (1998) 'Screening Out Men: Or "Has Mum Changed her Washing Powder Recently?"' In J. Popay, J. Hearn and J. Edwards (eds.) *Men, Gender Divisions and Welfare*. London: Routledge.

Elgar, M. and Head, A. (1999) 'An Overview of Siblings.' In A. Mullender (ed.) *We are Family: Sibling Relationships in Placement and Beyond*. London: BAAF.

Elkind, D. (1967) 'Egocentrism in adolescence.' *Child Development 38*, 1025–1034.

Erickson, M.F. and Egeland, B. (1996) 'Child Neglect.' In J. Briere, L. Berliner, J.A. Buckley, C. Jenny and T. Reid (eds.) *The APSAC Handbook on Child Maltreatment*. Thousand Oaks, CA, London and New Delhi: Sage Publications.

Erickson, M.F., Egeland, B. and Pianta, R.C. (1989) 'The Effects of Maltreatment on the Development of Young Children.' In D. Cicchetti and C. Carlson (eds.) *Child Maltreatment: Theory and Research on the Causes and Consequences of Child Abuse and Neglect*. New York: Cambridge University Press.

Erikson, E. (1959) 'Identity and the life cycle.' *Psychological Issues 1*, 1–7.

Fahlberg, V. (1988) *Fitting the Pieces Together*. London: BAAF.

Fahlberg, V. (1994) *A Child's Journey through Placement*. London: BAAF.

Farmer, E., Sturgess, W. and O'Neill, T. (2008) *The Reunification of Looked After Children with their Parents: Patterns, Interventions and Outcomes*. Report to the Department for Children, Schools and Families. Bristol: University of Bristol.

Feeney, J. and Noller, P. (1996) *Adult Attachment*. Thousand Oaks, CA, London and New Delhi: Sage Publications.

Fife Council (unpublished 2006) *Permanency Training Manual*. Glenrothes: Fife Council.

Flavell, J.H. (1985) *Cognitive Development* (2nd edition). Englewood Cliffs, NJ: Prentice-Hall.

Flood, M. and Hamilton, C. (2003) *Youth and Pornography in Australia: Evidence on the Extent of Exposure and Likely Effects*. Canberra: The Australia Institute.

Fonagy, P., Steele, M., Steele, H., Higgit, A. and Target, M. (1994) 'The theory and practice of resilience.' *Journal of Child Psychology and Psychiatry 35*, 2, 231–257.

Franklin, A. and Sloper, P. (2005) *Participation of Disabled Children and Young People under Quality Protects*. York: University of York.

Friborg, O., Hjemdal, O., Rosenvinge, J.H. and Martinussen, M. (2003) 'A new rating scale for adult resilience: What are the central protective resources behind healthy adjustment?' *International Journal of Methods in Psychiatric Research 12*, 65–76.

Gagnon, J.H. and Simon, W. (1973) *Sexual Conduct: The Social Sources of Human Sexuality*. Chicago: Aldine.

Gambe, D., Gomes, J., Kapur, V., Rangel, M. and Stubbs, P. (1992) *Anti-racist Social Work Education: Improving Practice with Children and Families*. London: CCETSW.

Garbarino, J.M. (1980) 'Defining emotional maltreatment: The meaning is the message.' *Journal of Psychiatric Treatment and Evaluation 2*, 105–110.

Garbarino, J. and Garbarino, A. (1986) *Emotional Maltreatment of Children*. Chicago: National Committee for Prevention of Child Abuse.

Gass, K., Jenkins, J. and Dunn, J. (2007) 'Are sibling relationships protective? A longitudinal study.' *Journal of Child Psychology and Psychiatry 48*, 167–175.

Gaudin Jr, J.M. (1993) 'Effective intervention with neglectful families.' *Criminal Justice and Behaviour 20*, 1, 66–89.

Geiger, B. (1996) *Fathers as Primary Caregivers.* Westport, CN: Greenwood Press.

German, G. (2002) 'Antiracist Strategies for Educational Performance: Facilitating Successful Learning for all Children.' In K.N. Dwivedi (ed.) *Meeting the Needs of Ethnic Minority Children.* London: Jessica Kingsley Publishers.

Ghate, D. and Hazel, N. (2002) *Parenting in Poor Environments.* London: Jessica Kingsley Publishers.

Gibbons, J., Gallagher, B., Bell, C. and Gordon, D. (1995) *Development After Physical Abuse in Early Childhood: A Follow-up Study of Children on Protection Registers.* London: HMSO.

Giedd, J.N., Blumenthal, J., Jeffries, N.O., Castellanos, F.X. *et al.* (1999) 'Brain development during childhood and adolescence: A longitudinal MRI study.' *Nature Neuroscience 2*, 10, 861–863.

Gil, E. and Cavanagh Johnson, T. (1993) *Sexualised Children: Assessment and Treatment of Sexualised Children and Children who Molest.* Rockville, MD: Launch Press.

Gilbert, R., Spatz Widom, C., Browne, K., Fergusson, D., Webb, E. and Janson, S. (2009) 'Burden and consequences of child maltreatment in high-income countries.' *The Lancet 373*, 9657, 68–81.

Gilligan, C. (1993) *In a Different Voice: Psychological Theory and Women's Development* (2nd edition). Cambridge, MA, and London: Harvard University Press.

Gilligan, R. (1997) 'Beyond permanence? The importance of resilience in child placement practice and planning.' *Adoption and Fostering 21*, 1, 12–20.

Gilligan, R. (1999) 'Children's Own Social Networks and Network Members: Key Resources in Helping Children at Risk.' In M. Hill (ed.) *Effective Ways of Working with Children and their Families.* London: Jessica Kingsley Publishers.

Gilligan, R. (2001) *Promoting Resilience.* London: BAAF.

Gilligan, R. (2008) 'Promoting resilience in young people in long term care – The relevance of roles and relationships in the domains of recreation and work.' *Journal of Social Work Practice 22*, 1, 37– 50.

Gilligan, R. (2009a) *Promoting Resilience: Supporting Children and Young People who are in Care, Adopted or in Need.* London: BAAF.

Gilligan, R. (2009b) 'Positive Turning Points in the Dynamics of Change over the Life Course.' In J.A. Mancini and K.A. Roberto (eds) *Pathways of Human Development: Explorations of Change.* Lanham, MD: Lexington Books.

Goldman, L. (1994) *Life and Loss: A Guide to Helping Grieving Children.* Muncie, IN: Accelerated Development Inc.

Goldsmith, E.B. (1990) 'In support of working parents and their children.' *Journal of Social Behaviour and Personality 5*, 6, 517–520.

Goleman, D. (1996) *Emotional Intelligence.* London: Bloomsbury Publishing.

Golombok, S. (2000) *Parenting: What Really Counts?* London: Routledge.

Golombok, S. and Fivush, R. (1994) *Gender Development.* Cambridge: Cambridge University Press.

Gottman, J.M. and Parker, J.G. (1987) *Conversations of Friends.* New York: Cambridge University Press.

Grossbard, J.R., Lee, C.M., Neighbors, C. and Larimer, M.E. (2009) 'Body image concerns and contingent self-esteem in male and female college students.' *Sex Roles 60*, 198–207.

Hakuta, K. and Garcia, E.E. (1989) 'Bilingualism and education.' *American Psychologist 44*, 374–379.

Hartman, A. (1984) *Working with Adoptive Families Beyond Placement.* New York: Child Welfare League of America.

Hayden, C. (2007) *Children in Trouble.* Basingstoke: Palgrave Macmillan.

Heider, F. (1958) *The Psychology of Interpersonal Relations.* New York: Wiley.

Herbert, M. (1987) *Conduct Disorders of Childhood and Adolescence.* New York: Wiley.

Herbert, M. (2005) *Developmental Problems of Childhood and Adolescence.* Oxford: Blackwell Publishing.

Hess, P.M. and Proch, K.O. (1993) *Contact: Managing Visits to Children Looked After Away from Home.* London: BAAF.

Hester, M. (2009) 'Not silos but planets.' Presentation at ESRC-funded seminar series *Interrogating Harm and Abuse.* Stirling: University of Stirling.

Hester, M. and Pearson, C. (1993) 'Domestic violence, mediation and child contact arrangements: Issues from current research.' *Family Mediation 3,* 2, 3–6.

Hester, M. and Radford, L. (1992) 'Domestic violence and access arrangements for children in Denmark and Britain.' *Journal of Social Welfare and Family Law 1,* 57–70.

Hester, M. and Radford, L. (1996) *Domestic Violence and Child Contact Arrangements in England and Denmark.* Bristol: Policy Press.

Hester, M., Pearson, C. and Harwin, N. with Abrahams, H. (2000) *Making an Impact: Children and Domestic Violence. A Reader.* London: Jessica Kingsley Publishers.

Hester, M., Pearson, C. and Harwin, N. with Abrahams, H. (2007) *Making an Impact: Children and Domestic Violence. A Reader* (2nd edition). London: Jessica Kingsley Publishers.

Hetherington, E.M. (1989) 'Coping with family transitions: Winners, losers and survivors.' *Child Development 60,* 1–14.

Hillier, L., Warr, D. and Haste, B. (1996) *The Rural Mural: Sexuality and Diversity in Rural Youth.* Carlton: National Centre in HIV Social Research, La Trobe University.

HM Government (2005) *Common Core of Skills and Knowledge for the Children's Workforce.* London: DfES.

HM Treasury and Department for Education and Skills (2007) *Aiming High for Disabled Children: Better Support for Families.* London: DfES.

Holmes, J. (1993) 'Attachment theory: A biological basis for psychotherapy.' *British Journal of Psychiatry 163,* 430–438.

Holt, S. (2010) *The Contact Conundrum: Exploring Children's Experiences of Post-separation Contact with Domestically Abusive Fathers.* Thesis submitted in fulfilment of the requirements for the degree of PhD. Dublin: Trinity College Dublin.

Home Office (2003) *A Guide to Anti-social Behaviour Orders and Acceptable Behaviour Contracts.* London: Home Office.

Horwath, J. (2007) *Child Neglect: Identification and Assessment.* Basingstoke: Palgrave Macmillan.

Horwath, J. and Morrison, T. (2001) 'Assessment of Parental Motivation to Change.' In J. Horwath (ed.) *The Child's World: Assessing Children in Need.* London: Jessica Kingsley Publishers.

Howe, D. (1995) *Attachment Theory for Social Work Practice.* Basingstoke: Macmillan.

Howe, D. (1996) *Attachment and Loss in Child and Family Social Work.* Aldershot: Avebury.

Howe, D., Brandon M., Hinings, D. and Schofield, G. (1999) *Attachment Theory, Child Maltreatment and Family Support: A Practice and Assessment Model.* Basingstoke: Macmillan.

Hughes, D.A. (1997) *Facilitating Developmental Attachment: The Road to Emotional Recovery and Behavioural Change in Foster and Adopted Children.* North Vale, NJ and London: Jason Aronson Inc.

Hughes, D.A. (2006) *Building the Bond of Attachment: Awakening Love in Deeply Troubled Children.* North Vale, NJ and London: Jason Aronson Inc.

Hughes, D.A. (2009) *Attachment-Focussed Parenting: Effective Strategies to Care for Children.* New York and London: W.W. Norton and Co.

Humphreys, C. and Stanley, N. (eds.) (2006) *Domestic Violence and Child Protection: Directions for Good Practice.* London: Jessica Kingsley Publishers.

Jack, G. (2000) 'Ecological influences on parenting and child development.' *British Journal of Social Work 30,* 703–720.

Jack, G. (2001) 'Ecological Perspectives in Assessing Children and Families.' In J. Horwath (ed.) *The Child's World: Assessing Children in Need.* London: Jessica Kingsley Publishers.

Jackson, S. and McParlin, P. (2006) 'The education of children in care.' *The Psychologist 19,* 2, 90–93.

Jackson, S. and Sachdev, D. (2001) *Better Education, Better Futures: Research Practice and the Views of Young People in Public Care.* Essex: Barnardo's.

Jefferis, B.J.M.H.; Power, C. and Hertzman, C. (2002) 'Birth weight, childhood socioeconomic environment, and cognitive development in the 1958 British birth cohort study.' *British Medical Journal 325*, 7359, 305–310.

Jewett, C. (1984) *Helping Children Cope with Separation and Loss*. London: BAAF.

Jones, K.L. and Smith, D.W. (1973) 'Recognition of the fetal alcohol syndrome in early infancy.' *The Lancet 2, 302*, 7836, 999–1001.

Jones, L., Atkin, K. and Ahmad, W.I.U. (2001) 'Supporting Asian deaf young people and their families: The role of professionals and services.' *Disability and Society 16*, 1, 51–70.

Katchadourian, H. (1990) 'Sexuality.' In S.S. Feldman and G.R. Elliot (eds.) *At the Threshold: The Developing Adolescent*. Cambridge, MA: Harvard University Press.

Katz, I. (1996) *The Construction of Racial Identity in Children of Mixed Parentage: Mixed Metaphors*. London: Jessica Kingsley Publishers.

Katz, P. (1982) 'Development of children's racial awareness and intergroup attitudes.' In L.G. Katz (ed.) *Current Topics in Early Childhood Education, Vol. 4*. Norwood, NJ: Ablex.

Kennedy, M. and Wonnacott, J. (2005) 'Neglect of disabled children.' In J. Taylor, and B. Daniel (eds.) *Child Neglect: Practice Issues for Health and Social Care*. London: Jessica Kingsley Publishers.

Kohlberg, L. (1966) 'A Cognitive-developmental Analysis of Children's Sex-role Concepts and Attitudes.' In E.E. Maccoby (ed.) *The Development of Sex Differences*. Stanford, CA: Stanford University Press.

Kohlberg, L. (1969) 'Stages and Sequence: The Cognitive-developmental Approach to Socialization.' In D.A. Goslin (ed.) *Handbook of Socialization Theory and Research*. Chicago: Rand McNally.

Kosonen, M. (1997) 'Sibling abuse: A hidden misery. Children's perceptions of their relationships with their siblings.' Paper presented at BAPSCAN Congress *Approaching the Millennium: The Future Shape of Child Protection*, Centre for the Study of Child and Society, University of Glasgow.

Kosonen, M. (1999) 'Core and Kin Siblings: Foster Children's Changing Families.' In A. Mullender (ed.) *We are Family: Sibling Relationships in Placement and Beyond*. London: BAAF.

Lacher, D., Nichols, T. and May, J. (2005) *Connecting with Kids Through Stories*. London: Jessica Kingsley Publishers.

Lamb, M.E. (ed.) (2004) *The Role of the Father in Child Development* (4th edition). New York: Wiley.

Lees, S. (1993) *Sugar and Spice: Sexuality and Adolescent Girls*. Harmondsworth: Penguin.

Levine, M.P. and Smolak, L. (2002). 'Body Image Development in Adolescence.' In T.F. Cash and T. Pruzinsky (eds.) *Body Image: A Handbook of Theory, Research and Clinical Practice*. London: Guilford Press.

Lewis, M. (1994) 'Does attachment imply a relationship or multiple relationships?' *Psychological Inquiry 1*, 47–51.

Lindsay, J., Smith, A.M.A. and Rosenthal, D.A. (1997) *Secondary Students, HIV/AIDS and Sexual Health 1997*. Melbourne: Centre for the Study of Sexually Transmissible Diseases, La Trobe University.

Littner, N. (1975) 'The importance of natural parents to the child in placement.' *Child Welfare 54*, 175–181.

Lord, J. and Borthwick, S. (2001) *Together or Apart? Assessing Brothers and Sisters for Permanent Placement*. London: BAAF.

Luckock, B. and Lefevre, M. (2008) *Direct Work: Social Work with Children and Young People in Care*. London: BAAF.

Luthar, S. (1991) 'Vulnerability and resilience: A study of high-risk adolescents.' *Child Development 62*, 600–612.

Luthar, S. (2005) 'Resilience in Development: A Synthesis of Research across Five Decades.' In D. Cicchetti and D.J. Cohen (eds.) *Development Psychopathology: Risk, Disorder and Adaptation* (2nd edition, Vol. 3). New York: Wiley.

Luthar, S.S., Sawyer, J.A. and Brown, P.J. (2006) 'Conceptual issues in studies of resilience: Past, present, and future research.' *Annals of the New York Academy of Sciences 1094*, 105–115.

Maccoby, E.E. (1998) *The Two Sexes: Growing up Apart, Coming Together*. Cambridge, MA: Harvard University Press.

Maccoby, E.E. (2002) 'Gender and group process: A developmental perspective.' *Current Directions in Psychological Science 11*, 2, 54–58.

Macdonald, J. and Lugton, J. (2006) 'Helping parents to understand and communicate with their babies from birth: An evaluation of an antenatal VIG teaching session.' *Veroc Online Journal.* Available at www.cpdeducation.co.uk/veroc/conference/journal.php 1-30, accessed on 31 January 2010.

MacMillan, H.L.,Wathen, C.N., Barlow, J., Fergusson, D.M., Leventhal, J.M. and Taussig, H.N. (2009) 'Interventions to prevent child maltreatment and associated impairment.' *The Lancet 373*, 9659, 250–266.

Main, M. (1991) 'Meta Cognitive Knowledge, Meta Cognitive Monitoring and Singular (Coherent) versus Multiple (Incoherent) Model of Attachment: Findings and Directions for Future Research.' In C.M. Parkes, J. Stevenson-Hinde and P. Marris (eds.) *Attachment Across the Life Cycle.* London: Tavistock/Routledge.

Main, M. and Goldwyn, R. (1984) 'Predicting rejection of her infant from mother's representations of her own experience: Implications for the abused–abusing intergenerational cycle.' *Child Abuse and Neglect 8*, 203–217.

Malik, N.M. and Furman, W. (1993) 'Practitioner review. Problems in children's peer relations: What can the clinician do?' *Journal of Child Psychology 34*, 8, 1303–1326.

Mama, A. (1989) *The Hidden Struggle: Statutory and Voluntary Sector Responses to Women and Children Escaping from Violence in the Home.* Bristol: Women's Aid Federation England and University of Bristol School of Applied Social Studies.

Marcia, J.E. (1966) 'Development and validation of ego-identity status.' *Journal of Personality and Social Psychology 3*, 551–558.

Marcia, J.E. (1980) 'Identity in adolescence.' In J. Adelson (ed.) *Handbook of Adolescent Psychology.* New York: Wiley.

Masten, A. (1994) 'Resilience in Individual Development.' In M.C. Wang and E.W. Gordon (eds.) *Educational Resilience in Inner-city America.* Hillsdale, NJ: Erlbaum.

Masten, A.S., and Coatsworth, J.D. (1998) 'The development of competence in favorable and unfavorable environments.' *American Psychologist 53*, 2, 205–220.

Maxime, J. (1986) 'Some psychological models of black self-concept.' In S. Ahmed, J. Cheetham and J. Small (eds.) *Social Work with Black Children and their Families.* London: BAAF.

Maxime, J. (1994) *'Black Like Me' Workbooks 1–3.* Beckenham: Emani Publications.

McCabe, M.P. and Collins, J.K. (1990) *Dating, Relating and Sex.* Sydney: Horowitz Grahame.

McClung, M. (2008) *Could Do Better.* Unpublished PhD thesis. Stirling: University of Stirling.

McDonald, L., Billingham, S., Conrad, T., Morgan, A., Nancy, O. and Payton, E. (1997) 'Families and Schools Together (FAST): Integrating community development with clinical strategies.' *Families in Society: The Journal of Contemporary Human Services 78*, 2, 140–155.

McDonald, S. (1991) *All Equal Under the Act: A Practical Guide to the Children Act 1989 for Social Workers.* London: Race Equality Unit.

McFadden, E. (1986) *The Child who is Physically Battered and Abused.* Ypsilanti, MI: University of Michigan.

McFadden, E. (1996) *Fostering the Child who has been Sexually Abused.* Ypsilanti, MI: University of Michigan.

Meadows, S. (1986) *Understanding Child Development.* London: Routledge.

Miller, D. (2002) *Disabled Children and Abuse.* NSPCC Inform Available at www.nspcc.org.uk/inform/research/briefings/disabledchildrenandabuse_wda48224.html, accessed on 23 January 2010.

Miller, D. and Daniel, B. (2007) 'Competent to cope, worthy of happiness? How the duality of self-esteem can inform a resilience-based classroom environment.' *School Psychology International 28*, 5, 605–622.

Miller, D.J. and Moran, T.R. (2006) 'Positive self-worth is not enough: Some implications of a two-dimensional model of self-esteem for primary teaching.' *Improving Schools 9*, 1, 7–16.

Moffit, T.E. (1997) 'Adolescence – Limited and Life-course Persistent Offending: A Complementary Pair of Developmental Theories.' In T.P. Thornberry (ed.) *Developmental Theories of Crime and Delinquency.* New Brunswick, NJ: Transaction.

Montgomery, P., Gardner, F., Bjornstad, G. and Ramchandani, P. (2009) *Systematic Review of Interventions Following Physical Abuse: Helping Practitioners and Expert Witnesses Improve the Outcomes of Child Abuse.* Research Brief DCSF-RBX-09-08A. Available at www.dcsf.gov.uk/research/data/uploadfiles/DCSF-RBX-09-08A.pdf, accessed on 29 January 2010.

Mooney, E., Farley, H. and Strugnell, C. (2009) 'A qualitative investigation into the opinions of adolescent females regarding their body image concerns and dieting practices in the Republic of Ireland (ROI).' *Appetite 52,* 485–491.

Moore, S. and Rosenthal, D. (1991) 'Adolescents' perceptions of friends' and parents' attitudes to sex and sexual risk-taking.' *Journal of Community and Applied Psychology 1,* 189–200.

Moore, S. and Rosenthal, D. (2006) *Sexuality in Adolescence.* London and New York: Routledge.

Moran, P. (2009) *Research Evidence to Inform Practice.* London: Action for Children.

Morrison, T. (1998) 'Partnership, Collaboration and Change under the Children Act.' In M. Adcock and R. White (eds.) *Significant Harm: Its Management and Outcome* (2nd edition). Croydon: Significant Publications.

Mostyn, W. (1996) *Childhood Matters: Report of the National Commission of Inquiry into the Prevention of Child Abuse.* London: The Stationery Office.

Mruk, C. (1999) *Self-esteem: Research, Theory and Practice.* London: Free Association Books.

Munro, E. (2007) *Child Protection.* London, Thousand Oaks and New Delhi: Sage Publications.

National Scientific Council on the Developing Child (2004) *Young Children Develop in an Environment of Relationships: Working Paper No. 1.* Available at www.developingchild.harvard.edu, accessed 21 July 2010.

National Literacy Trust (2009) 'Literacy and education levels by ethnic group and populations.' Available at www.literacytrust.org.uk/Database/STATS/EALstats.html#schools, accessed on 5 December 2009.

NCH Action for Children (1994) *The Hidden Victims: Children and Domestic Violence.* London: NCH Action for Children.

NCH Action for Children (1997) *Making a Difference: Working with Women and Children Experiencing Domestic Violence.* London: NCH Action for Children.

Newman, T. (2004) *What Works in Building Resilience.* London: Barnardo's.

NSPCC (2008) *Children Talking to ChildLine about Bullying: ChildLine Casenote November 2009.* London: NSPCC. Available at www.nspcc.org.uk/Inform/publications/casenotes/children_talking_to_childline_about_sexual_abuse_wda69414.html, accessed on 10 December 2009.

Office for National Statistics (2009) *Teenage Conception Statistics for England, 1998–2007.* London: DH.

O'Hagan, K. (1993) *Emotional and Psychological Abuse of Children.* Thousand Oaks, CA, London and New Delhi: Sage Publications.

O'Hara, M. (1993) 'Child Protection and Domestic Violence: Changing Policy and Practice.' In *The Links between Domestic Violence and Child Abuse: Developing Services.* London: London Borough of Hackney.

O'Hara, M. (1994) 'Child Deaths in Contexts of Domestic Violence: Implications for Professional Practice.' In A. Mullender and R. Morley (eds.) *Children Living with Domestic Violence: Putting Men's Abuse of Women on the Child Care Agenda.* London: Whiting and Birch.

Olsen, R. and Tyers, H. (2004) *Think Parent: Supporting Disabled Adults as Parents.* London: National Family Parenting Institute.

Osler, A., Whatling, R., Busher, H., Cole, T. and White, A. (2001) *Reasons for Exclusion from School.* Research Brief No. 244. London: Department for Education and Employment.

Owusu-Bempah, J. and Howitt, D. (1997) 'Socio-genealogical connectedness, attachment theory, and childcare practice.' *Child and Family Social Work 2,* 199–207.

Parton, N. (1995) 'Neglect as child protection: The political context and the practical outcomes.' *Children and Society 9,* 1, 67–89.

Patterson, J. (2005) *Lesbian and Gay Parenting.* Washington, DC: American Psychological Association.

Perry, B. (1995) *Maltreated Children: Experience, Brain Development and the Next Generation.* New York: W.W. Norton.

Petersen, C. and Seligman, M.E.P. (1985) 'The learned helplessness model of depression: Current status of theory and research.' In E. Beckham (ed.) *Handbook of Depression, Treatment Assessment and Research.* Homewood, IL: Dorsey Press.

Phillips, M. and Dutt, R. (1990) *Towards a Black Perspective in Child Protection.* London: Race Equality Unit.

Phinney, J.S. (1993) 'A Three-stage Model of Ethnic Identity Development in Adolescence.' In M.E. Bernal and G.P. Knight (eds.) *Ethnic Identity: Formation and Transmission Among Hispanics and Other Minorities.* Albany, NY: State University of New York Press.

Phoenix, A. (1991) *Young Mothers?* Cambridge: Polity Press.

Piaget, J. (1932) *The Moral Judgement of the Child.* Harmondsworth: Penguin.

Piaget, J. (1952) *The Origins of Intelligence in Children.* New York: International Universities Press.

Piaget, J. (1954) *The Construction of Reality in the Child.* New York: Basic Books.

Plant, M.L. (2000) 'Drinking During Pregnancy.' In M.A. Plant and D. Cameron (eds.) *The Alcohol Report.* London: Free Association Books.

Prior, V. and Glaser, D. (2006) *Understanding Attachment and Attachment Disorders.* London: Jessica Kingsley Publishers.

Prochaska, J.O., DiClemente, C.C. and Narcross, J.C. (1992) 'In search of how people change.' *American Psychologist 47,* 9, 1102–1114.

Rashid, S.P. (1996) 'Attachment Reviewed through a Cultural Lens.' In D. Howe (ed.) *Attachment and Loss in Child and Family Social Work.* Aldershot: Ashgate.

Reder, P. and Duncan, S. (1995) 'The Meaning of the Child.' In P. Reder and L. Lucey (eds.) *Assessment of Parenting: Psychiatric and Psychological Contributions.* London: Routledge.

Reder, P. and Lucey, C. (1995) *The Assessment of Parenting: Psychiatric and Psychological Contributions.* London: Routledge.

Rice, K. (1990) 'Attachment in adolescence: A narrative and meta-analytic review.' *Journal of Youth and Adolescence 19,* 511–538.

Rigsby, L.C. (1994). 'The Americanization of Resilience: Deconstructing Research Practice.' In M. Wang and E. Gordon (eds.) *Educational Resilience in Inner-city America.* Hillsdale, NJ: Lawrence Erlbaum.

Robinson, J.L., Zahn-Waxler, C. and Emde, R. (1994) 'Patterns of development in early empathic behaviour: Environmental and child contributional influences.' *Social Development 3,* 125–145.

Robinson, L. (2007) *Cross-cultural Child Development for Social Workers.* Basingstoke: Palgrave Macmillan.

Rodriguez, J., Cauce, A.M. and Wilson, L. (2002) 'A Conceptual Framework of Identity Formation in a Society of Multiple Cultures.' In K.N. Dwivedi (ed.) *Meeting the Needs of Ethnic Minority Children.* London: Jessica Kingsley Publishers.

Rogoff, B. (1990) *Apprenticeship Training.* New York: Oxford University Press.

Rosenman, S. and Rodgers, B. (2004) 'Childhood adversity in an Australian population.' *Social Psychiatry and Psychiatric Epidemiology 39,* 9, 695–702.

Rosenthal, D.A. and Collis, F. (1997) 'Parents' belief about adolescent sexuality and HIV/AIDS.' *Journal of HIV Education and Prevention in Children and Adolescents 1,* 57–72.

Rowe, J., Hundleby, M. and Garnett, L. (1989) *Child Care Now,* Research Series 6. London: British Agencies for Adoption and Fostering.

Ruble, D.N., Taylor, L.J., Cyphers, L., Greulich, F.K., Lurye, L.E. and Shrout, P.E. (2007) 'The role of gender constancy in early gender development.' *Child Development 78,* 4, 1121–1136.

Rutter, M. (1981) *Maternal Deprivation Reassessed* (2nd edition). Harmondsworth: Penguin.

Rutter, M. (1987) 'Psychosocial resilience and protective mechanisms.' *American Journal of Orthopsychiatry 57,* 316–331.

Rutter, M. (1991) 'Pathways from childhood to adult life: The role of schooling.' *Pastoral Care,* Sep., 3–10.

Rutter, M. (2000) 'Resilience Reconsidered: Conceptual Considerations.' In J.P. Shonkoff and S.J. Meisels (eds.) *Handbook of Early Childhood Intervention* (2nd edition). Cambridge: Cambridge University Press.

Rutter, M. and Quinton, D. (1984) 'Parental psychiatric disorder: Effects on children.' *Psychological Medicine 14,* 853–880.

Rutter, M. and Rutter, M. (1993) *Developing Minds: Challenge and Continuity across the Life Span.* Harmondsworth: Penguin.

Rutter, M., Giller, H. and Hagel, A. (1998) *Antisocial Behaviour by Young People.* Cambridge: Cambridge University Press.

Rutter, M., Tizard, C. and Reads, P. (1986) *Depression and Young People: Developmental and Clinical Perspectives.* Guilford Press: New York.

Ryan, P. (1979) *Training Foster Parents to Handle Lying and Stealing.* Ypsilanti, MI: Eastern Michigan University.

Santrok, J.W. (1994) *Child Development.* Madison, WI and Dubuque, IA: W.C.B. Brown and Benchmark.

Santrok, J.W. (2001) *Child Development* (8th edition). Boston, MA: McGraw Hill.

Saywitz, K.J. and Goodman, G.S. (1996) 'Interviewing Children in and out of Court: Current Research and Practice Implications.' In J. Briere, L. Berliner, J.A. Buckley, C. Jenny and T. Reid (eds.) *The APSAC Handbook on Child Maltreatment.* Thousand Oaks, CA: Sage Publications.

Scales, P. and Gibbons, J. (1996) 'Extended family members and unrelated adults in the lives of young adolescents: A research agenda.' *Journal of Early Adolescence 16,* 4, 365–389.

Scarr, S. (1990) 'Mother's proper place, children's needs and women's rights.' *Journal of Social Behaviour and Personality 5,* 6, 507–515.

Schaffer, H.R. (1996) *Social Development.* Oxford: Blackwell.

Schaffer, H.R. (1998) *Making Decisions about Children: Psychological Questions and Answers* (2nd edition). Oxford: Blackwell.

Schlesinger, H.S. and Meadow, K.P. (1972) *Sound and Sign.* Berkeley: University of California Press.

Schofield, G. and Beek, M. (2006) *Attachment Handbook for Foster Carers and Adoption.* London: BAAF.

Schore, A.N. (1994) *Affection Regulation and the Origin of the Self.* Hillsdale, NJ: Erlbaum.

Scottish Executive (2005) *Getting it Right for Every Child: Proposals for Action.* Edinburgh: Scottish Executive.

Seaman. P., Turner, K., Hill, M., Stafford, A. and Walker, M. (2005) *Parenting and Children's Resilience in Disadvantaged Areas.* York: Joseph Rowntree Foundation.

Seligman, M.E.P. and Peterson, C. (1986) 'A Learned Helplessness Perspective on Childhood Depression: Theory and Research.' In M. Rutter, C. Tizard and P. Reads (eds.) *Depression and Young People: Developmental and Clinical Perspectives.* Guilford Press: New York.

Seligman, R. (1995) *The Optimistic Child: A Proven Program to Safeguard Children Against Depression and Build Lifelong Resilience.* New York: HarperCollins.

Sinclair, I. and Gibbs, I. (1996) *Quality of Care in Children's Homes: A Short Report and Issues Paper.* York: University of York, Social Work Research and Development Unit.

Sinclair, I., Baker, C., Lee, J. and Gibbs, I. (2007) *The Pursuit of Permanence: A Study of the English Care System.* London: Jessica Kingsley Publishers.

Slee, P.T. (2002) *Child, Adolescent and Family Development.* Cambridge: Cambridge University Press.

Smetana, J. (1989) 'Adolescents' and parents' reasoning about actual family conflict.' *Child Development 60,* 1052–1067.

Smith, A.M.A., Agius, P., Dyson, S., Mitchell, A. and Pitts, M. (2003) *Secondary Students and Sexual Health 2002: Results of the 3rd National Survey of Australian Secondary Students, HIV/AIDS and Sexual Health.* Melbourne: Australian Research Centre in Sex, Health, and Society, La Trobe University.

Smith, G. (1992) 'The Unbearable Traumatogenic Past: Child Sexual Abuse.' In V. Varma (ed.) *The Secret Life of Vulnerable Children.* London: Routledge.

Smith, P.K. and Cowie, H. (1991) *Understanding Children's Development.* Oxford: Blackwell.

Smith, P.K., Cowie, H. and Blades, M. (2003) *Understanding Children's Development* (4th edition). Oxford: Blackwell Publishing.

Smith, V. and Ellis, S. (2005) *A Curriculum for Excellence: Review of Research for Language and Literacy.* SEED website (2005) Available at www.acurriculumforexcellencescotland.gov.uk/ images/Language%20 Literacy_tcm4-252173.pdf, accessed 5 December 2009.

Social Exclusion Unit (2003) *A Better Education for Children in Care.* London: SEU.

Sroufe, L.A. and Fleeson, J. (1988) 'The coherence of family relationships.' In R. Hinde and J. Stevenson (eds.) *Relationships within Families*. Milton Keynes: Open University Press.

Stainton Rogers, W. (2001) 'Constructing Childhood, Constructing Child Concern.' In P. Foley, J. Roche and S. Tucker (eds.) *Children in Society*. Basingstoke and New York: Palgrave with the Open University.

Stalker, K., Green Lister, P., Lerpiniere, J. and McArthur, K. (2009) *Child Protection and the Needs and Rights of Disabled Children: Abridged Report*. Strathclyde: University of Strathclyde, Faculty of Education.

Stanley, N., Penhale, B., Riordan, D., Barbour, R.S. and Holden, S. (2003) *Child Protection and Mental Health Services: Interprofessional Responses to the Needs of Mothers*. Bristol: The Policy Press.

Stein, M. (2009) *Quality Matters in Children's Services: Messages from Research*. London: Jessica Kingsley Publishers.

Stein, M., Rhys, G., Hicks, L. and Gorin, S. (2009) *Neglected Adolescents: Literature Review*. Research Brief, DCSF-RBX-09-04. London: DCSF.

Steinberg, L. (1993) *Adolescence*. New York: McGraw-Hill.

Stevenson, O. (2007) *Neglected Children and their Families*. Oxford: Blackwell Publishers.

Stone, M. (1989) *Young People Leaving Care: A Study of Management Systems, Service Delivery and User Evaluation*. Westerham, Kent: The Royal Philanthropic Society.

Stopford, V. (1993) *Understanding Disability: Causes, Characteristics and Coping*. London: Edward Arnold.

Sullivan, P. and Knutson, J. (2000) 'Maltreatment and disabilities: A population-based epidemiological study.' *Child Abuse and Neglect 24*, 10, 1257–1273.

Summit, R. (1983) 'The child sexual abuse accommodation syndrome.' *Child Abuse and Neglect 7*, 177–193.

Swift, K.J. (1995) *Manufacturing 'Bad Mothers': A Critical Perspective in Child Neglect*. Toronto: University of Toronto Press.

Tasker, F. (1999) 'Children in lesbian-led families: A review.' *Clinical Child Psychology and Psychiatry 4*, 2, 153–166.

Tasker, F. and Golombok, S. (1997) *Growing Up in a Lesbian Family: Effects on Child Development*. Hove: Guilford Press.

Taylor, J. and Daniel, B. (2005) *Child Neglect: Practice Issues for Health and Social Care*. London: Jessica Kingsley Publishers.

Thoburn, J., Chand, A. and Procter, J. (2005) *Child Welfare Services for Minority Ethnic Families*. London: Jessica Kingsley Publishers.

Thompson, R. (1995) *Preventing Child Maltreatment Through Social Support*. Thousand Oaks, CA, London and New Delhi: Sage Publications.

Trevarthen, C. (1991) 'Cognitive and co-operative motives in infancy.' Symposium, *Early Development: Current Theories and Research Findings*, Crete.

Trevarthen, C. and Aitken, K.J. (2001) 'Infants into subjectivity: Research, theory and clinical applications.' *Journal of Child Psychology and Psychiatry 42*, 3–48.

Trinke, S. and Bartholomew, K. (1997) 'Hierarchies of attachment relationships in young adulthood.' *Journal of Social and Personal Relationships 14*, 5, 603–625.

Triseliotis, J., Borland, M., Hill, M. and Lambert, L. (1995) *Teenagers and the Social Work Services*. London: HMSO.

Unger, R. and Crawford, M. (1992) *Women and Gender: A Feminist Psychology*. Philadelphia: Temple University Press.

Utting, D. (1995) *Family and Parenthood: Supporting Families, Preventing Breakdown*. York: Joseph Rowntree Foundation.

Utting, D., Monteiro, H. and Ghate, D. (2007) *Interventions for Children at Risk of Developing Antisocial Personality Disorder*. London: Policy Research Bureau.

van der Veer, R. and Valsiner, J. (1991) *Understanding Vygotsky: A Quest for Synthesis*. Cambridge, MA, and Oxford: Blackwell.

Webster-Stratton, C. (1999) 'Researching the Impact of Parent Training on Child Conduct Problems.' In E. Lloyd (ed.) *Parenting Matters – What Works in Parenting Education?* Barkingside: Barnardos.

Weir, A. (2003) 'A Framework for Assessing Parents with Mental Health Problems.' In M.C. Calder and S. Hackett (eds.) *Assessment in Childcare: Using and Developing Frameworks for Practice.* Dorset: Russell House.

Werner, E. (1990) 'Protective Factors and Individual Resilience.' In S. Meisels and J. Shonkoff (eds.) *Handbook of Early Childhood Intervention.* Cambridge: Cambridge University Press.

Werner, E. and Smith, R. (1992) *Overcoming the Odds: High Risk Children from Birth to Adulthood.* Ithaca: Cornell University Press.

Westcott, H.L. (1993) *Abuse of Children and Adults with Disabilities.* London: NSPCC.

Westcott, H.L. and Jones, D.P.H. (1999) 'Annotation: The abuse of disabled children.' *Journal of Child Psychology and Psychiatry 40,* 4, 497–506.

Whiting, B.B. and Edwards, C.P. (1988) *Children of Different Worlds: The Formation of Social Behaviour.* Cambridge, MA: Harvard University Press.

Williams, L. (2010) 'Harm and resilience among prostituted teens: Broadening our understanding of victimization and survival.' *Social Policy and Society 9,* 2, 243–254.

Yates, T.M. and Masten, A. (2004) 'Prologue: The Promise of Resilience Research for Practice and Policy.' In T. Newman (ed.) *What Works in Building Resilience?* Barkingside: Barnardo's.

Young, A.M., Green L. and Rogers K.D. (2008) 'Resilience and deaf children: A literature review.' *Deafness and Education International 10,* 1, 40–55.

Yuille, J.C., Hunter, R., Joffe, R. and Zaparniuk, J. (1993) 'Interviewing Children in Sexual Abuse Cases.' In G. Goodman and B. Bottoms (eds.) *Understanding and Improving Children's Testimony: Clinical, Developmental and Legal Implications.* New York: Guilford Press.

Zahn-Waxler, C., Radke-Yarrow, M. and King, R.A. (1979) 'Child-rearing and children's prosocial initiations towards victims of distress.' *Child Development 50,* 319–330.

Zeitlin, H. (2002) 'Adoption of Children from Minority Groups.' In K.N. Dwivedi (ed.) *Meeting the Needs of Ethnic Minority Children.* London: Jessica Kingsley Publishers.

Zimmerman, R.B. (1988) 'Childhood depression: New theoretical formulations and implications for foster care services.' *Child Welfare 67,* 1, 37–47.

Subject Index

Author Index